Adobe® Muse®

CLASSROOM IN A BOOK®

The official training workbook from Adobe Systems

Adobe

Adobe Press books are published by Peachpit, a division of Pearson Education located in Berkeley, California. For the latest on Adobe Press books, go to www.adobepress.com. To report errors, please send a note to errata@peachpit.com. For information on getting permission for reprints and excerpts, contact permissions@peachpit.com.

Printed and bound in the United States of America

ISBN-13: 978-0-321-82136-2
ISBN-10:   0-321-82136-X

9 8 7 6 5 4 3 2 1

WHAT'S ON THE DISC

Here is an overview of the contents of the Classroom in a Book disc

The *Adobe Muse Classroom in a Book* disc includes the lesson files that you'll need to complete the exercises in this book, as well as other content to help you learn more about Adobe Muse and use it with greater efficiency and ease. The diagram below represents the contents of the disc, which should help you locate the files you need.

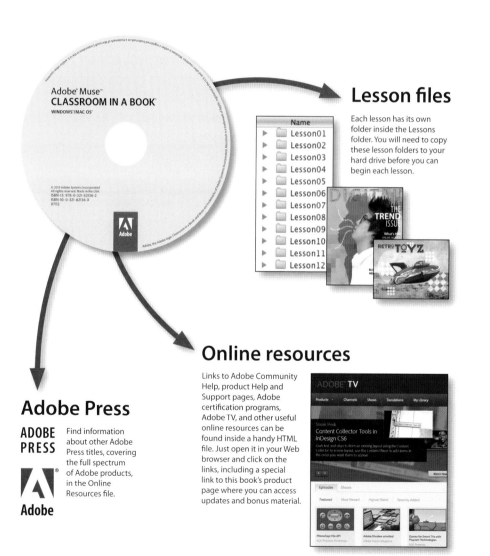

Lesson files

Each lesson has its own folder inside the Lessons folder. You will need to copy these lesson folders to your hard drive before you can begin each lesson.

Name
▶ Lesson01
▶ Lesson02
▶ Lesson03
▶ Lesson04
▶ Lesson05
▶ Lesson06
▶ Lesson07
▶ Lesson08
▶ Lesson09
▶ Lesson10
▶ Lesson11
▶ Lesson12

Online resources

Links to Adobe Community Help, product Help and Support pages, Adobe certification programs, Adobe TV, and other useful online resources can be found inside a handy HTML file. Just open it in your Web browser and click on the links, including a special link to this book's product page where you can access updates and bonus material.

Adobe Press

Find information about other Adobe Press titles, covering the full spectrum of Adobe products, in the Online Resources file.

CONTENTS

GETTING STARTED

If you are a graphic designer, business owner, or anyone who wants to design and create professional, original websites without ever touching code, Muse is the program you've been waiting for.

With Muse, you can quickly and easily design and create user-friendly, interactive websites, without the help of a developer. You just design your site in Muse using design-savvy graphic tools that leverage the same skills as Adobe InDesign and Photoshop. Then, after creating your site in Muse, you can take your site live using Adobe hosting or export to a provider of your choice, publishing your site as original HTML pages that conform to the latest web standards.

Muse really is that easy and that powerful, and *Adobe Muse Classroom in a Book*® will help you make the most of it.

About Classroom in a Book

Adobe Muse Classroom in a Book is part of the official training series for Adobe graphics and publishing software developed with the support of Adobe product experts. The lessons are designed so that you can learn at your own pace. If you're new to Adobe Muse, you'll learn the fundamentals you need to master to put the application to work. If you are an experienced user, you'll find that *Classroom in a Book* teaches many advanced features, including tips and techniques for using the latest version of Adobe Muse.

Although each lesson provides step-by-step instructions for creating a specific project, there's room for exploration and experimentation. You can follow the book from start to finish, or do only the lessons that correspond to your interests and needs. Each lesson concludes with a review section summarizing what you've covered.

Prerequisites

Before beginning to use *Adobe Muse Classroom in a Book*, you should have working knowledge of your computer and its operating system. Make sure that you know how to use the mouse and standard menus and commands, and also how to open, save, and close files. If you need to review these techniques, see the printed or online documentation included with your Microsoft Windows or Mac OS software.

Installing Muse

Before you begin using *Adobe Muse Classroom in a Book*, make sure that your system is set up correctly and that you've installed the required software and hardware.

The Adobe Muse software is not included on the *Adobe Muse Classroom in a Book* CD; you must purchase the software separately. For complete instructions on installing the software, see the Adobe Muse Read Me file on the application DVD or on the web at www.adobe.com/support.

Fonts used in this book

The fonts used with the *Adobe Muse Classroom in a Book* lesson files can be found on the *Adobe Muse Classroom in a Book* CD in the Fonts folder. These fonts can be installed in the following locations:

• Windows: [startup drive]\Windows\Fonts\

• Mac OS X: [startup drive]/Library/Fonts/

For more information about fonts and installation, see the Adobe Muse Read Me file on the application DVD or on the web at www.adobe.com/support.

Copying the Classroom in a Book files

The *Adobe Muse Classroom in a Book* CD includes folders containing all the electronic files for the lessons. Each lesson has its own folder. You must install these folders on your hard disk to use the files for the lessons.

To install the Classroom in a Book files

1 Insert the *Adobe Muse Classroom in a Book* CD into your CD-ROM drive.

2 Do one of the following:

- Copy the entire Lessons folder onto your hard disk (recommended).

- Copy only the specific lesson folder that you need onto your hard disk.

Restoring default program preferences

The preference files control how command settings appear on your screen when you open the Adobe Muse program. Each time you quit Adobe Muse, the position of the panels and certain command settings are recorded in different preference files. If you want to restore the tools and settings to their original default settings, you can delete the current Adobe Muse preference files. Adobe Muse creates new preference files, if they don't already exist, the next time you start the program and save a file.

To save current Muse preferences

If you would like to restore the current preferences for Muse after completing the Lessons, you can do so by following these steps:

1 Exit Adobe Muse.

2 Locate the AdobeMuse preferences folder as follows:

- (Windows) The AdobeMuse folder is located in the folder [startup drive]\Users\[username]\AppData\Roaming\AdobeMuse.

- (Mac OS X) The AdobeMuse folder is located in the folder [startup drive]/Users/[username]/Library/Preferences/AdobeMuse.

Keep in mind that your folder name may be different depending on the language version you have installed. If you can't find the file, you either haven't started Adobe Muse yet or you have moved the preferences folder. The preferences folder is created after you open Muse the first time and is updated thereafter.

3 Copy the folder, and save it to another folder on your hard disk.

4 Start Adobe Muse.

Note: If you cannot locate the preferences folder, use your operating system's Find command and search for AdobeMuse.

Note: The AppData folder may be hidden on Windows.

To delete current Muse preferences

Tip: To quickly locate and delete the Adobe Muse preferences folder each time you begin a new lesson, create a short-cut (Windows) or an alias (Mac OS) to the AdobeMuse folder.

If you are entering the Lessons using Jumpstart, you need to delete the current preference files for Muse by following these steps:

1 Exit Adobe Muse.

2 Locate the AdobeMuse folder as follows:

- (Windows) The AdobeMuse folder is located in the folder [startup drive]\Users\[username]\AppData\Roaming\AdobeMuse.

- (Mac OS X) The AdobeMuse folder is located in the folder [startup drive]/Users/[username]/Library/Preferences/AdobeMuse.

Note: If you cannot locate the preferences folder, use your operating system's Find command and search for AdobeMuse.

Remember, the folder name may be different depending on the language version you have installed.

3 Delete the preferences folder.

4 Start Muse.

To restore saved preferences

After completing the lessons, you can restore your personalized preferences you saved in the "To save current Muse preferences" section, in two steps.

1 Exit Adobe Muse.

2 Find the original AdobeMuse preferences folder that you saved and replace the AdobeMuse folder found here:

- (Windows) The AdobeMuse folder is located in the folder [startup drive]\Users\[username]\AppData\Roaming\AdobeMuse.

- (Mac OS X) The AdobeMuse folder is located in the folder [startup drive]/Users/[username]/Library/Preferences/AdobeMuse.

Again, the folder name may be different depending on the language version you have installed.

Recommended lesson order

Adobe Muse Classroom in a Book is designed to take you from A to Z in basic to intermediate website design and creation. Each new lesson builds on previous exercises, using the files and assets you create to develop an entire website. To achieve a successful result and the most complete understanding of all aspects of web design, the ideal training scenario is to start in Lesson 1, and perform each lesson in sequential order through the entire book to Lesson 9. Because each lesson builds essential files and content for the next, you shouldn't skip any lessons or even individual exercises. While ideal, this method may not be a practicable scenario for everyone.

Jumpstart

If you don't have the time or inclination to perform each lesson in the book in order, or if you're having difficulty with a particular lesson, you can work through individual lessons using the jumpstart method with the files supplied on the book's CD. Each lesson folder includes staged files (files that are completed to that point in the Lessons).

To jumpstart a lesson, follow these steps:

1 Install the fonts used in the Lessons. See the section "Fonts used in this book" on page 2.

2 Restore the program preferences as explained in the "To restore saved preferences" section on page 3.

> **Note:** If you see a dialog box indicating modified, missing, or upsampled images, click OK.

3 Copy the Lessons folder from the *Adobe Muse Classroom in a Book* CD onto your hard drive.

4 Open Muse.

5 Choose File > Open Site and navigate to the Lessons folder on your hard drive, then to the specific lesson folder you are starting from. For instance, if you are jumpstarting Lesson 3, navigate to the Lesson03 folder in the Lessons folder and open the file named L3_start.muse.

   For most of the lessons, you will need to open the _start file for your operating system due to font differences. For instance, if you are on Mac OS and want to jump into Lesson 8, you will open the lesson file named L8_start_mac.muse.

These simple steps will have to be repeated for each lesson you wish to jumpstart. If you choose the jumpstart method once, however, you do not have to continue using it for all subsequent lessons. For example, if you want to jumpstart Lesson 6, you can simply continue on to Lesson 7, and so on.

Windows versus Mac OS

When instructions differ by platform, Windows commands appear first and then the Mac OS commands, with the platform noted in parentheses. For example, you might see "press Alt (Windows) or Option (Mac OS) and click away from the artwork." In some instances, common commands may be abbreviated with the Windows commands first, followed by a slash and the Mac OS commands, without any parenthetical reference. For example, "press Alt/Option" or "press Ctrl/Command+click."

Additional resources

Adobe Muse Classroom in a Book is not meant to replace documentation that comes with the program or to be a comprehensive reference for every feature. Only the commands and options used in the lessons are explained in this book. For comprehensive information about program features and tutorials, refer to these resources:

Adobe Community Help: Community Help brings together active Adobe product users, Adobe product team members, authors, and experts to give you the most useful, relevant, and up-to-date information about Adobe products.

To access Community Help: To invoke Help, choose Help > Adobe Muse Help.

Adobe content is updated based on community feedback and contributions. You can contribute in several ways: add comments to content or forums, including links to web content; publish your own content using Community Publishing; or contribute Cookbook Recipes. Find out how to contribute at www.adobe.com/community/publishing/download.html.

See community.adobe.com/help/profile/faq.html for answers to frequently asked questions about Community Help.

Adobe Muse Help and Support: www.adobe.com/support/Muse is where you can find and browse Help and Support content on Adobe's site.

Adobe Forums: forums.adobe.com lets you tap into peer-to-peer discussions, questions, and answers on Adobe products.

Adobe TV: tv.adobe.com is an online video resource for expert instruction and inspiration about Adobe products, including a How To channel to get you started with your product.

Adobe Design Center: www.adobe.com/designcenter offers thoughtful articles on design and design issues, a gallery showcasing the work of top-notch designers, tutorials, and more.

Adobe Developer Connection: www.adobe.com/devnet is your source for technical articles, code samples, and how-to videos that cover Adobe developer products and technologies.

Resources for educators: www.adobe.com/education offers a treasure trove of information for instructors who teach classes on Adobe software. Find solutions for education at all levels, including free curricula that use an integrated approach to teaching Adobe software and can be used to prepare for the Adobe Certified Associate exams.

Also check out these useful links:

Adobe Marketplace & Exchange: www.adobe.com/cfusion/exchange is a central resource for finding tools, services, extensions, code samples, and more to supplement and extend your Adobe products.

Adobe Muse product home page: www.adobe.com/products/muse.html

Adobe Labs: labs.adobe.com gives you access to early builds of cutting-edge technology, as well as forums where you can interact with both the Adobe development teams building that technology and other like-minded members of the community.

Adobe Certification

The Adobe training and certification programs are designed to help Adobe customers improve and promote their product-proficiency skills. There are four levels of certification:

- Adobe Certified Associate (ACA)
- Adobe Certified Expert (ACE)
- Adobe Certified Instructor (ACI)
- Adobe Authorized Training Center (AATC)

The Adobe Certified Associate (ACA) credential certifies that individuals have the entry-level skills to plan, design, build, and maintain effective communications using different forms of digital media.

The Adobe Certified Expert program is a way for expert users to upgrade their credentials. You can use Adobe certification as a catalyst for getting a raise, finding a job, or promoting your expertise.

If you are an ACE-level instructor, the Adobe Certified Instructor program takes your skills to the next level and gives you access to a wide range of Adobe resources.

Adobe Authorized Training Centers offer instructor-led courses and training on Adobe products, employing only Adobe Certified Instructors. A directory of AATCs is available at http://partners.adobe.com.

For information on the Adobe Certified programs, visit www.adobe.com/support/certification/main.html.

1 OVERVIEW OF THE WORKSPACE

Lesson overview

In this lesson, you'll familiarize yourself with the Adobe Muse program interface and learn how to

- Work with the Welcome screen
- Navigate modes
- Work with panels
- Zoom and pan
- Preview your site

 This lesson takes approximately 30 minutes to complete. Before beginning, make sure you have copied the Lessons folder to your hard drive as described on page 3 of "Getting Started."

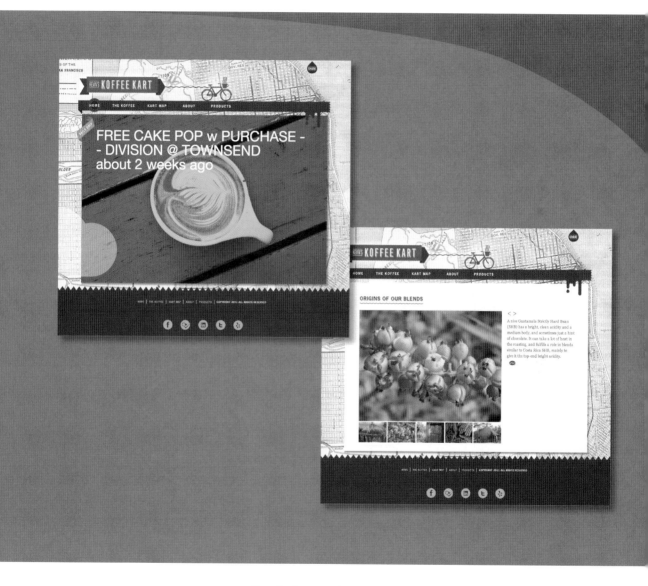

To make the most of Adobe Muse, you need to know how to navigate the workspace. The workspace consists of the menu bar, Toolbox, Control panel, Document window, default panels, and modes.

A typical Muse web workflow

Before you get started with Muse, it's a good idea to understand the typical Muse workflow. In a print design workflow, you use Adobe InDesign as a page layout tool and a combination of Adobe Photoshop and Adobe Illustrator for creating graphics. The same holds true for creating sites in Muse, except that Muse replaces InDesign for the website design and creation process.

As you step into Muse, you will quickly learn that its easy-to-follow workflow is similar to your print design workflow, with just a few adjustments. As with most creative programs, the Muse workflow is flexible and easily adapts to your own work style. The typical Muse workflow from concept to published website is

Note: These workflow steps are a general guide, and may not be the same for every website you create. Your process may be different. As you will learn, the bigger or more complex a site is, the more planning and preparation is typically needed.

1 Create a site concept.

2 Create your Muse site file.

3 Plan your site. Typically, this step includes

   • Editing your site map (adding, organizing pages)

   • Wireframing (determining content positioning)

4 Design your pages.

5 Test your pages.

6 Publish your site.

To get a sense of what you'll be learning in the lessons that follow, take a closer look at each of the workflow steps.

Create a site concept

At the outset of the creation process, you need to determine the purpose of the site. To do so, ask those involved (like the client) such questions as

Tip: For suggestions on the type of questions to ask clients in the initial stages of the website creation process, check out the PDF file named client_questions.pdf in the Lesson01 folder on the companion disc.

• What does your company do?

• Why are you building this site?

• What are our/my deliverables?

• Who are some competitors, and what do you like and dislike about their sites?

Obtaining answers to these questions (and more) in advance can make your creative process more efficient and ensure that you achieve all the site's objectives. For most websites, investing time in some forethought and preplanning will go a long way toward avoiding unnecessary issues later in the process.

With the site scope, function, and goals defined, you can begin to create the site file in Muse.

Create your Muse site file

After coming up with the concept for your site, the first step within Muse is as easy as creating a new document in a program like Adobe InDesign or Illustrator.

To begin, you create a site file, which has the file extension of .muse. The site file is similar to an InDesign file, because it contains the pages as well as master pages for your entire website.

Plan your site

When you open your site in Muse, you enter Plan mode, where you can generate a site map. Your site map shows the number of pages in your site, how the pages will be ordered, and how they connect to each other in the site navigation.

Set up the Site Map

Creating your site map is a critical step in the website creation process, but Muse makes it easy. In Muse, your site map is structured like a flowchart so you can quickly see the relationship between parent pages, which are accessible through the main site navigation, and child pages, which are often available through second-tier menus or other navigation. In Plan mode, you see thumbnails of the pages in your site as well as a master page that you can use to control the consistent elements in your design, like header and footer content. Using simple tools in Plan mode, you can add and remove pages, connect pages to each other, work with master pages, and rearrange pages.

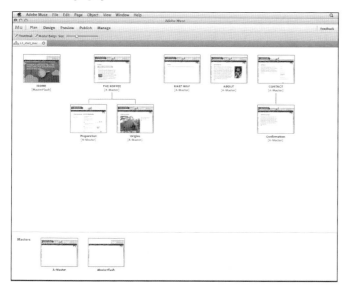

You can organize your site however you feel will benefit the end user the most. Suppose you were building a site for Kevin's Koffee Kart. The parent pages could be the home page, contact page, products page, and so on. The child pages for the products parent page could be the types of products that Kevin's Koffee Kart sells, like coffee, brewers, grinders, and the rest. It always helps to go out on the Web and look around for how companies are organizing pages in their sites. Keep in mind that you can edit your site map later, if your needs change, but it will guide your process and determine the site navigation.

Wireframe your concept (recommended)

With your site map created, your next major step is to create your site design, but don't jump into the designing process just yet. Taking some time now to wireframe your layout may ultimately save you time and make creating your site in a team environment easier.

A wireframe is basically the designer's version of an outline. It shows the site structure, the positioning of such basic elements as the header, footer, sidebar, navigation, and others. The benefit of starting with a wireframe is that it gives everyone involved (including the client) a simple way to envision the site layout, and decide where content should be placed. The actual design, including fonts, colors, and styles, are not visible in a wireframe.

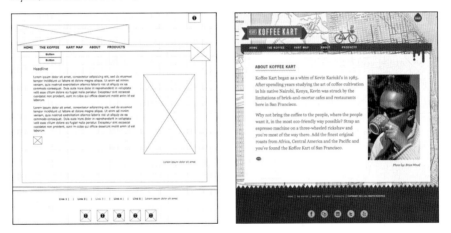

Generally speaking, you should make one wireframe for each unique page or section on a website. You can create them in several ways from simply sketching on paper to using dedicated wireframing software or a program like Adobe Photoshop, Illustrator, or Fireworks. Once your wireframes are created and approved, you can more confidently add flesh to the bones of your site.

Design your pages

After you plan your site, set up a site map and, ideally, wireframe your pages, you can approach the page design from either of two routes. For one, you can start your design in a program like Photoshop or Illustrator, slice up the content, save it in the desired format, .jpg, .gif, or .png, then assemble the pieces in Muse (even pasting them directly from Photoshop).

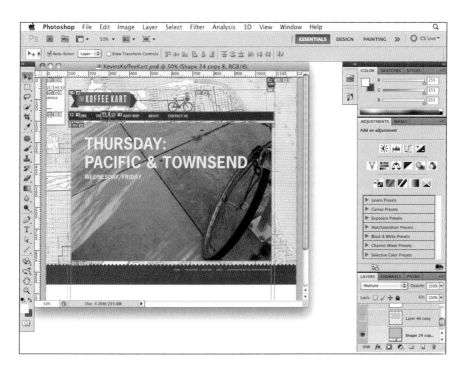

Alternately, you can start the design stage right in Muse like you approach page layout in InDesign. You can then place web-supported images like .gif, .jpg, .png, or .psd (Photoshop) files as you design your pages. You can add text, format that text using familiar formatting options, and even create character and paragraph styles to control the text formatting throughout your site. Muse also supplies lots of prebuilt, but fully customizable, widgets you can drag and drop onto your pages, such as navigation bars, slideshows, lightboxes, and much more that you will learn how to use in the lessons.

Preview your pages

As you design and add content to your pages, you can use Preview mode in Muse to see how your site will look to visitors. In addition, you can test it in various browsers to ensure that your site displays and functions the way you intended.

Publish your site

The last step in the process is publishing your site. When your site is ready, you can share it with the world by either hosting it using Adobe hosting or exporting your site as HTML and hosting it with a different vendor of your choice.

Now that you've seen a general process for creating a Web site in Muse, it's time to explore the Muse workspace.

Touring the Workspace

In this lesson, you will learn the fundamentals of the Muse workspace by touring key features and getting familiar with some commonly used tools.

The Muse workspace shows toolbars and panels that let you view, create, and edit Muse documents. You can also display multiple documents in a single window with tabs for each document.

The workspace is an integrated document layout with panel sets that float on the side (or wherever you drag them on your desktop). Panel groups are initially docked together in default groups, but can be undocked from each other if you want to customize your workspace.

The Welcome screen

● **Note:** If you have not already done so, copy the Lessons resource folder onto your hard disk, on the *Adobe Muse Classroom in a Book* CD. See "Copying the Classroom in a Book files" on page 3.

Before you interact with the workspace, however, you see the Welcome screen, which appears when you first open Muse. You can use the Welcome screen to learn more about Muse and access resources, such as videos, files, and more. The Welcome screen also lets you create a new site file, open a recent site file, or browse to open a site file.

1 Double-click the Adobe Muse icon to start the program. Muse opens and displays the Welcome screen.

> ▶ **Tip:** The Welcome screen appears when no site files are open. If you don't want to see this dialog box when you launch Muse in the future, select Don't Show Again in the lower-left corner of the Welcome screen. To have the Welcome screen appear again when you relaunch the program, choose Edit > Preferences (Windows) or Muse > Preferences (Mac OS) and select Show for the Welcome Screen option.

Understanding Modes

In the upper-left corner of the Muse Application window, notice the links for three main modes: Plan, Design, and Preview. When you select a mode, Muse displays it in the Document window. Each of these modes represents a step in the website creation process, as the section "A typical Muse web workflow" explained.

Next, you will open an existing site and explore the Muse workspace. You will use the L1_start.muse file that corresponds to your operating system to practice navigating, zooming, and previewing a Muse document and work area.

1   Choose File > Open Site, and open the L1_start_mac.muse (Mac OS) or L1_start_win.muse (Windows) file in the Lesson01 folder, located in the Lessons folder on your hard disk.

When you open a .muse site file, Muse displays Plan mode by default. You can tell that Plan mode is showing because the word "Plan" is highlighted in blue in the upper-left corner of the Application window.

Plan mode displays your *site map* (also called a site plan), which shows the pages in your site and how they are connected to each other. It also displays your *master pages*, which serve as templates for the pages of your site. Plan mode also has options that enable you to remove thumbnail previews, the master badge indicator, and resize thumbnails. You will explore Plan mode and its options further in Lesson 2 when you create your own site file.

Note: To see the final site that you will create in these lessons, open the KoffeeKart_end_win.muse (Windows) or KoffeeKart_end_mac.muse (Mac OS) site file in the Lessons folder.

Note: The thumbnails you see in Plan mode may be different than what is shown in the figure. That's okay.

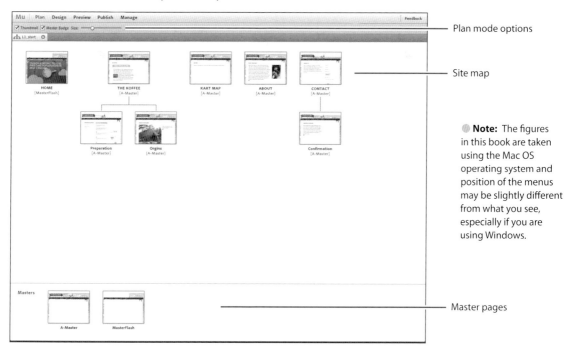

Plan mode options

Site map

Note: The figures in this book are taken using the Mac OS operating system and position of the menus may be slightly different from what you see, especially if you are using Windows.

Master pages

Tip: You can also enter Design mode by pressing Ctrl+I (Windows) or Command+I (Mac OS).

2 Click the Design mode link in the upper-left corner of the Application window.

When you click the Design mode link, the first page of the website opens, and appears in a separate tab at the top left of the Document window. In this case, the tab for the page shows HOME. That is the name and the title of the page, which you will learn more about in later lessons. Design mode is where you create the layout for each page of your site by adding text, images, links, and more.

Notice that more options, tools, and panels now appear as well. Take a moment to familiarize yourself with the names of these workspace components.

Menus ⎯
Links to modes and publishing options ⎯
Control panel ⎯
Document tabs ⎯

Toolbox

Panels

Document window ⎯

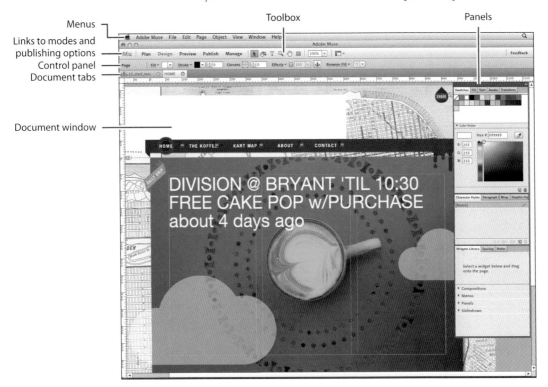

Tip: You can also enter Plan mode by choosing View > Plan Mode or by pressing Ctrl+M (Windows) or Command+M (Mac OS).

3 Click the Plan mode link in the upper-left corner of the Application window to return to Plan mode. Notice that the page called HOME is still open as a tab at the top of the Document window.

Similar to Adobe InDesign, where you need the InDesign file open to edit the pages in it, you must always have the .muse site file open in order to edit pages of the site in Design mode. If you find yourself needing to work on more than one site at a time, you can also open multiple .muse site files and the pages of those sites.

4 Click the HOME page tab to return to Design mode and see the page in the Document window.

5 Click the Preview mode link in the upper-left corner of the Application window. The active page (HOME) opens in Preview mode.

Note: If a font warning dialog box appears, click OK.

The final mode, Preview, shows you what your page looks like in a browser. In Preview mode, you can essentially browse your site like your visitors will, including clicking and testing links, as well as viewing such interactive content as slideshows.

6 Click around on the page, and notice that the interactive content, like the animated logo at the top of the page and the image slideshow in the main area of the page, is working.

7 Choose View > Design Mode.

Next, you will further explore the components of Design mode.

Working in Design mode

In Design mode, you see the Toolbox, Control panel, and panel groups that float independently in the Application window. All of these features make up the Muse workspace. As with other Adobe applications, you can customize the workspace in Muse by manipulating some of the panels. That's what you'll do next.

The Toolbox

In Design mode, the Muse Toolbox appears above the Control panel, and contains selection, cropping, type, viewing, and drawing tools. It's an abbreviated version of the toolboxes from other Adobe Creative Suite components, such as InDesign CS6 and Photoshop CS6. As you work through the lessons, you'll learn more about the functions of each tool, which are

A **Selection tool**: Selects objects on a web page

B **Crop tool**: Crops images that you insert into your pages

C **Text tool**: Creates a text area so that you can place text on a page

D **Zoom tool**: Zooms in on or out from the page

E **Hand tool**: Pans around a page by dragging

F **Rectangle tool**: Creates rectangle shapes that can be used as design elements

By default, the Toolbox appears as a single horizontal row of tools and cannot be edited or moved. As in other Adobe applications, you can select a tool from the Toolbox by clicking it or pressing a keyboard shortcut.

1 Position the pointer over the Zoom tool ( ) in the Toolbox. Notice that Muse displays the tool's name and keyboard shortcut. Click to select the Zoom tool. Every tool in the Toolbox has a keyboard shortcut associated with it.

2 Press the V key to select the Selection tool.

The keyboard shortcuts in Muse, like those in Adobe InDesign CS6 and Adobe Photoshop CS6, are spring-loaded tool shortcuts. This means that you can hold down a tool's shortcut key to switch to that tool temporarily. When you are finished using the tool, you can simply release the shortcut key to return to the previously selected tool.

3 With the Selection tool selected, press and hold the H key. Notice that the pointer in the Document window changes to a Hand tool ( ). Without releasing the H key, click and drag the page up or down.

4 Release the H key to return to the Selection tool once again.

Spring-loaded tool shortcuts can help you work faster, saving you time that adds up over the life of a project.

The Control panel

The Control panel offers quick access to options and commands related to the current page item or objects you select. By default, Muse displays the Control panel horizontally across the top of the Document window; you cannot edit or move it. You can, however, open and close it by choosing Window > Control, if necessary. In the Window menu, a check mark to the left of the word "Control" indicates that the Control panel is open in the workspace.

Options displayed in the Control panel vary depending on the type of object you select. As you progress through each lesson, you will also notice that some of the options displayed in the Control panel are also found within other panels in Muse.

When you first open a page, with nothing selected, you see the word "Page" on the left end of the Control panel. This is called the Selection Indicator. When you select content on the page, the currently selected object is named here. For example, Page indicates that the options currently showing in the Control panel will affect the large, white page box in the Document window (you will learn more about the page area in a later lesson).

1   With the Selection tool still selected, click to select the Daily Drip image in the upper-left portion of the page.

On the left end of the Control panel, you now see the words "Image Frame" to indicate that you selected an image frame on the page. Notice also that the options in the Control panel have changed. Any changes you make in the Control panel will affect the selected image.

► **Tip:** As the options in the Control panel change, you can get more information about each option by hovering over an icon or option label with the pointer to view its tool tip.

2   Choose Edit > Deselect All to deselect the image.

Throughout the lessons in this book, you will be using the Control panel to format content on your pages and learn more about those options.

Working with panels

Panels, which are listed in the Window menu, give you quick access to many tools that make modifying content easier.

Panels live in the panel dock on the right side of the workspace. The panel dock is a collection of Muse panels displayed together in a vertical orientation. Within the panel dock, there are three main groups of panels. You can see the division between the groups as darker gray lines. Muse lets you collapse, open, and close panels, as well as move them around between groups within the panel dock to make more important panels easier to see or access.

Next, you will experiment with moving, hiding, opening, and closing panels in the panel dock.

1   Click the Fill panel tab on the right side of the workspace to open the panel, if it's not yet open, or choose Window > Fill.

2 Click the Swatches panel tab to display the Swatches panel.

Notice that the Swatches panel appears with four other panels—the Fill panel, Text panel, the Assets panel, and the Transform panel. These five panels are all part of the same panel group.

3 Drag the panel dock to the left by clicking and holding down on the dark gray panel dock bar at the top, making sure to avoid the double arrow on the right side of the panel dock bar when you click. (Clicking the double arrow will collapse the panel dock to icons.)

4 Drag the panel dock back to the right side of the workspace.

5 Click the Text panel tab to view the Text panel.

6 Click the Text panel tab again, and notice that the panel height decreases.

▶ **Tip:** A quick way to open a collapsed panel is to choose Window > Open All. You can also close all panels simultaneously by choosing Window > Close All. When you choose Close All, the panel dock minimizes to a single dark gray bar in the workspace.

7 Click the Text panel tab once more to reveal the contents of the Text panel.

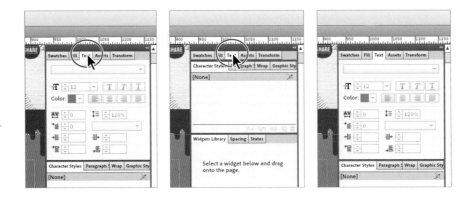

You can also rearrange the order in which the panels appear in a group. That's what you'll do next.

8 Click the Swatches panel tab to show the panel. Click and drag the Swatches panel tab to the right of the Transform panel.

9 Drag the Swatches panel back to the left of the Fill panel.

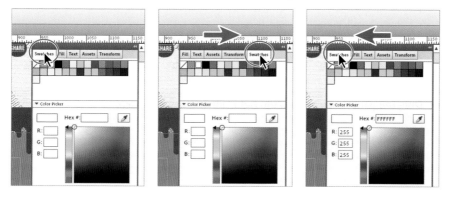

Next, you will change the height of a panel group, making it easier to see more of the panel contents.

10 With the Swatches panel showing, drag down the dark gray dividing line between the Swatches panel group and the Character Styles panel group to resize the group. Drag the dividing line back up.

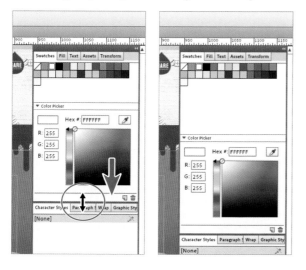

● **Note:** You may not be able to drag the divider very far, depending on your screen size, screen resolution, and the panel showing.

Next, you will drag a panel from one group to another in the docked panels. This can help you organize like panels with each other.

Note: The position of the mouse (rather than the position of the panel), activates the drop zone, so if you can't see the drop zone, ensure that the mouse is positioned over the place where you want to move the panel.

11 Click and drag the Transform panel by the panel tab into the panel group below that contains the Character Styles and Paragraph Styles panels. Release the mouse button when the pointer is within the bounds of the panel group and when you see a blue outline around the entire panel group.

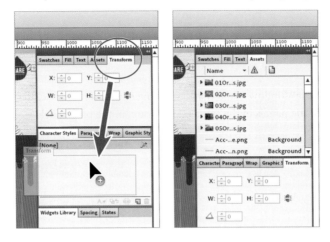

As you move panels, you will see blue highlighted drop zones, which are areas where you can move the panel. When moving panels you can also create new panel groups.

12 Drag the Transform panel by its tab back into the Swatches panel group.

13 Click and drag the States panel by the panel tab up to the dark gray bar between the panel group that contains the Swatches panel and the panel group below it. Release the mouse button when you see a blue line between the panel groups, which indicates the drop zone.

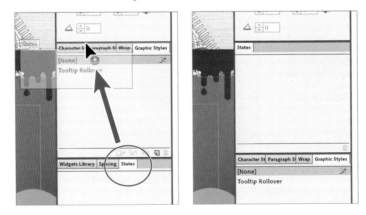

The States panel is now docked in its own group above the Character Styles panel group. Creating lots of panel groups, however, can also clutter your workspace. One solution is to close unneeded panels.

14 Click and drag the States panel by the panel tab down into the panel group that contains the Widgets Library.

15 Choose the Window menu, and you will see a listing of all of the available panels. The panels with a check mark to the left of their name are already open in the workspace.

16 Make sure that the Swatches panel is selected in the panel dock on the right side of the workspace and that its contents are showing. Choose Window > Swatches.

Selecting a panel in the Window menu that is showing in the workspace closes that panel, and all of the panels in the same panel group, in the panel dock.

17 Choose Window > Swatches to reopen the Swatches panel and all the other panels in that same panel group.

18 Choose Window > Character Styles.

When you choose a panel in the Window menu that isn't currently showing in the panel dock, that panel's contents are revealed in the panel dock.

19 Click the double arrow in the upper-right corner of the dock (in the dark gray bar) to collapse the panels to icons.

Much like in other Adobe applications, collapsing the panel dock to icons reduces clutter in your Muse workspace.

▶ **Tip:** When the panel dock is collapsed to icons, you can reposition it by dragging it by the dark gray dock bar at the top of the dock.

20 Click the double arrow at the top again or any of the panel icons in the dock to expand the entire panel dock again.

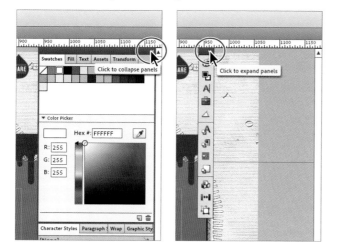

21 Click the Widgets Library panel tab to show the panel.

● **Note:** By default, *all* of the available panels in Muse are in the workspace already. If there is no check mark next to the panel name in the Window menu, it is in the panel dock and not currently showing (the Control panel is the only exception).

▶ **Tip:** If you want to close a panel in a group, you can drag that panel by the tab to the dark gray bar between any two panel groups to create another panel group in the dock. Then you can choose that panel name from the Window menu and it will only close that panel.

▶ **Tip:** To hide all the of the panels in the dock, you can choose Window > Hide Panels. To show them again, choose Window > Show Panels.

Zooming and panning

When you're working in pages in a site, you'll often need to change the magnification level and navigate between pages. To the right of the Toolbox, the zoom view menu displays the magnification level, which can range from 10% to 4000%. Using any of the viewing tools and commands affects only the display of the page, not the actual size of the page and contents.

▶ **Tip:** Zoom in using the keyboard shortcut Ctrl+= (Windows) or Command+= (Mac OS).

1   Choose View > Zoom In to enlarge the display of the page.

2   Choose View > Zoom Out to reduce the view of the page.

▶ **Tip:** Zoom out using the keyboard shortcut Ctrl+– (Windows) or Command+–(Mac OS).

Each time you choose a Zoom option, the view of the page is resized to the closest preset zoom level. The preset zoom levels appear in the zoom view drop-down menu to the right of the Toolbox, identified by a down arrow next to a percentage.

3   Choose 200% from the zoom view menu.

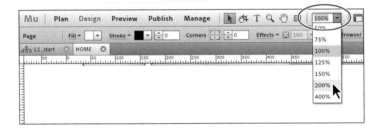

4   Select the 200% in the zoom view menu field and type **20**. Press Enter or Return.

You can type values in the zoom view menu that range from 10% to 4000%. Also, notice that you do not need to type the %.

▶ **Tip:** You can also use the keyboard shortcuts Ctrl+0 (Windows) or Command+0 (Mac OS) to fit the page in the Document window.

5   Choose View > Fit Page In Window to display a reduced view of the page in the Document window.

The View menu is a quick route to fitting a page to your screen or viewing the page at actual size.

6 Choose View > Actual Size to display the page at actual size.

The page displays at 100%, which is the most accurate reflection of what your site will look like to visitors. The actual size of your page determines how much of it you can see onscreen at 100%.

> **Tip:** You can also use the keyboard shortcuts Ctrl+1 (Windows) or Command+1 (Mac OS) to view the page at actual size (100%).

7 Choose View > Fit Page In Window before continuing to the next section.

Using the Zoom tool

In addition to the View options, you can use the Zoom tool to magnify and reduce the view of your pages. The Zoom tool allows you to zoom into and out of specific areas of your pages.

1 Click the Zoom tool (🔍) in the Toolbox to select the tool, and then move the pointer into the Document window. Notice that a plus sign (+) appears at the center of the Zoom tool pointer.

2 Position the Zoom tool over the Daily Drip banner on the left side of the Home page and click once. The artwork displays at a higher magnification.

3 Click two more times on the Daily Drip banner to increase the view again.

Notice that the specific area you clicked is magnified. You can reduce the view of the page in a similar manner.

4 With the Zoom tool still selected, position the pointer over the Daily Drip banner and hold down Alt (Windows) or Option (Mac OS). A minus sign (−) appears at the center of the Zoom tool pointer (🔍).

5 With the Alt or Option key still pressed, click the artwork twice to reduce the view of the artwork.

For a more controlled zoom, you can drag a marquee around a specific area of your artwork. This magnifies only the selected area. You'll try that next.

6 Choose View > Fit Page In Window.

7 With the Zoom tool still selected, click and drag across the Daily Drip banner. When you see the aqua box, called a *marquee*, around the area you are dragging, release the mouse button. The marqueed area is now enlarged to fit the Document window.

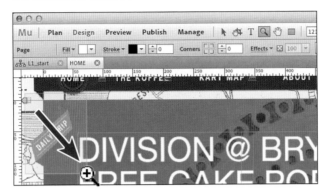

8 Choose View > Fit Page In Window.

The Zoom tool is used frequently during the editing process to enlarge and reduce the view of the page. Because of this, Muse allows you to select it using the keyboard at any time without first deselecting any other tool you may be using.

9 Before selecting the Zoom tool using the keyboard, select any other tool in the Toolbox and move the pointer into the Document window.

10 Now hold down Control+spacebar (Windows) or Command+spacebar (Mac OS) to use the Zoom tool. Click or drag to zoom in on any area of the artwork, and then release the keys.

11 To zoom out using the keyboard, hold down Control+Alt+spacebar (Windows) or Command+Option+spacebar (Mac OS). Click the desired area to reduce the view of the page, and then release the keys.

12 Choose View > Fit Page In Window.

Note: In certain versions of Mac OS, the keyboard shortcuts for the Zoom tool open Spotlight in the Finder. If you decide to use these shortcuts in Muse, you may want to turn off or change those keyboard shortcuts in the Mac OS System Preferences.

Scrolling through a document

In Muse, much like other Adobe applications, you can use the Hand tool to pan to different areas of a document. Using the Hand tool allows you to push the page around much like you would a piece of paper on your desk.

1 Select the Hand tool (🖑) in the Toolbox.

2 Drag down in the Document window. As you drag, the page moves with the hand.

3 Click any other tool except the Text tool (T) in the Toolbox and move the pointer into the Document window.

4 Hold down the spacebar to select the Hand tool from the keyboard, and then drag up to bring the page back into the center of your view.

As with the Zoom tool ($\mathbb{Q}$), you can select the Hand tool with a keyboard shortcut without first deselecting the active tool.

⬤ **Note:** The spacebar shortcut for the Hand tool does not work when the Text tool is active and your cursor is in text. To access the Hand tool while the Text tool is selected, press Alt (Windows) or Option (Mac OS).

Preview mode

As you create your designs in Muse, you can use Preview mode to see what your page will look like in a browser (without guides), test your links, view video and widget content, and more. As you will learn in later lessons, you can also preview a page or your entire site in a browser on your hard drive.

Why do we preview our websites?

Unlike the print world, where you output to a single printing device, on the Web there are many different browsers, and multiple versions of each browser—not to mention different platforms like Mac OS and Windows. Typically, you'll want to test your websites in all of these different environments.

You can preview your site in Muse by clicking the Preview link in the upper-left corner of the Application window. Preview uses WebKit as a rendering engine—the same engine that powers the Apple Safari browser and a host of other applications such as Google Chrome and Adobe AIR.

The code that Muse generates is automatically cross-browser compatible. This lets you focus on your design and use Preview as a way to test your links and other content by browsing through it the way site visitors would.

As of the writing of this book, the Muse team tests and optimizes output for the following browsers:

- Firefox 11 for Mac OS and Windows
- Internet Explorer 7, 8, and 9 for Windows
- Safari 5 for Mac
- Chrome for Mac OS and Windows

1   With the HOME page showing in Design mode, click the Preview link in the upper-left corner of the Application window.

Notice that any animations, such as .SWF content, links, slideshows, videos, and others are fully active in the preview.

▶ **Tip:** You can also preview a page by pressing Ctrl+P (Windows) or Command+P (Mac OS).

2   Click the KART MAP link in the navbar at the top of the page. Notice that the KART MAP page appears. Preview lets you test links between pages and navigate the site as you would in a browser.

Note: You cannot make edits to your pages while previewing them. You must return to Design mode to continue editing.

3   Click the Design mode link in the upper-left corner of the Application window to return to Design mode.

No matter which page is showing in Preview, when you return to Design mode, the same pages that were open remain open.

4   Choose File > Close Site to close the .muse site file and any open pages associated with that site without saving changes.

Review questions

1　How do you select tools in Muse?

2　Name the modes and briefly describe each.

3　Describe two ways to change the view of a document.

4　Name two things that the Welcome screen allows you to do.

5　Which menu command allows you to hide all panels temporarily?

Review answers

1　To select a tool, you can either click the tool in the Toolbox or press the keyboard shortcut for that tool. For example, you can press V to select the Selection tool.

2　The three modes in Muse are Plan, Design, and Preview. Plan mode is used to edit your site map by adding and organizing pages and working with master pages. Design mode is used to edit your pages, and Preview mode is used to test your site.

3　You can choose commands from the View menu to zoom in or out of a document, or fit it to your Document window; you can also use the Zoom tool in the Toolbox, and click or drag over a document to enlarge or reduce the view. In addition, you can use keyboard shortcuts to magnify or reduce the display of artwork. You can also use the zoom view menu to change the magnification of the page within the Document window.

4　The Welcome screen allows you to create a new site, open a recent or existing site file, learn more about the program, and get news about program features.

5　By choosing Window > Hide Panels, you can temporarily hide the panel dock. To show the panel dock when hidden, choose Window > Show Panels.

2 CREATING YOUR SITE

Lesson overview

In this lesson, you'll take the first steps in creating your website and learn how to

- Create a new site

- Edit site properties

- Work in Plan mode

- Add, edit, and organize pages

- Set page specific properties

- Add metadata

 This lesson takes approximately 45 minutes to complete. Before beginning, make sure you have copied the Lessons folder to your hard drive as described on page 3 of "Getting Started." If you are starting from scratch in this lesson, use the method described in the "Jumpstart" section on page 5.

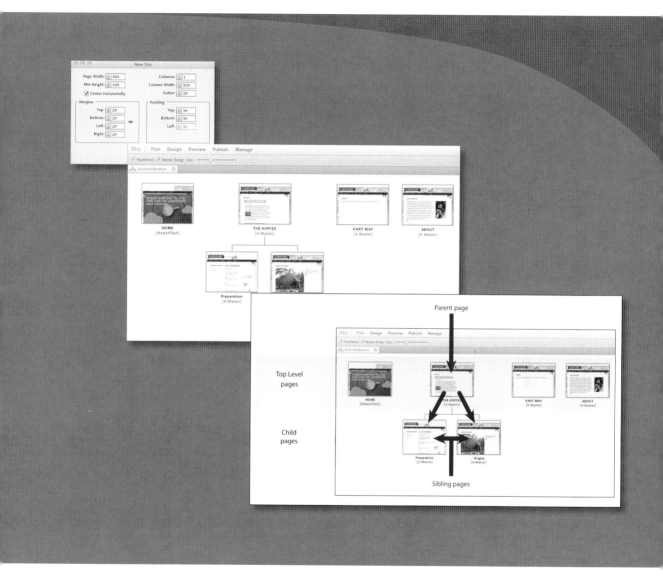

After creating your site file in Muse, you will take advantage of Plan mode to quickly and visually add, delete, and organize pages in your site as well as add information about your pages, called metadata, for search engines to use.

Note: If you have not already done so, copy the Lessons folder onto your hard disk, from the *Adobe Muse Classroom in a Book* CD. See "Copying the Classroom in a Book files" on page 2.

Creating a new site

In this lesson, you will learn the fundamentals of creating a Muse site, adding and organizing pages in Plan mode, and adding metadata to your pages.

Note: To see the final site that you will create in these lessons, open the KoffeeKart_end_win.muse (Windows) or KoffeeKart_end_mac.muse (Mac OS) site file in the Lessons folder.

When you begin to work in Muse, you first create a site file with the extension .muse. That site file contains all of the pages, master pages, colors, styles, and more that you will use in your website. Muse provides an environment where you can easily plan, design, and organize all of your web documents.

You need to create a Muse site before you can begin creating pages that belong to that site, and that's what you'll do first.

1   Launch Adobe Muse. When the Welcome screen appears, click Site in the Create New section. Alternately, you can close the Welcome screen and choose File > New Site.

The New Site dialog box appears. Here you will set page dimensions, margins, columns, and other page properties that you can edit later if necessary.

Note: Going forward, the units you will use in Muse will be in pixels, unless otherwise indicated.

2   In the New Site dialog box, set the following options:

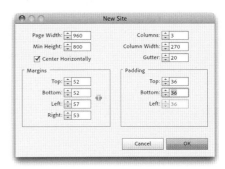

- Page Width: **960**

- Min Height: **800**

- Center Horizontally: **Selected** (default setting)

- Make All Margin Settings The Same: **Deselected** (⬚)

- Top and Bottom Margins: **52**

- Left Margin: **57**

- Right Margin: **53**

- Top and Bottom Padding: **36**

Set these last:

- Columns: **3**

Tip: To learn more about the New Site dialog box settings, see the "Site_settings.pdf" file in the Lesson02 folder.

- Column Width: **270** (default setting)

- Gutter: **20** (default setting)

Notice that you cannot edit the Left padding value (it is dimmed). That is because the page is set to center horizontally in the browser window.

3 Click OK.

Muse opens the new site you created in Plan mode.

4 Choose File > Save Site As. In the Save Adobe Muse File As dialog box, navigate to and open the Lessons folder. Type **KevinsKoffeeKart.muse** in the Save As text field, and click Save.

● **Note:** Muse allows you to save as only one file type (.muse) as of the writing of this book.

Edit the site properties

You don't always get it right the first time, and you easily can edit the options you originally set for your site as well as add some new ones at any point later on.

1 With the KevinsKoffeeKart.muse site file still open, choose File > Site Properties.

The Site Properties dialog box opens, displaying the layout settings you specified when you created the site. You can change their values at any time from this dialog, as well as specify other optional properties by clicking the Hyperlinks button (more on that in step 4) or the Favicon Image setting. A *favicon* is a small image in the .ico format that displays to the left of your site's address in a browser's Address bar and the site's name in history and bookmark lists. Although it doesn't affect your site's functioning, a favicon image can give visitors a visual cue that it is your site.

2 Click the folder icon to the right of Favicon Image in the Site Properties dialog box to browse for an image to use as your site favicon. As you consider potential images, keep in mind that favicons must be square.

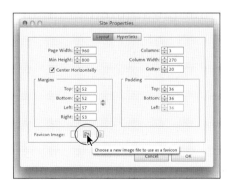

▶ **Tip:** If you want to make your own favicon in a program like Adobe Illustrator or Adobe Photoshop, make a new document that is 32 pixels by 32 pixels with a resolution of 72 ppi (pixels per inch). Add your content, and save it as a .jpg, .gif, or .png file.

3 Navigate to the images folder in the Lessons folder, choose favicon.png, and click Select.

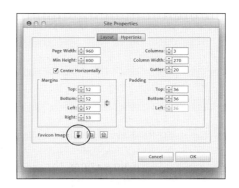

A small, red coffee cup icon appears to the right of the Favicon Image to indicate the new setting. When the site is published, Muse converts the image to the .ico format that most browsers use as the favicon image type.

● **Note:** If you want to remove the favicon, you can click the Delete Current Favicon button.

4 Click the Hyperlinks option at the top of the Site Properties dialog box.

When you create text links to other pages, sites, and so on, Muse allows you to create multiple styles for the various states of those links. You can set and adjust the colors and other formatting options for those styles here. You will create hyperlink styles in Lesson 7, "Working with Links and Buttons."

5 Click OK to close the Site Properties dialog box.

6 Choose File > Save Site.

● **Note:** To see the favicon in the address bar of a web browser, you must preview the page in a browser on your machine, rather than preview the page by clicking the Preview link above the Control panel in Muse.

7 Choose File > Preview Page In Browser to open the page in the default browser installed on your machine, such as Internet Explorer (Windows) or Safari (Mac OS). Notice the favicon that appears next to the Address bar in the browser.

8 Close the browser and return to Muse.

Now you will begin to explore Plan mode and the site map by adding and organizing pages in your site.

Creating and editing your site map

The best way to begin working on your site is by editing your site map. Refining a site map is a critical first step because the map shows the number of pages in your site, how the pages will be ordered, and how they connect to each other in the site navigation. In the exercises that follow, you will edit your site map in Plan mode.

With the KevinsKoffeeKart.muse site file open, make sure Plan mode is selected in the upper-left corner of the Application window. As you can see, Plan mode is divided into two main sections: the site plan area and the masters area. The site plan area contains thumbnail images of your website's pages organized into a site map that shows how those pages relate to each other. Below each page thumbnail are the page's name and, in blue brackets, the name of the master page associated with that page. The masters section, below the site plan area, contains the default master page that every Muse site starts with. A master page is essentially a template that you use to maintain consistency across the pages in your website. You will learn more about master pages in Lesson 3, "Working with Master Pages."

▶ **Tip:** Muse gives you lots of flexibility when creating your website. You can add blank pages to your site map and then apply masters to them later, or you can create your website by starting with the master, applying it to a single page (the Home page), and then creating new pages based on that.

Site plan (contains the site map)

Masters

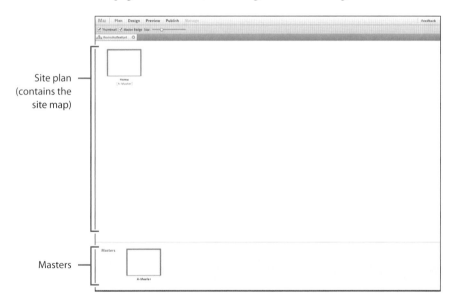

When you create a new site, Muse creates one blank home page and one blank master page by default. These pages are the starting point for your site map and website itself. The next step is to begin adding pages to your site and determine how users will navigate your site.

Adding and deleting pages in your site

In a Muse site, the web pages you create in your site map follow a basic family hierarchy and are displayed in levels that reinforce their relationships. Sibling pages appear on the same level in the site plan. Child pages appear a level below and are usually linked from a particular Parent page. Parent and sibling pages may appear on the Home-page level or another level of the site map, while child pages reside below the Home-page level. Any page on any level of the site plan can have sibling pages or child pages.

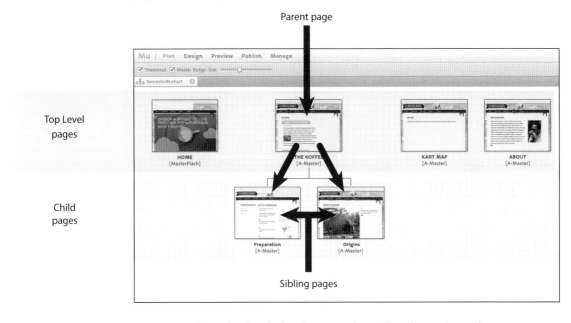

Note: For more information on sibling and child pages, see the "Set up the Site Map" section in Lesson 1 on page 11.

The site map's top level includes the pages that will make up the site's main navigation. For example, the page named Home is always a top-level page. Any pages that you create to the right or left of the Home page are considered siblings to Home and are also in the top level of the site navigation. The next figure illustrates how a Muse site map later translates into a navigation menu for the site.

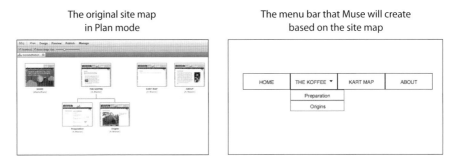

The original site map
in Plan mode

The menu bar that Muse will create
based on the site map

Adding sibling pages

You'll learn more about the relationship between the site map and menus in Lesson 3, "Working with Master Pages." For now simply concentrate on adding top-level pages to your site.

1 Position the cursor over the Home page thumbnail in the site plan area.

   Notice a series of plus signs (+) appear on the right, bottom, and left sides of the thumbnail. Clicking the plus sign to the right or left of a page thumbnail adds a sibling page. Clicking the plus sign beneath the page thumbnail adds a child page.

2 Click the plus sign (+) to the right of the Home page thumbnail to add a new sibling page to the right of the Home page.

   After inserting a page, you can immediately change the title of the page.

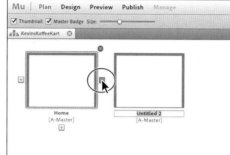

▶ **Tip:** You can also choose Page > Add New Top Level Page to add a new page to the top level of the site map. Don't forget, a top-level page is any page that appears to the right or left of the Home thumbnail in the site map.

3 Select the text "Untitled 2" beneath the new thumbnail to rename the page, and type **THE KOFFEE** in all capital letters.

   When the site is published, by default Muse uses the name that appears beneath each site map thumbnail as the page's title at the top of the browser window. Muse also automatically fills these names into the navigation menu you create to access the pages. You'll learn more about menus in Lesson 3, "Working with Master Pages."

● **Note:** If you cannot select the text "Untitled 2" beneath the page thumbnail, try slowly clicking the text twice. You can also right-click (Windows) or Control-click (Mac OS) the page thumbnail and choose Rename Page from the resulting context menu to select the text.

4 Choose File > Preview Page In Browser to open the home page in the default browser installed on your machine.

   Notice that Muse used the thumbnail's name, Home, as the title of the page at the top of the browser window. You'll learn how to specify more descriptive titles for pages in "Adding page metadata" on page 42.

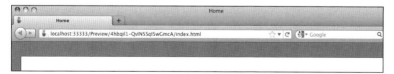

5 Close the browser window, and return to Muse.

6 Position the cursor over the thumbnail labeled THE KOFFEE, then click the plus sign (+) to its right to add a new sibling page to the right of the THE KOFFEE page.

Tip: Another way to add another sibling page is to right-click (Windows) or Ctrl-click (Mac OS) a page thumbnail and choose New Sibling Page from the context menu. This command adds a new sibling page to the right of the active page thumbnail.

7   Change the name of the page to ABOUT using the technique from step 3.

8   Position the cursor over the THE KOFFEE thumbnail, then click the plus sign (+) to the right

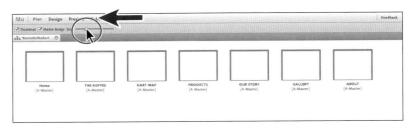

four more times. You now have a total of seven pages, including the Home, THE KOFFEE, and ABOUT pages.

9   Beneath each of the new page thumbnails, click twice slowly to edit the title of each page. Starting from the left, name them KART MAP, PRODUCTS, OUR STORY, and GALLERY, respectively.

The page thumbnails may not fit in the visible site plan area. If they don't, a horizontal scroll bar will appear at the bottom of the site plan area, above the masters area.

10 In the upper-left corner of the Application window, drag the Size slider to the left to resize the page thumbnails until they all fit horizontally in the site plan area and the scroll bar disappears.

Adding child pages

With top-level pages created, you turn them into parent pages by adding child pages to your site map, if necessary. Child pages are typically lower-level pages that are accessible on a web page via a pop-up menu that appears when you position the pointer over the top-level navigation. You can add child pages to help further organize the pages in your site.

Once published, the KevinsKoffeeKart site will showcase several products. Each product will have its own page, all of which will be child pages to the PRODUCTS page.

1   Position the pointer over the PRODUCTS page thumbnail, and click the plus sign (+) that appears beneath it.

2   Select the default name of the new child page, and type **Grinders**.

Notice that a line now connects the PRODUCTS (parent) and Grinders (child) pages, indicating their relationship.

3   Position the pointer over the Grinders page thumbnail, and then click the plus sign (+) to the right two more times to add two sibling pages to the right of the Grinders page.

4   Slowly double-click the text "Untitled 10" to select it (if not already selected) and enter **Coffee** for the page's new name. Your page name may be different from "Untitled 10." Just make sure it's the middle child page beneath the PRODUCTS page.

▶ **Tip:** Another way to add a child page is to right-click (Windows) or Ctrl-click (Mac OS) a page thumbnail and choose New Child Page from the context menu. This command adds a new child page beneath the active page thumbnail.

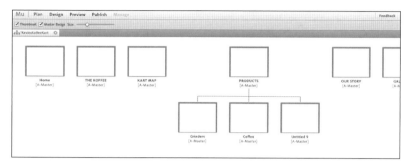

Notice that the three new pages—Grinders, Coffee, and Untitled 9—are now sibling pages of each other and are also child pages of the parent page PRODUCTS. (If the addition of the child pages made the page thumbnails spread out too much to be seen, drag the Size slider to the left until all the page thumbnails fit in the visible the site plan area.)

5   Position the pointer over the Untitled 9 page thumbnail (the third page from the left in the child pages). Notice the delete button (x) that appears off the upper-right corner of the thumbnail. Just as you can add pages to your site map with a click, you can delete them as easily.

6   Click the delete button to remove the page from the site map.

▶ **Tip:** Another way to delete a page is to right-click (Windows) or Ctrl-click (Mac OS) a page thumbnail and choose Delete Page from the context menu.

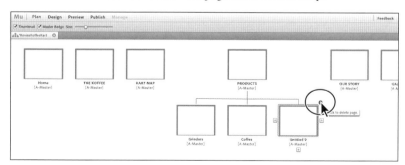

As you add and delete pages to create your site map, know that you don't have to have the site map finalized before you begin adding content to existing pages. You can always add, delete, and rearrange pages later.

● **Note:** When you delete a parent page, such as PRODUCTS, Muse does not delete the children of the page, but instead raises them to the level of the former parent page.

Arranging pages in the site map

A well-organized site map will help you immensely when you begin to insert a menu system into your pages. Rearranging the pages in your site map in Plan mode is easy.

1   Drag the Size slider to the left until all the page thumbnails fit in the visible the site plan area, if necessary.

2   Click and drag the ABOUT page thumbnail to the right of the KART MAP page. When you see a blue drop zone between the pages, release the mouse.

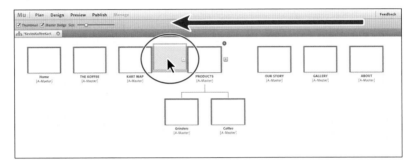

The ABOUT page thumbnail now resides to the right of the KART MAP page thumbnail in the site map. As you drag pages in the site map, you can also easily drag and duplicate them.

3   Press and hold the Alt (Window) or Option (Mac OS) key and drag the ABOUT page thumbnail to the right until you see a blue drop zone between the pages. Release the mouse button and then the key. You just created a page copy.

4   Position the pointer over the ABOUT copy page thumbnail and click the delete button to remove the page from the site map.

5   Click and drag the Coffee child page thumbnail to the left until it is directly on top of the Grinders page thumbnail. When a blue drop zone appears beneath the Grinders thumbnail, release the mouse button.

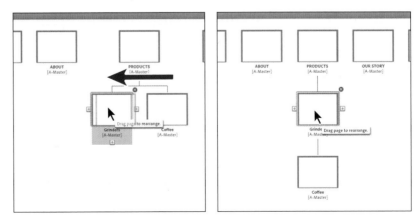

Rearranging child pages is as simple as dragging: The Coffee page is now a child of the Grinders page.

6 Choose Edit > Undo Rearrange Page to put the child pages back in the previous order.

7 Drag the Coffee page thumbnail to the left of the Grinders page thumbnail, directly over the plus sign (+). When you see the small blue drop zone to the left of Grinders, release the mouse button to relocate Coffee.

Note: Instead of choosing to undo the previous operation, you could have instead dragged the Coffee thumbnail back to the right of the Grinders thumbnail and released the mouse button when the blue drop zone appeared.

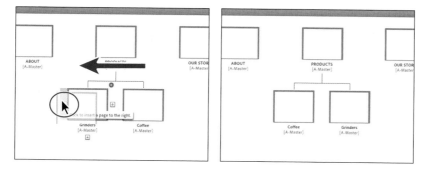

8 Position the pointer over the PRODUCTS page thumbnail, then drag it between the KART MAP and ABOUT pages. When the blue drop zone appears between the thumbnails, release the mouse button.

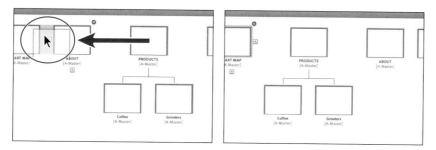

Notice the Coffee and Grinders pages moved as well. Relocating a parent page moves all of its child pages at the same time.

9 Choose File > Save Site.

Setting page properties

When you created your site and edited the site properties, you set default properties for every page in your site. In addition to editing those properties for the entire site, you can also edit them on a page-by-page basis, which is what you'll do in this exercise.

1   In Plan mode, position the pointer over the Home page thumbnail and double-click to open that page in Design mode.

2   Choose Page > Page Properties.

In the Page Properties dialog box that opens, you will see the same familiar options. This time, however, any changes you make will affect the Home page only. Any options you change also will override the default properties set when you first created the site or edited later by choosing File > Site Properties.

Tip: Another way to access the page properties without opening the page in Design mode is to right-click (Windows) or Control-click (Mac OS) the Home thumbnail in Plan mode and choose Page Properties from the context menu.

3   Change the columns to **1**. The column guides disappear; only the margin guides around the inside edge of the page edge remain. Leave the dialog box open for the next section.

Tip: To learn more about using the columns and guides to your advantage when designing, see the "Grid_design.pdf" file in the Lesson02 folder.

Adding page metadata

In addition to setting standard page properties in the Page Properties dialog box, you can also add metadata to each of your pages. Consisting of key information about your site, metadata is a great way for you to provide search engines, such as Google and Bing, with a summary of your page.

Adding metadata is also a first step on the long road of search engine optimization, (SEO), the process of trying to improve the visibility of a website in search engines in unpaid search results. The goal is to get ranked higher by search engines, meaning search engines perceive your site as more relevant to the search terms someone enters and place it higher in their returned lists of results.

In Muse, you can add three types of metadata to describe the page content to a search engine:

- The **title** appears at the top of the browser window when you preview a page or visit it on the Web. For instance, when you visit adobe.com, you can see the title of the page at the top of the browser window.

By default, Muse uses a page's name (the name you edited under the page's thumbnail in Plan mode) as its title. As you'll see in the following exercise, you can use Page Properties to change the title to a more descriptive phrase. Your title provides visitors and search engines with useful information about your site.

- The **description** briefly describes the page content or provides information about a blog post such as author and date or byline information. In some cases, search engines show a portion of this description in their results. If you search for Adobe at google.com, for instance, in the search results you would see the site title and a description below that. Some search engines also display the description metadata that you add to each page.

It's a good idea to write descriptions that accurately reflect the specific content on a given page. A description can be as long as you wish, but most sites keep it within 150 characters to avoid being cut off in search engine results.

- **Keywords** are words and phrases that relate directly to the content on your site and that someone is likely to type in when searching for your business or website in a search engine.

Adding metadata to your pages doesn't guarantee that your site will be ranked higher by a search engine, but using a relevant title, description, and keywords in your pages typically doesn't hurt and is considered the best practice. In addition, search engines display some of this metadata information to users in their search results, which might draw in some extra visitors.

1   Click the Metadata option at the top of the Page Properties dialog box to view the metadata options.

2   In the Description field, type **Kevin's Koffee Kart is the best San Francisco coffee vendor specializing in great local gourmet coffee, coffee roasting, and bagged coffee**.

3   In the Keywords field below, enter **coffee**, **San Francisco**, **roasting**, and **gourmet**. Be sure to list keywords in priority, from most to least important, and to separate each keyword or key phrase with a comma. Choose keywords that are relevant to the specific page you're working on.

● **Note:** Some search engines give certain metadata less importance when ranking a page in search results. Google, for instance, currently doesn't add weight to metadata keywords in its page rankings but does suggest that you add a good title and relevant description to your pages.

Skip over the HTML for <head> field. It is used to add code to a section of the HTML page that is generated when you preview, publish, or export a site. Continue to the next field, Page Name. Muse automatically fills in the name you gave the page in Plan mode. You can change the name, but remember that Muse will use this name in the menu bar you'll create later. For this site, you want Home to appear in the menu bar, so don't change the page name setting.

4   Under the Page Title field, deselect Same As Page Name.

By default, Muse sets the Page Title field to be the same as the Page Name field. Deselecting Same as Page Name enables you to enter a unique, more descriptive title in the Page Title field.

5 In Page Title, type **KevinsKoffeeKart, a San Francisco gourmet coffee cart |
Home**.

Remember, the title of a page displays at the top of the browser window and
can appear in the search results for search engines. By specifying a relevant title
and adding the text "| Home" to the end, you give the search engine information
about the page and indicate to visitors which page they are on.

● **Note:** Below the Page Title field in the Page Properties dialog box is the Filename field. The name
of the HTML file that Muse generates when you publish the site will be the same as the page name.
For a page named PRODUCTS in the site map, for example, Muse names the HTML file products.
html. The exception to this rule is the Home page. Conventionally, the first page of a website, which
is usually the Home page, has a filename of index.html. You cannot edit the file name for the home
page, so this option is dimmed. Editing the filename is necessary only under special circumstances,
such as when the web developer you're working with asks you to do so.

Writing good descriptions and page titles

Because the metadata descriptions aren't displayed in the pages visitors see, you
might be tempted to let this content slide. Resist the urge, however. Because
high-quality descriptions are more likely to be displayed in Google search results,
taking the time to write this content can go a long way to improving the quality and
quantity of your search traffic.

To make your page titles and descriptions for effective, remember to

• Write unique, specific descriptions for each page of your site.

• Include facts about the content on the page that are not represented in the title.

• Make the descriptions easy to read.

• Make sure your descriptions represent the content on the page.

Tip: After setting the page properties, you might later realize that you don't want those properties (like metadata or columns) to be different from other pages in your site. You can always reset the page properties to the default site properties by choosing Page > Reset Page Properties.

6 Click OK.

7 Choose File > Preview Page In Browser to see that the title at the top of the browser window now reads "KevinsKoffeeKart, a San Francisco gourmet coffee cart | Home."

8 Close the browser and return to Muse.

9 Choose File > Close Page to close the page named Home and return to Plan mode. Alternatively, you can click the X in the Home tab to close the Home page and return to Plan mode.

10 Choose File > Save Site, leaving the KevinsKoffeeKart.muse site file open for the next lesson.

As you progress through the lessons, you can add title, description, and keywords to each of the pages if you like.

In the next lesson, you will learn about working with master pages, which make it easier and faster to apply consistent content and formatting to multiple pages.

Review questions

1 Describe how the Min Height setting affects pages.

2 Where can you set the favicon for the entire site?

3 Name the two main parts of Plan mode.

4 What is the purpose of a site map?

5 What is a top-level page?

6 What are three types of metadata that can be added in the page properties?

Review answers

1 Min height is the minimum height that a page will be in the browser. As you add content to a page, the page height will increase to fit the new content.

2 The favicon is an image that appears in a browser's Address bar next to your site's address. It is square and typically 32 pixels x 32 pixels or 16 x 16 pixels in dimension. You can set the favicon for the entire site in the Site Properties dialog box (File > Site Properties). Muse lets you use a .jpg, .gif, or .png image as the favicon.

3 The two parts of Plan mode are the site plan area and masters area.

4 The site map in Plan mode is a critical first step in the website creation process because it shows the number of pages in your site, how the pages will be ordered, and how they relate to each other in the site navigation.

5 A top-level page is a page that appears in Plan mode at the top level of the site map. These pages are the main sections of the site and automatically appear in the site's menu bar. In the case of the Kevin's Koffee Kart site, the top-level pages are, Home, THE KOFFEE, KART MAP, PRODUCTS, ABOUT, OUR STORY, and GALLERY.

6 Three types of metadata that Muse allows you to insert into your pages in the Page Properties dialog box (Page > Page Properties) are a title, a description, and keywords. The page name and filename can also be used by search engines to help improve the ranking of your page and can be considered metadata as well.

3 WORKING WITH MASTER PAGES

Lesson overview

In this lesson, you'll work with master pages and learn how to

- Edit master page properties
- Edit master page guides
- Add header and footer content
- Edit the page appearance
- Create and duplicate master pages
- Insert and style a menu widget
- Test your pages

This lesson takes approximately 90 minutes to complete. If you are starting from scratch in this lesson, use the method described in the "Jumpstart" section on page 5 of "Getting Started."

Working with master pages in Muse allows you to control the appearance of pages, set up consistent areas of your pages, such as headers and footers, and maintain design consistency across the pages in your website.

Web design versus print design

As you begin to design your pages in Muse, you'll discover quickly that web design relies on many familiar print design concepts regarding text, graphics, color, and more. Soon after that, you'll also realize that web design offers its own set of challenges and design parameters that aren't so familiar. To help you navigate them, this section explores some of the biggest differences between print and the Web.

Resolution

Resolution refers to the number of pixels that fit in 1 linear inch and is expressed as PPI, or *pixels per inch*. In print, the optimal resolution is 300ppi for images, whereas on the Web, the standard image resolution is 72ppi. Unlike in the print world, on the Web you must also be concerned with how resolution affects your finished page's file size. Keeping most web image files at this lower resolution increases download speed, which is important for site performance.

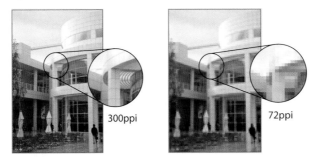

300ppi   72ppi

Fixed, yet fluid design

For a print design job, one of the first pieces of information you get is the physical dimensions of the final piece.

When you're designing for the Web, however, the dimensions of your site are less cut-and-dried. In fact, you're ideally building a site that works within a range of monitor and device screen resolutions. As a result, you have to consider how your web pages will look when viewed in a variety of different resolutions. Most websites have vertical scrolling content, meaning the height of the page is dictated by its content (as opposed to horizontally scrolling content).

As for width, at the time of this writing, Muse creates what are commonly called *fixed width* pages. That means that your pages are a set width and are centered in the browser window. To avoid horizontal scrolling, design your web page in Muse to fit the width of the smallest monitor resolution, which is typically 1024 × 768 pixels.

Although you can set certain content to be 100% of the width of the browser window, you cannot yet do that for an entire page. In the future, you may be able to design your pages in Muse to fit variable monitor resolutions, in order to accommodate smaller devices like tablets and smartphones.

File size

When you design for print, file sizes can balloon quickly, but as long as you can fit your files on a disc, upload them via FTP, or push them through the RIP, large file sizes aren't an obstacle. When you design for the Web, however, file size is important enough to steer your design decisions. No one likes to wait and wait while a site loads large bulky files, and remember, all the images on your site have to download to a visitor's machine before they can be viewed. Download times can, and will, impact how your website performs. For instance, suppose a site visitor opens a really simple web page, which contains only text and three images. The visitor's browser will have to make a series of connections to the server that hosts your page: one to locate the page itself and the three additional connections to retrieve each of the images on the page. That time adds up quickly. To keep your site as lean and quick to download as possible, reuse images on a web page when you can. Even if your logo appears ten times on the page, for example, a visitor's browser has to download it only once.

Understand web navigation

Site navigation determines how visitors get around, or navigate, the pages of your site and is a vital consideration. If visitors find your site difficult to navigate, they will quickly leave and not return. As a result, early in the planning process make designing effective navigation for

your site a priority. As you will see, your site navigation is tied directly to the design of your pages.

When you're planning your site navigation, consider

- **Consistency is key.** Changing the colors or location of your navigation system between pages can quickly frustrate site visitors. For example, if menu items are blue on the home page but the same menu items are green on different site pages, your visitors will likely get annoyed or lost and leave your site in frustration. Determine a single style and placement for your site navigation, and keep it consistent throughout your pages.

- **Clearly label your navigation elements**. Simple images or icons aren't always enough to guide site visitors. In fact, visitors might not even recognize some icons as navigational elements. Use clear section labels so your site visitors can quickly and easily navigate to different parts of your site.

Design with interactivity in mind

When you design a web page, you consider how users will interact with the content. When designing a button, for example, you need to also consider the states of that button—how it appears initially, when hovered over, and when clicked. Typically, when you hover over a button, its appearance changes to indicate that the button is connected to an action, like taking you to another page, and when you click it changes again, to indicate an action will occur when you release the button. You need to design the button states as well. You will learn more about button states in Lesson 7, "Working with Links and Buttons."

Building a master page

● **Note:** If you have not already done so, copy the Lessons folder onto your hard disk, from the *Adobe Muse Classroom in a Book* disc. See "Copying the Classroom in a Book files" on page 3.

When you create a site in Muse, you start with a single master page, which is essentially a template you can apply to other pages. Using a single master page, or even using a few master pages to target different site sections, makes it easier to create consistent pages and a cohesive site. For example, if you add content to the master page such as a logo and a navigation menu, any page you apply the master to will contain those elements in the same positions. When you change a master page, all pages based on that master reflect those changes.

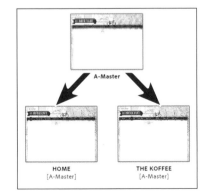

In Plan mode, the masters section, located below the site plan area, contains the default master page that every Muse site starts with. A master page is essentially a design that contains all of the common site elements that you use to maintain consistency across the pages in your website. In this next section, you will learn how to create, delete, apply, and add content to a master page in your site.

Editing the page area and browser fill

When you design for the Web, you must consider not only the page design and contents, but also the area outside of the page area, called the *browser fill* in Muse. The browser fill is the area that surrounds your page when a visitor's browser window's width exceeds the width you specified for your page. Remember, Muse uses fixed layouts, so if a visitor resizes the browser window, your page won't widen to fill it. You will need to specify something, such as a background color or image to fill the space.

When you open a page or master page, Muse divides the Document window into a white page area and two gray areas outside of that white box. The white box is the page area, which contains the content for your page. The dark gray area outside the page area is the browser fill area. It can contain a color, an image, or both, which appear behind the page area's contents. The lighter gray zone outside of the browser fill area is beyond the edge of the browser and cannot be edited.

Note: You may need to zoom out to see the page area and gray areas beyond by choosing View > Zoom Out.

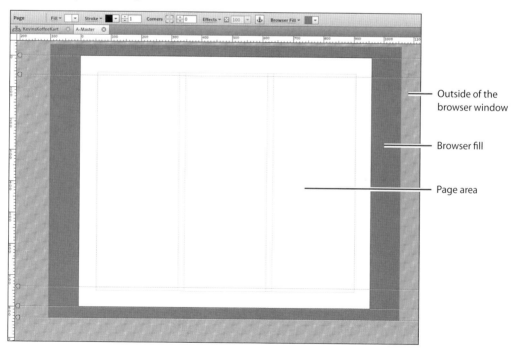

Outside of the browser window

Browser fill

Page area

1 With your KevinsKoffeeKart site open in Plan mode, look at the page thumbnails in the site map. Below each thumbnail you see [A-Master] in blue, which indicates that the A-Master master page is applied to the thumbnail's page. As a result, any elements on A-Master appear on the related page.

2 Double-click the A-Master thumbnail in the masters area at the bottom of the Application window to open the A-Master page.

The A-Master page opens as a new tab in the Document window in Design mode. As you saw in the first chapter, with a page or master page open the workspace shows a lot more features, including the Control panel, Toolbox, and panels.

3 Choose View > Fit Page In Window, then Choose View > Zoom Out.

The first step in creating your page design is adding content to the master page. In most cases, you will add header content, such as a logo and menu bar, and footer content, such as social media links and more, to the master page, because those elements should appear on every page.

In the Control panel, notice that the Selection Indicator on the left end of the panel shows Page. As you learned in Lesson 1, this indicates that nothing is selected on the page and that any formatting options you change in the Control panel will affect the page area.

The Browser Fill menu in the Control panel is the exception to this rule. The Browser Fill menu allows you to add a color and image to the background of the browser window, which resides behind the page area.

Note: You will learn more about creating and saving colors in Lesson 5, "Working with Shapes and Color."

4 Click the Color box to the right of the Browser Fill menu in the Control panel. Click the white color in the panel that appears.

Notice that the color behind the page area changes to white. That white color will now fill the browser window, regardless of screen size (screen resolution).

5   Click Browser Fill in the Control panel to see the fill options for the browser.

    The preview area at the top of the options previews the color and/or image you set within the browser area. Here you can change the color, as well as add or adjust a background image.

6   Click the folder to the right of the Image option. Navigate to the Lessons folder and in the images folder, select the image bk-map.gif. Click Open (Windows) or Select (Mac OS).

    This step inserts an image, bk-map.gif, into the background of the browser window, where it appears behind the page area. You will typically create the background image in a separate application, such as Adobe Photoshop or Adobe Illustrator, and save it in an accepted web format (.jpg, .gif, or .png). You will learn more about image types in Lesson 6, "Adding Images to Your Site."

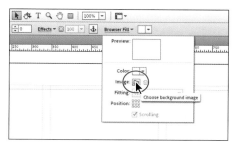

7   In the Browser Fill options, choose Original Size from the Fitting menu, and select the center point of the Position reference point indicator (⊞).

    Muse now inserts the image in the browser background at the same pixel dimensions as you created it and positions it in the center of the browser window, no matter the size of the browser window.

8   Deselect the Scrolling option.

    With Scrolling deselected, the background image stays in place if the user scrolls the page content using the scroll bars in the browser. The page content scrolls on top of the fixed background image. If you'd rather have the image scroll with the page, leave Scrolling selected.

9   Choose View > Preview Mode to preview the background image. If scroll bars appear in the Application window, try scrolling the page to see the effect. If you don't see scroll bars in the application, your screen resolution may be large enough to fit the entire page, and that's okay.

Background image tips

If you are going to create your own background image, you should consider a few points:

- If you want a single background image to fill the browser window, make sure that you make it large enough to fill a larger screen resolution.

- Consider the file size of the background image. One larger image can be much larger and take longer to load into a browser compared to one small, repeating image.

- If you are going to create a background image that contains texture, use a low-contrast, subtle texture or pattern.

- If an image is to repeat in the background, make sure that the edges line up perfectly. You can do this within the program you use to create the background image.

- For an image that you want to repeat, remove objects that stand out from the rest of the image, otherwise your image will not blend into a unified texture when repeated.

Setting the page area's appearance

Next, you will edit the appearance of the page area. As you did for the browser fill area, you can assign a background color and image for the page area along with other options to match your design. In addition, you can adjust the opacity of the page area to allow the browser fill, a busy map, to be visible behind it. To ensure that there is a high level of contrast between the page content and the background content, you can adjust the opacity, color, and other formatting options of the page area. By default, the page area has a white color fill and a black, 1-pixel stroke (border).

1 Click the Design mode link in the upper-left corner of the Application window to return to Design mode.

2 With Page showing in the Selection Indicator, click the word "Fill" in the Control panel to show the Fill options.

Notice the choices for Fill Type, Solid and Gradient, are dimmed. The page area can't have a gradient, only a solid color, which is why you can't change this setting.

3 In the Fill options, click the arrow to the right of the Opacity option and drag the slider to the left until **94** appears in the field. (You could also simply enter the value.) This makes the page area very slightly transparent.

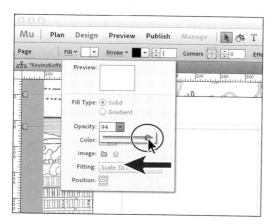

If you want to change the color fill of the page area, you can do so in the Fill options as well.

The Fill options also include an option for a background image for the page area. The options are similar to the options for the browser fill, only the image would appear in the page area, on top of the page fill color.

4 Click away from the Fill options in the page area to hide the options.

5 Click the down arrow to the right of the Stroke Color so that the stroke is 0 (zero). That removes the default black stroke around the edge of the page area, indicated by the arrow in the figure.

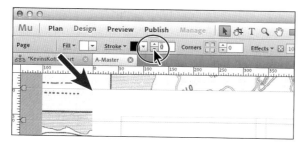

6 Choose File > Save Site.

Now that the page area is set, you can start to edit other properties for the master page.

Editing master page properties

In the previous lesson, you set up the site file and edited the page properties. Just as you can for a single page, you can also edit those same properties for a master page. The difference is that any page that has that master page applied will have the same properties as the master page by default. Setting page properties on a master page can save time because it lets you set properties across multiple pages simultaneously, instead of editing them page by page.

Tip: To edit the page properties for the A-Master page, you could also stay in Plan mode and right-click (Windows) or Control-click (Mac OS) the A-Master thumbnail and choose Page Properties to edit them.

1 Choose Page > Page Properties with the A-Master page open in Design mode.

2 In the Page Properties dialog box, which should start to look familiar, change the Min Height value to **640**. Click OK.

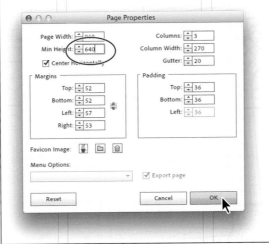

Note: Clicking Reset in the Page Properties dialog box or choosing Page > Reset Page Properties will set the page properties to mirror the site properties and remove any page/browser fill changes you made.

That setting decreases the minimum height of all the pages with A-Master applied to them. Of course, you can make changes to the properties of your master pages later, if needed.

Editing the master page guides

Like other websites designed with HTML and CSS, individual pages in your Muse website can have varying heights based on the unique content on each page, but all can feature the same header and footer regions. These regions ensure that the header content, such as your logo, always remains in place at the top of the page and the footer content, such as copyright information, always displays directly below the page content, regardless of the height of a given page. By adjusting the blue page guides on a master page in Design mode, you can easily specify consistent header and footer sizes across multiple pages.

Using the page guides on the master, you can control not only the size of the header and footer, but also set the padding on the top and bottom of the page (the distance between the browser window edge and the page edge), and the minimum height of the page (called the Min Height). Some of these are settings you already saw when you edited the page properties. The master page guides simply give you a visual way to edit those same properties.

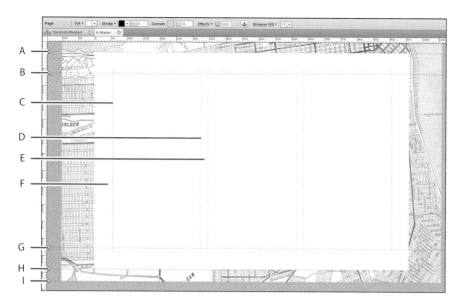

Here's a quick guide to page guides:

A **Top of Page:** Defines padding above the page and is the same as the Padding Top setting in the page properties.

B **Header:** Delineates the bottom of the header area. Items inserted on a master page above the header guide appear at the top of the page and are locked (cannot be selected or edited) on the pages of the site.

C **Margin guides:** Define a safe area of the page in which to lay out page content. Objects snap to the margin guides as you lay out your page. Margins, columns, and gutters in Muse are similar to margins and columns you use when designing layouts in Adobe InDesign.

D **Column guides:** Divide the page area into columns of content.

E **Gutters:** Specify the distance between columns.

F **Page area:** Indicates where you can add the unique content for each page.

G **Footer:** Delineates the top of the footer area. Items below the footer guide appear at the bottom of the page. Elements associated with the footer stay at the bottom of the page, regardless of content height, and elements placed in the footer on a master page are locked (cannot be selected or edited) on the pages of the site.

H **Bottom of Page:** Defines the minimum page height. This is the same as the Min Height setting in the page properties. You set the minimum height in an earlier step when you edited the master page properties. This guide is a visual way to edit that value.

I **Bottom of Browser:** Defines padding below the page and is the same as the Padding Bottom setting in the page properties.

The next exercise gives you some practice working with guides. You'll add padding to the top of the A-Master page, which pushes the page area (the white box) down, then use this extra room to increase the header region enough to hold a larger logo and menu bar. Finally, you'll adjust the three guides in the lower portion of the page.

Tip: If 210px is difficult to achieve by dragging, you can zoom into the page to see finer increments in the measurement label as you drag the page guides.

1 With A-Master page open in Design mode, locate the Top of Page blue guide handle off the left side of the page. Drag the handle down, noticing the measurement label as you do so. When the Y: value is approximately 210px, release the mouse. The Y: value is a pixel value that indicates how far from the top edge of the browser the page area starts.

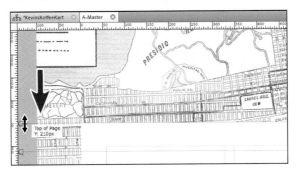

Note: If you don't see the master page guide handles, you may need to scroll over to the upper-left part of the page using the Document window scroll bars, or choose View > Show Guides to display them again.

2 Off the left side of the page, click and drag the Header guide handle up until the Y: value shows 0 in the measurement label, then release the mouse.

The Y value, in this case, indicates how far from the top edge of the page area the header guide is located. Setting it to 0 puts the Top of Page guide and the Header guide on top of each other so that the header area is above the page area.

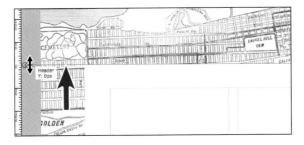

The header and footer area in your design

The design for the KevinsKoffeeKart site called for header content that includes a logo and menu bar to be above the white page area. That's why you dragged the Top of Page guide down: to leave a space for header content.

Some of your designs will require that the page area not have a gap between the top of the page and the browser window. You can accommodate this by setting the Top of Page guide at 0. You then drag the Header guide down into the page area and place the header content within the page area but above the Header guide. You could even choose Page > Page Properties and set the top margin to a large value that brings the Top of Page guide below the Header guide. This frames the positioning of the text and content on the page.

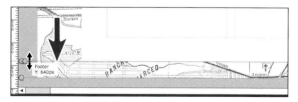

You can adjust the Footer and Bottom of Page guides to have similar relationships.

3 Click and drag the Footer guide down until the measurement label reads 640px to overlap the Footer guide and the Bottom of Page guide. You may need to scroll down in the Document window.

● **Note:** Although you can edit the Header and Footer guides on master pages only, you can adjust all other page guides on individual pages in the site as well.

4 Leave the Bottom of Page guide at the current location. Don't forget, this sets the minimum height of the page.

Note: The bottom of the browser window dictates the lowest part of the display area when a visitor views the site in a browser. If you want a strip of browser fill to appear below the lowest page content, set the Bottom of Page guide above the Bottom of Browser guide. If you do not want the browser fill to display below the page content, drag both the Bottom of Page guide and the Bottom of Browser guide to the same location.

5   Drag the Bottom of Browser guide down until the measurement label shows a value of approximately 320px.

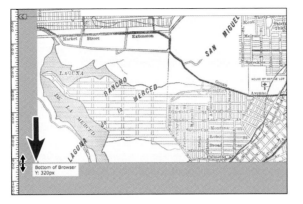

The Bottom of Browser guide gives you room to insert footer content below the page area and measures the distance from the bottom of the page.

6   Choose File > Save Site.

With the key areas of the master page mapped out, you can start adding content to them.

Adding a logo to the header

The header of most websites contains a variety of content: a company logo, a menu bar (also called a navigation or nav bar), possibly social media links, and more. For now, you'll concentrate on adding a logo to the KevinsKoffeeKart site's header.

1   With A-Master still open in Design mode, choose View > Fit Page In Window, then scroll up using the scroll bars on the right side of the Document window to see the header area.

Fitting the A-Master page in the Document window fits only the white page area in the window. For this site, that cuts off the header and footer areas so you needed to scroll.

2   Choose File > Place. Navigate to the images folder in the Lessons folder. Browse to the image called logo.png, and click Open (Windows) or Select (Mac OS).

Like InDesign, placing an image gives you the Place Gun (⊢) in Muse. With the Place Gun, you click to place an image on the page at 100% its original size or click and drag to size the image as you place it.

3 Position the Place Gun just below the top ruler in the Document window, and align it with the left edge of the page area. Remember, the image's upper-left corner will sit where you click. See the figure for placement help.

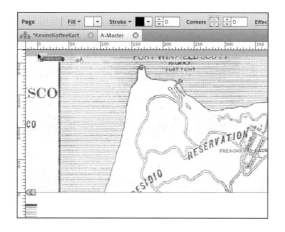

4 Click to place the logo. You will reposition the image later, so don't worry if it doesn't match the figure exactly.

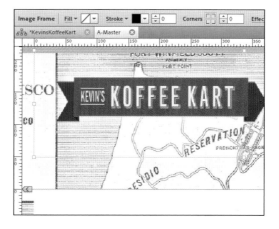

When you place images, Muse, like InDesign, creates a frame and places the image within it. You can use the frame to crop the image, and you can move the image within the frame.

You will learn more about working with images in Lesson 6, "Adding Images to Your Site."

5 Click the Plan link in the upper-left corner of the Application window to show Plan mode again.

Notice that each page thumbnail now shows the content you added to the A-Master page, including the background image and logo.

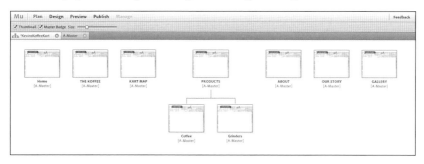

6 Double-click the Home page thumbnail to open that page in Design mode.

7 With the Selection tool, try clicking on the company logo in the header.

You won't be able to select or edit master content on your pages, and currently there is no way around that, as in InDesign.

Note: If you don't see the A-Master page in the Document window, click the A-Master tab below the Control panel to show the page.

8 Choose File > Close Page to return to the A-Master page.

With the A-Master page guides set and some of the header content in place, you will now add a menu bar to the header to help users navigate between the pages in your site.

Adding a navigation menu

When designing for the Web, the site navigation plays a key role in your design process, and the prime navigation system of any website is its menu bar.

To help you create one, Muse offers menu widgets. Although you can create a series of links to connect the pages manually, the widgets are a fast and flexible way to add navigation and more.

Widgets are ready-made objects that you can drag into your pages to add such functionality as slideshow controls or a menu. Widgets live in the Widgets Library panel (Window > Widgets Library), which offers several categories of widgets to choose from. To add a widget, like a menu widget, simply drag it onto your page in Design mode. From there, you can customize it with your own content and formatting.

In this section, you will focus on the Menus category of the Widgets Library panel.

Exploring the different menus

Muse offers three menu widgets that you can use in your designs. Take a look at your choices:

Note: If the Widgets Library panel isn't in the workspace, choose Window > Widgets Library to open it.

1 In Design mode, click the Widgets Library panel tab to see the panel.

2 Double-click the Menus category in the Widgets Library panel to reveal those widgets.

▶ **Tip:** You can also click the arrow to the left of the category name to reveal the widgets in the category.

3 Click the Bar widget and notice that a preview appears in the top portion of the Widgets Library panel.

The Bar menu widget lists the menu items (links to your pages) horizontally. By default, it has a gradient fill in the background of each menu item and each menu item is the same width.

4 Click the Horizontal menu bar, then the Vertical menu bar listed in the Widgets Library panel and look at the previews for each. The Horizontal menu widget lists the menu items horizontally. By default, its menu items have no background color and the text they contain determines their widths.

The Vertical menu widget lists the menu items vertically. By default, items have a gradient fill in the background and are the same width and height.

The menu widgets are just a starting point, which means that you can change a widget's appearance in almost any way you want after dragging it onto your page.

Inserting a menu widget

The next step, after deciding which menu bar you want to use on your page, is to drag it onto the page. The Horizontal widget works best for the KevinsKoffeeKart site.

1 Choose the Selection tool, if it's not already selected, and make sure you can see the logo above the page area in the Document window. You are going to drag the menu widget to just below the logo.

2 From the Widgets Library panel, drag the Horizontal menu bar into the page area. Release the mouse when the pointer is positioned in the upper-left corner of the margin guides on the page. See the figure for help in placement, but don't worry about exact placement. You'll reposition the menu later in the lesson.

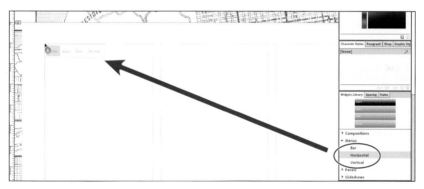

With the menu widget on the page, notice that Muse automatically filled in the names of your pages in the menu, following the same order as the page thumbnails in Plan mode. Muse creates the menu bar with links to all of the top-level pages in your site map. Be careful and accurate when naming those thumbnails; any errors in the site map names will appear in your menu!

Now that the menu is on the A-Master page, it shows up on all of the pages with A-Master applied.

3 Choose File > Save Site.

Excluding pages from the menu

Every time you create a new top-level page in Plan mode, Muse automatically adds it to the menu. Sometimes, however, you may want to test a page before opening it to visitors or hide a seasonally specific page during the offseason. From Plan mode you can specify pages to exclude from the navigation (to leave out of the menu bar).

1 Click the Plan mode link above the Control panel to return to Plan mode.

2 Position the pointer over the GALLERY thumbnail, and click the plus sign (+) to the right of the thumbnail to add another page.

3 Name the page **GALLERYb**.

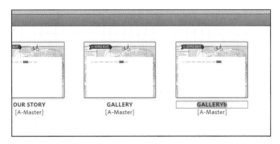

This page will be another design option for the gallery page. Later, you can choose which of the two designs you prefer to use.

4 Drag the Size slider to the left so the page thumbnails are smaller and all fit in the plan area, if necessary.

5 Click the A-Master page tab above the site plan area to show the A-Master page in the Document window. Notice that the new page, GALLERYb, was automatically added to the menu.

In the menu, each page listed is called a *menu item*. Muse automatically creates links to those pages so you won't have to do so later. The GALLERYb page is just for testing design ideas, however, so it doesn't need to appear in the menu bar.

6 Choose View > Plan Mode.

7 Right-click (Windows) or Control-click (Mac OS) the GALLERYb page thumbnail and choose Menu Options > Exclude Page From Menus so that the page no longer appears in the menu.

By default, any new pages are added to the menu, but by selecting Exclude Page From Menus for GALLERYb, only that single page is excluded from the menu.

8 Double-click the Home page name below the page thumbnail. Change the name to **HOME**.

If you discover a typo or otherwise need to adjust a page name for a consistent look in your menu, you can easily change it later in Plan mode. In this case, the Home page needed to become HOME to match the rest of the uppercase names in the menu.

9 Click the A-Master page tab below the Control panel to return to the master page and see the change in the menu bar.

10 Choose File > Save Site.

Editing the menu widget parameters

After placing a menu widget onto a page, you can define how the menu behaves.

1 Choose Edit > Deselect All with the A-Master page showing in the Document window.

2 With the Selection tool, click to select the menu widget on the page.

Notice the blue circle with the white arrow appear in the upper-right corner of the menu. By clicking that arrow, you will reveal the Options menu.

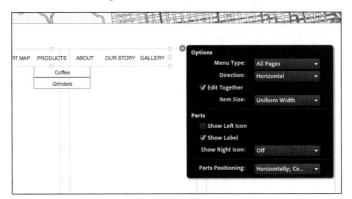

● **Note:** To learn more about the menu options, see the "Menu_options.pdf" file in the Lesson03 folder.

3 Click the arrow to reveal Options menu, and set the following for the KevinsKoffeeKart site:

- Menu Type: **All Pages**

- Direction: **Horizontal** (the default setting)

- Edit Together: **Selected** (the default setting)

- Item Size: **Uniform Width**

- Show Left Icon: **Deselected** (the default setting)

- Show Label: **Selected** (the default setting)

- Show Right Icon: **Off**

- Parts Positioning: **Horizontally; Center-Aligned** (the default setting)

It is usually a good idea to set these basic options first, before you add your own styling to the menu bar.

4 Click the Preview link above the Control panel. Move the pointer over the menu items, especially the PRODUCTS menu item in Preview to see the submenu.

5 Click the PRODUCTS link, and notice that the PRODUCTS menu item has a darker gray background color.

6 Click the Design mode link above the Control panel to return to the A-Master page in Design mode.

7 Choose File > Save Site to save the page and the site.

Include pages in the menu without a link

When creating a menu that has submenu content, like the PRODUCTS section of your menu, you may not want visitors to click the parent page (PRODUCTS). You may prefer that visitors are able to click only the child pages in the submenu. In Plan mode, you can include a page in the menu, but without a hyperlink to a page.

In Plan Mode, you can right-click (Windows) or Control-click (Mac OS) a page thumbnail, like the PRODUCTS page thumbnail, and choose Menu Options > Include Page Without Hyperlink so that the page still appears in the menu, but no longer links anywhere.

When you preview the site, position the pointer over the menu item, and click, nothing happens. The submenu links (if there are any for that page), however, will still link to their respective pages. If you tried this, set the page to Include Page with Hyperlink again before continuing.

The menu has default formatting and some of the menu items aren't fitting very well. Don't worry; you'll start to edit the appearance of the menu next.

Understanding the parts of a menu widget

You can set a lot of different formatting options for a menu widget, including background and border colors, text formatting, rounded corners, effects, and much more. That said, it's important to understand how a menu widget is built and how to select its various parts before you add your favorite color.

The menu widget is a larger container that surrounds a series of inner containers. It's a nested "group" of container objects, but not a group in the same sense as other Adobe applications. You can't ungroup a menu. As you select a part of the menu widget, Muse displays a bounding box around that container to indicate which one is currently selected.

The figure shows the different containers, color coded and with exaggerated gaps between the containers to help you see them. (Those gaps do not show in the menu by default.)

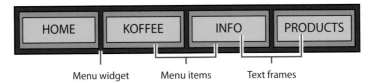

Menu widget   Menu items   Text frames

Now that you understand how a menu widget is built in Muse, you are going to practice selecting and maneuvering amongst the various parts.

1　Choose Edit > Deselect All.

2　With the Selection tool, click the menu bar widget on the page to select it. On the left end of the Control panel, notice that the Selection Indicator displays the words "Menu Widget."

3　Position the pointer over the word "HOME" in the menu, and you will see an outline appear around the smaller container. Click on the word "HOME."

Notice that the words "Menu Item" appear on the left end of the Control panel in the Selection Indicator.

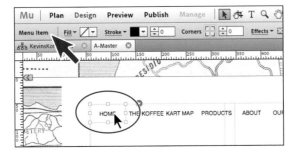

4 Click once more on the word "HOME," and the words "Text Frame" appear in the Selection Indicator in the Control panel.

5 Press the Escape key to select the container (called Menu Item) that the HOME text frame is in.

The Escape key lets you back up the hierarchy of nested elements.

6 Press the Escape key once more to select the menu widget.

Note: You can also click away from the widget, and click to select the menu bar again.

Single-clicking repeatedly allows you to drill down into the menu content hierarchy, while pressing the Escape key moves you back up the hierarchy. As you start to style the menu bar, it's important to select the correct part of the menu.

Next, you will edit the appearance of the menu bar using fills, strokes, and more.

Edit the appearance of the menu bar

You can change the look of your menu bars by changing appearance settings. When an entire widget is selected, you can change its dimensions, appearance, and location. With the subelements of a widget selected, you can format the contents (such as insert other objects, like images, text, and rectangles) as well as update each element's appearance and dimensions within the confines of the widget itself. First, you will edit the size and appearance of the entire widget.

1 Choose View > Fit Page In Window.

2 With the entire menu selected and the Selection tool selected in the Toolbox, drag the right-middle point of the container to the right until the measurement label shows a width of approximately 720px.

Because you selected Uniform Width for the Item Size in the menu bar options previously, Muse lets you manually resize the width of the entire menu. If you had selected Fit Width, you would not be able to resize the menu using this method.

Note: Notice that the white arrow for the menu options is off the upper-right corner of the selected text frame. Clicking that options menu arrow reveals the same menu options you saw in the beginning.

Note: Depending on your screen resolution, the panels on the right side of the workspace may get in the way. You may need to either scroll the page horizontally using the scroll bar at the bottom of the Document window or zoom out.

3　Choose Window > Transform. In the Transform panel, change the Height to 38 by selecting the value in the Height (H) field and entering **38**. Press Enter or Return to accept the value.

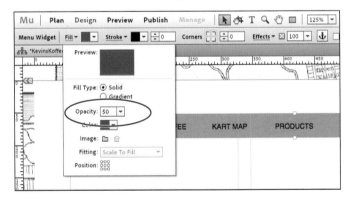

The Transform panel is just another way to edit the width or height of the menu. You'll learn more about the Transform panel in Lesson 5, "Working with Shapes and Color."

4　With the menu still selected, click the word "Fill" in the Control panel to reveal the fill options.

These options are the same as those you saw previously when adjusting the fill of the page area. Notice that you can now, however, select the Gradient option. Currently, the menu bar has no color fill (it is transparent), but you can change its appearance.

5　With Solid selected, click the arrow next to Color and select any red color. The background of the menu bar is now filled with the red color.

6　Change the Opacity value to 50 by selecting 100 in the Opacity field and typing **50**. Press Enter or Return to accept the value.

Changing the opacity is a great way to add unique design treatments.

7 Select Gradient, and notice that the menu bar background features a color gradient that incorporates the red from the previous steps.

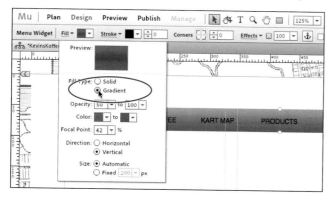

A gradient is a linear blend from one color to another. You can adjust gradients in several different ways, including changing the colors. You will learn all about creating and manipulating gradient colors in Chapter 5, "Working with Shapes and Color."

8 Select Solid, then click the arrow next to Color and select [None] (⊘) to remove the red color. Press the Escape key to hide the Fill options.

Now that the menu bar appearance is finished, you can edit each of the menu items.

9 Click the word "HOME" to select the individual menu item.

All of the appearance options you've applied up to this point can also be applied to each menu item.

10 Click the up arrow to the right of the Stroke Weight option in the Control panel to change the stroke to 1px. Notice that a stroke (border) is applied to every one of the menu items, separately.

Tip: You can also create an image in Adobe Photoshop, Illustrator, or similar program, save it in a web format, and then, using the Fill options, apply it as a background image to the entire menu bar.

Aside from a stroke, you can also apply fills, including gradients, solid colors, and background images in each of the containers. You will learn more about strokes, fills, and colors in Lesson 5, "Working with Shapes and Color." You can also apply effects like drop shadows or rounded corners to the menu containers. You'll learn about effects and rounded corners in Lesson 8, "Applying Effects, Graphic Styles, and Inserting HTML."

▶ **Tip:** If you want each of the menu item containers to look different, you can deselect Edit Together in the menu bar options. After deselecting Edit Together, you can then select each menu item within the menu bar widget, add different fills, strokes, background images, rounded corners, and more to each, independently.

11 Remove the stroke by setting the Stroke Weight to **0** in the Control panel.

With the menu containers formatted, you can also format the menu bar text using different fonts, sizes, and a host of text formatting options.

Format the menu bar text

▶ **Tip:** You can edit the text formatting like font family, size, and more without ever selecting the text in the menu. By selecting the entire menu bar widget, any changes you make to text formatting will affect all of the text in the menu bar.

When you insert a menu widget into your pages, the default font of the menu text is a sans-serif font like Helvetica or Arial. As easily as you formatted the containers, you can change the font of the text, as well as other appearance properties, such as the text's fill and stroke.

1 In Design view, click away from the menu bar to deselect it. Click three times, slowly, on the HOME text in the menu bar to select the HOME text frame.

The words "Text Frame" appear in the Selection Indicator of the Control panel.

2 Click the Text panel tab on the right side of the workspace to show it.

● **Note:** You cannot edit the text that appears in the menu. That is controlled by the name of the pages in the site map. If you create a manual menu in the menu options, however, you must enter the text for the menu items.

● **Note:** If you do not see News Gothic Std Bold in the list, you can choose any other font, or refer to the "Fonts Used in this Book" section on page 2 of "Getting Started" to learn how to access the fonts supplied on the Muse Classroom in a Book disc.

3 Click the Font Family menu in the Text panel, and choose News Gothic Std Bold from the System Fonts (Exports As Image) menu. On Windows, you can choose News Gothic Std and click the Bold button in the Text panel.

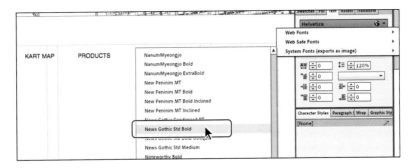

In the menu, notice that each of the menu items has changed font family. Also, the image icon that appears to the right of the text in the menu has changed. That image icon indicates that the text in the menu will be converted to an image when the site is published. You will learn all about working with font families and other text formatting in Lesson 4, "Adding and Styling Text."

4   In the Text panel, change the Size to **12**, by selecting it from the Size menu, clicking the arrows to the left of the size field, or typing the value directly into the field.

5   Change the Letter Space to **2**.

Letter Space, as you'll learn in the next lesson, adds 2 pixels of spacing between all characters in the menu bar.

6   Click the Color arrow, and select White as the color. Press the Escape key to close the Color Picker.

After changing the text to white, it will be difficult to see it. That's okay. You will fix that shortly.

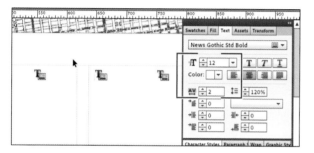

7   Click the word "Effects" in the Control panel to show the Effects options. Make sure that Shadow is selected at the top of the options. Select On to turn the shadow on, then set the shadow options as follows:

- Color: **Black** (default value)

- Opacity: **25**

- Size: **3**

- Angle: **45** (default value)

- Distance: **2**

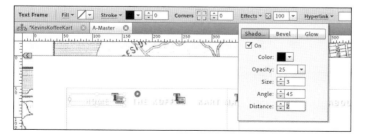

You can apply a lot of other formatting options to the text in the menu, including adding effects like bevel to create a 3D-like style of text. You will learn all about applying and editing Effects in Lesson 8, "Applying Effects, Graphic Styles, and Inserting HTML."

Next, you'll add an image to go behind the menu to make the menu text more readable.

8   Choose File > Place. Navigate to the images folder in the Lessons folder. Select the image named top-nav.png, and click Open (Windows) or Select (Mac OS). Click to place the image on top of the menu bar widget.

9   Press and hold the letter "H" to select the Hand tool temporarily. Drag down until you see the logo in the header area. Release the H key.

10 Drag the new image with the Selection tool until the bottom of the image snaps to the top of the page area. A red line appears along the bottom edge of the image when it is snapped. Drag it horizontally until a red guide appears in the center of the page running from top to bottom. See the figure for placement help.

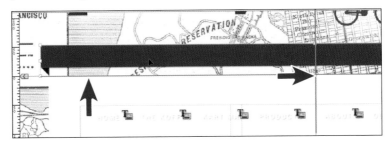

The red lines are part of the Smart Guides, which are turned on by default, and help you align content. You will learn more about working with Smart Guides in Lesson 4, "Adding and Styling Text."

11 Choose Object > Send Backward to put the new image behind the menu.

Visually, nothing will change. When you drag the menu on top of the image, however, you'll see that the menu is now on top of the image.

▶ **Tip:** If you need to nudge the menu bar, press an arrow key on your keyboard.

12 Drag the menu, centering it as best as you can vertically on the image with the menu bar aligned with the left edge of the new image. See the figure for placement help.

Because you made the text bigger and the letter spacing has spread the letters apart, the menu bar is a bit too narrow, but you'll fix that next.

13 With the menu widget still selected, click the Transform panel tab and change the width to **850px**.

14 Click the Preview link above the Control panel and position the pointer over the menu. Notice the background color change to gray. Click one of the links, and notice that the background color of the page link you clicked on is dark gray.

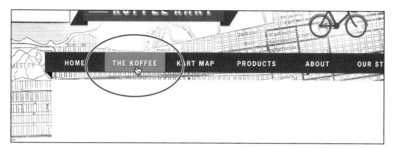

The appearance changes that you see when interacting with the menu are called the *states* of the menu. Editing the appearance of these states is an important part of designing your menu, and the task you'll work on next.

15 Click the Design mode link in the upper-left corner of the Application window to return to the A-Master page.

Edit the menu states

A *state* is the appearance of a rectangle (in this case, a menu item), text frames, and image frames on a web page. States can change with user interaction. For example, if a visitor positions the pointer over an item in the menu, a menu item's background color could change from none to blue.

You can edit the various states of Menu widget items by selecting the correct menu part and using the States panel.

1 In Design mode, click away from the menu bar to deselect it. Click twice, slowly, on the HOME link to select the HOME menu item.

2 Click the States panel tab (Window > States) on the right side of the workspace to show the States panel.

In the States panel, there are four states for every selected object.

3 Click the Rollover state, and Muse shows what the rollover state looks like on the page in the menu bar.

Once you select a state in the States panel, you can then edit the appearance of the state using any number of appearance options like fill, stroke, and more.

> **Note:** Remember that, by default, editing the appearance of one menu item will edit the rest in the menu.

4 Click the Fill Color in the Control panel and select the color [None] (⊘).

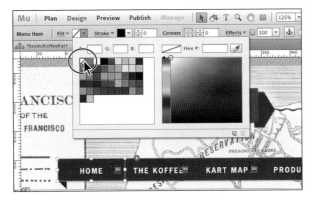

▶ **Tip:** In Lesson 8, "Applying Effects, Graphic Styles, and Inserting HTML" you will learn how to save formatting as a graphic style that you can easily use throughout your document, making changes like these easily.

5 Click the Mouse Down state, then click the fill color in the Control panel and select the color [None].

● **Note:** Clicking the Reset To Default button in the States panel (the trash can icon in the lower-right corner) with either the Rollover state or Active (Normal) state selected will make the selected state look like the Normal state. With the Mouse Down selected, clicking the Reset To Default button will make it look like the Rollover state. As of the writing of this book, this does not apply to every menu item, only to the menu item selected (in this case HOME).

6 Click the Active (Normal) state in the States panel.

The Active (Normal) state indicates the appearance of the menu item of the page currently showing in the browser window (it's a link in the menu bar).

7 Click the Fill option in the Control panel, and select None from the Color menu, leaving the Fill options showing.

8 Click the folder icon to the right of the Image option, and navigate to the images folder in the Lessons folder. Select the image named topnav-over.png, and click Open (Windows) or Select (Mac OS).

9 Make sure that Original Size is selected in the Fitting menu, and then select the center point of the Position reference point indicator (⊞) to align it to the center. Press Escape to hide the Fill options.

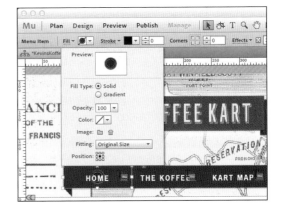

About the states in the States panel

It is important to understand the different states in the States panel when working with menu bars. The definitions of each state that follow use the word "object" in place of the menu "item" because states can apply to more than just menu widgets.

- **Normal:** Specifies the default appearance of the object when the web page loads in the browser.
- **Rollover:** Specifies the appearance of the object when a visitor rolls over the object with the mouse pointer.
- **Mouse Down:** Specifies the appearance of the object when a visitor clicks it.
- **Active (Normal):** Specifies the appearance of the object when a visitor activates a particular page. This option is normally specified for menu bar widgets and tabbed panel widgets. For example, when a visitor is viewing the Products page, the Products item in a Menu Bar widget might register a separate color to denote that the visitor is on that (active) page.

10 Click the Preview mode link and position the pointer over the menu items, clicking on a few to see the resulting states.

11 Click the Design mode link to return to the A-Master page.

Edit the submenu appearance

If you set the menu bar option to include the child pages as well, you will want to edit the appearance of the submenus in your menu, because the appearance properties you set for the menu top-level pages do not affect the submenu items. As you saw earlier in this lesson, the top-level pages in the site map appear in the menu and child pages appear as submenus.

1 While editing A-Master in Design mode, click away from the menu bar to deselect it. Click twice, slowly, on the PRODUCTS link to see the submenu appear.

2 Click once on the submenu to select the submenu container. The word "Container" appears in the Selection Indicator of the Control panel.

A submenu is similar in structure to the menu bar. Clicking once selects the main container. Clicking again on a menu item within the submenu selects that menu item. Clicking once more selects the text frame in that container. Pressing the Escape key moves you back up the hierarchy.

3 Drag the right-middle point of the submenu container to the left just a few pixels. The measurement label appears, showing you the width and height.

4 Drag the bottom-middle point of the submenu container down to make the submenu a few pixels taller.

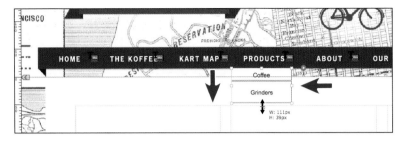

Notice that dragging the edge of the entire submenu container resizes only the bottom menu item, Grinders, not the entire container.

5 Choose Edit > Undo Resize Item twice to return the menu to the default size.

6 Click the Coffee submenu item to select that menu item.

7 Click the Fill color in the Control panel to open the color options. Click the Eyedropper tool, and click the brown bar beneath the main menu items to sample the brown color.

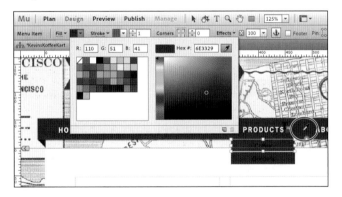

Just like with the top-level menu items, if you edit the appearance of one submenu container, they all change. By sampling a color, you fill the selected object with the color sampled. You will learn how to save and edit that sampled color in Lesson 5, "Working with Shapes and Color."

8 Click and drag the bottom-middle point of the Coffee container down until it's 30px in height.

9 Click the Grinders menu item, and drag the bottom-middle point of the container down until it is 30px in height as well.

10 Change the Stroke Weight in the Control panel to **0**, if necessary.

11 Click the Text panel tab, and change the color to White. Click the Font Family menu in the Text panel, and choose News Gothic Std Bold from the System

Fonts (Exports As Image) menu. On Windows, you can select News Gothic Std and click the Bold button in the Text panel.

12 In the States panel, click the Rollover state and click the Fill color in the Control panel to open the color options. Click the Eyedropper tool, and click the brown bar beneath the main menu items to sample the brown color. In the Text panel, click the Color box and select the orange color swatch with the tooltip that shows R=251 G=176 B=59.

13 Select the Mouse Down state, and make sure that the color fill and the text color match the Rollover state.

14 In the States panel, select the Active (Normal) state and repeat sampling the fill color in step 12. In the Text panel, click the Color box and select the orange color swatch with the tooltip that shows R=251 G=176 B=59.

15 Choose View > Hide Rasterized Text Frame Indicators to see the menu without the indicators.

16 Choose View > Show Rasterized Text Frame Indicators to show them again.

17 Choose File > Save Site.

Assigning content to the footer

The main navigation typically appears in the menu near the top of the page. In the footer, most sites also contain a repeat of the main navigation or links to other useful information, such as contact details, brief information about the site, or a statement of site ownership. Corporate sites often use the footer to provide links to driving directions, telephone number, a web form (like a contact form), or at least an e-mail.

1 Choose Edit > Deselect All.

2 With the Selection tool, click the menu widget, then choose Edit > Copy. Press and hold the H key, when the Hand cursor appears, drag the page up until you see the footer area at the bottom of the page. Release the H key. Choose Edit > Paste.

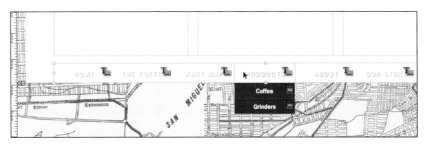

3 Attempt to drag the menu bar widget into the footer area, below the page area. Muse does not let you, because it considers the menu bar widget to be part of the page area. When you drag, the height of the page area simply increases instead.

To associate content with the footer and be able to drag that content into the footer area, you need to assign it as a Footer Item. Assigning an item to the footer also means that you cannot select it on the pages and that it will move with the footer if the page height grows or shrinks.

▶ **Tip:** You can also assign content to the footer by selecting the content on the page, right-clicking (Windows) or Control-clicking (Mac OS) and choosing Footer Item from the context menu or by choosing Object > Footer Item.

4 With the copied menu bar widget selected, select Footer in the Control panel.

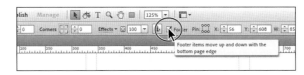

5 Drag the copied menu bar down below the page area below the footer guide. You will be adding more content to the footer in Lesson 5, "Working with Shapes and Color," but for now, leave the menu bar where it is.

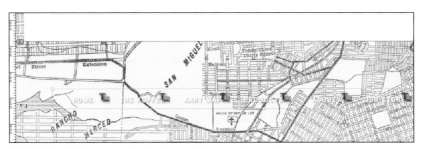

6 Choose File > Save Site.

Creating new master pages

Although a consistent, cohesive site design is important, that doesn't mean every page should look exactly alike. Sometimes a group of pages within a site need their own identity. For example, you may want to design the individual product pages or customer feedback pages with a slightly different look and feel from the main pages. Muse lets you create multiple master pages for just this reason. You can either create a new, blank master page based on the site properties or even duplicate an existing master page and make some changes to the copy.

Next, you will create a new, blank master page that you may use later on.

1 Click the Plan mode link above the Control panel.

2 In Plan mode, choose Page > Add New Master Page.

   Muse creates a new, blank master page in the Masters area, with the same properties (width, column, and so on) as the current site properties (File > Site Properties).

3 Name the new master page **Test**. Because this new master page is blank, you could double-click the master thumbnail in Plan mode and add content to the master page later. Instead, you will duplicate the A-Master page and make some changes.

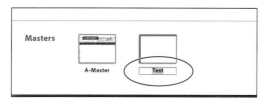

4 Position the pointer over the A-Master thumbnail in Plan mode. Right-click (Windows) or Control-click (Mac OS), and choose Duplicate Page from the context menu. Doing so creates a new master that is an exact copy of the A-Master page.

> **Tip:** Another way to duplicate a master page is to hold down the Alt (Windows) or Option (Mac OS) key while you drag a master thumbnail either between two master page thumbnails or to right of the master thumbnail farthest to the right. Release the mouse and then the key when the blue drop zone appears, and you've made a copy.

5 Name the new master page, **MasterFlash**.

6 Drag the MasterFlash thumbnail to the left, between the A-Master and Test thumbnails, if necessary. When the blue drop zone appears, release the mouse button.

> **Tip:** Just as you can delete pages in the site map, you can also easily delete a master page by positioning the pointer over its thumbnail and clicking the X that appears just off the upper-right corner of that same thumbnail.

You can easily reorder the master pages. This has no effect on the site, it can just be easier to either group similar master pages or put the most often used together.

7 Double-click the MasterFlash thumbnail to open the new master page in Design mode.

At this point, suppose you want this new master page to have two columns instead of three or to have a different page height. You could (but don't) choose Page > Page Properties to edit those properties. In this case, you are going to replace the static logo image with Flash (.swf) content.

8 With the Selection tool, select the logo image in the header area and delete it.

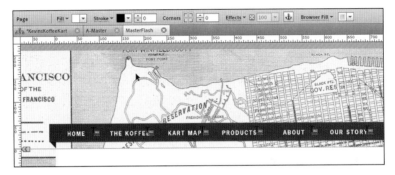

9 Choose File > Save Site, and choose File > Close Page to close the MasterFlash master page. In Lesson 6, "Adding Images to Your Site," you will add Flash content to the master page, making the static logo animated.

Applying master pages

▶ **Tip:** Another way to apply a master page is to right-click (Windows) or Control-click (Mac OS) a page thumbnail in the site map and choose Masters > [*name of the master to apply*]. Using this method, you will also see the No Master option in the context menu. You can apply No Master to a unique page that you don't want any master content on; the page will not associate with any master page.

When you create a new master page, either a blank master or by duplicating an existing master page, that new master page isn't applied to any of the pages in your site map. You can apply master pages to any number of pages, even having a unique master page for each page if you really wanted.

In the case of the KevinsKoffeeKart site, you will apply the MasterFlash master page to the HOME page. That way the SWF animation will play on the home page only and a static image (nonanimated), will appear on the rest.

1 In Plan mode, drag the Size slider in the Control panel, making sure that the page thumbnails still all fit in the Application window.

2 Drag the MasterFlash thumbnail onto the HOME page in the site map and release. Notice that the blue text beneath the page thumbnail, called the master badge, changed from A-Master to MasterFlash indicating that the Master Flash content is now on that page.

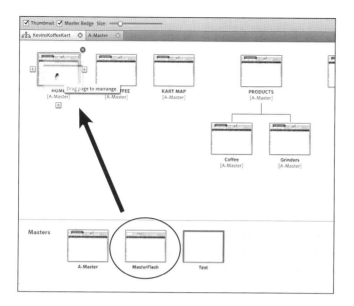

3 In the Control panel, deselect Master Badge. Notice that the master page names associated with the pages no longer show beneath the page thumbnails.

Sometimes, perhaps when you're discussing the site map with a client or colleague, you want to look at the site map and just see the page thumbnails. Muse lets you show and hide the master badge for all pages.

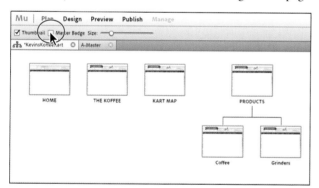

● **Note:** When you apply a different master page to a page in the site map, the previous master page content is removed from the page and replaced entirely by the new master page content.

4 Select Master Badge to show them again.

5 In the Control panel deselect Thumbnail, and you will see that the thumbnails turn into simple white boxes.

At times, you may also want to focus on the site map structure and not be distracted by a preview of the page in each thumbnail. You can also turn on and off the thumbnail preview.

6 Select Thumbnail again to see the previews once more.

7 Choose File > Save Site.

Testing your pages

During the course of the exercises, you've previewed the file by selecting Preview mode. This allows you to test links, hide all hidden items, and navigate the site like visitors will. While Preview mode is very useful, it does not show a few things in the site, such as the page title and favicon.

To give you the full user experience, Muse lets you test a page or your entire site in a browser outside of the program. That's what you'll do next.

1 Choose File > Preview Site In Browser.

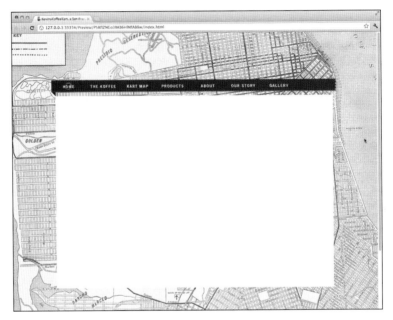

Preview Site In Browser allows you to navigate between pages for an overview of the site. Choosing Preview Page In Browser, the other alternative, allows you to see only the current page in the Document window or the first page of the site if there are no open pages. If you click any of the links in the page, they will not work because you are only previewing the appearance of that single page.

2 Click the links in the menu bar to navigate to other pages.

The pages all look the same at this point, except for the HOME page, but in the next lesson, you will start to add page content to each page.

3 Close the browser window, and return to Muse.

4 Close all open pages, but leave the KevinsKoffeeKart.muse site file open for the next lesson.

Review questions

1 What purpose do master pages serve?

2 What resolution are images typically in your website?

3 What purpose do the header and footer page guides serve on the master pages?

4 Where on a page does a background image in the browser fill appear?

5 Name the two ways that you can apply master pages to pages in Plan mode.

6 How do you assign content that is not in the footer area to the footer?

Review answers

1 A master page in Muse contains content that is consistently on each page of your site, like a menu or logo. You can use just one default master page throughout your website, or you can create multiple master pages and apply them individually to other pages.

2 When designing for the web, the optimal resolution for images is 72ppi.

3 The header and footer page guides frame where the header and footer content appear on the page. They also determine how large either of those areas is. Content that is placed on a master page and appears above the header guide or below the footer guide is locked on each page (cannot be selected or edited).

4 When you insert a background image using the Browser Fill option in the Control panel, the image appears in the background of the browser window, behind the page area.

5 You can apply master pages to pages in your site by dragging a master page thumbnail in Plan mode onto a page in the site plan area. You can also apply a master page to a page in the site map by right-clicking (Windows) or Control-clicking (Mac OS) a page thumbnail in the site plan area and choosing Masters > [*name of the master to apply*].

6 Select the content on the page and select Footer in the Control panel, right-click (Windows)/Control-click (Mac OS) the content, and choose Footer Item from the context menu, or select the content and choose Object > Footer Item.

4 ADDING AND STYLING TEXT

Lesson overview

In this lesson, you'll begin to add more content to your pages and learn to

- Type and place text
- Change text attributes
- Work with fonts
- Create and edit paragraph styles
- Create and edit character styles
- Paste text between Muse sites
- Format text frames

This lesson takes approximately 45 minutes to complete. If you are starting from scratch in this lesson, use the method described in the "Jumpstart" section on page 5 of "Getting Started."

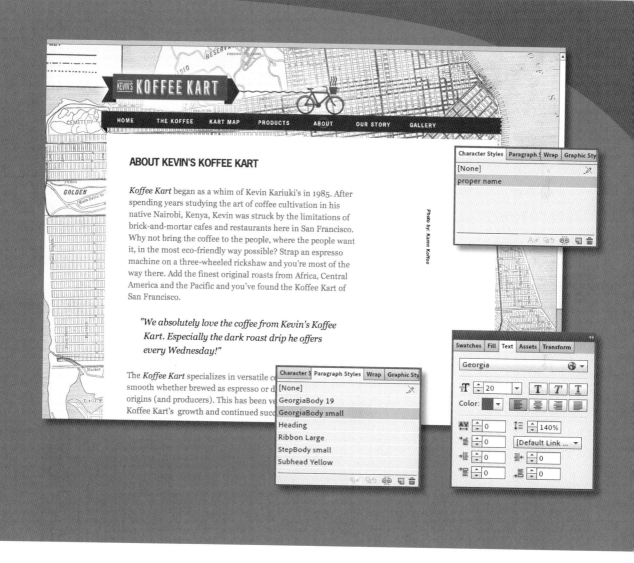

Muse provides numerous tools for creating, editing, and formatting text, whether it's created within the program or imported from another source.

Inserting text

In this lesson, you will explore the text formatting and the style options available to you in Muse.

Muse offers several ways to add text to your web pages. From typing text directly on your page to placing or pasting text from other applications, adding text to your design is simple.

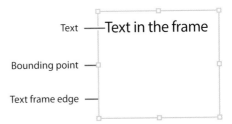

Like in Adobe InDesign, text that you insert into your pages in Muse is contained within a text frame. You can resize, reposition, rotate, and transform those text frames and their content (which can include text *and* images), almost any way you like.

In this first section, you will insert text in various ways, then move on to formatting that same text.

Typing text

The first method you'll use to insert text into your pages is to create a text frame and simply type a page heading into it.

1   With the KevinsKoffeeKart.muse site file still open and Plan mode showing, double-click the ABOUT page thumbnail to open the page in Design mode.

2   Choose View > Fit Page In Window.

3   Select the Text tool in the Toolbox. Position the pointer in the upper-left corner of the first column on the page, click and drag down and to the right to the right edge of the column. When the measurement label shows a height of approximately 40px, release the mouse button. A blinking cursor will appear within the text frame.

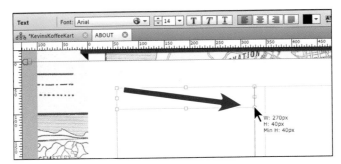

Note: If you are starting from scratch using the Jumpstart method described in the "Jumpstart" section of "Getting Started," your workspace may look different from the figures you see in this Lesson.

Note: The exercises in this Lesson, like others in this book, require that you have the fonts supplied on the *Muse Classroom in a Book* disc installed on your machine. For more information on installing the necessary fonts, see "Fonts used in this book" on page 2.

Note: If you have not already done so, copy the Lessons folder onto your hard disk, from the *Adobe Muse Classroom in a Book* CD. See "Copying the Classroom in a Book files" on page 3.

As you create the text frame, if the cursor comes close to a guide on the page, the frame you are drawing will snap to that guide and a red line will appear indicating that it is snapped.

Note: When creating or editing frames in Muse, the more you zoom into the content, the finer the increments will appear in the measurement label.

4 Type **About Koffee Kart** in the text frame.

Muse uses Arial as the default font and 14 pixels as the default font size, whether you type or place your text onto your pages. You can change these settings easily and will do so in the "Formatting text" section on page 94.

5 Select the Selection tool in the Toolbox, and notice that the text frame, which is still selected, now has bounding points around it. Later, you'll use these points to resize the text frame.

6 Click the center of the text frame and drag it toward the middle of the page.

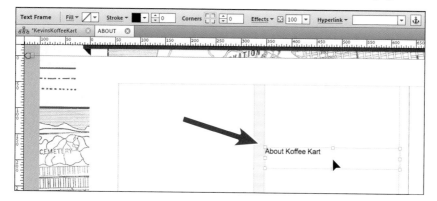

Notice that the frame snaps to guides, and red lines and other visual aids display, depending on where you drag the frame and what its edges touch. The snapping feature and visual aids are part of Smart Guides and are turned on by default. In a later lesson, you will turn them off to reposition content when you don't want it snapping to guides or other content.

7 Again from its center, drag the text frame into the upper-left corner of the first column guides, ensuring that the top and left edges of the frame snap into the guides.

About Smart Guides

Smart Guides are temporary snap-to guides and pop-ups that appear when you create or manipulate objects. They help you align, edit, and transform objects relative to other objects, page guides, or both by snap-aligning and displaying gap measurements to help with consistent spacing between objects.

Smart Guides are turned on by default, but you can easily turn them off by choosing View > Smart Guides. Be aware, however, that when you turn off Smart Guides, you also turn off the snapping feature and visual aids.

Note: When the pointer is over the bounding point, the cursor will change to a double arrow, indicating that you can resize the frame.

8 With the frame selected, drag the bottom-middle bounding point of the frame down until the measurement label shows a height (H) of approximately 50px.

9 With the Selection tool, double-click the text frame to select the Text tool in the Toolbox and enable text editing.

10 Insert the cursor before the word, "Koffee" and type **Kevin's** and then a space.

Note: You may want to zoom in to see the text more clearly.

11 Choose File > Save Site.

Placing text

In Muse, you can place text (File > Place) from a file that was created in another application, provided it was saved as a .txt file. Because .txt files typically do not contain formatting, Muse applies default formatting to the text when you place the file.

1 Select the Selection tool in the Toolbox, and click away from the text frame to deselect it.

Note: You cannot place (File > Place) text into an existing text frame in Muse.

2 Choose File > Place. Navigate to the Lesson04 folder in the Lessons folder. Select the file called TextAbout.txt, and click Open (Windows) or Select (Mac OS).

You see the Place Gun cursor, which indicates that you can either click to create a text frame and place the text in it or you can click and drag to draw the frame to the proportions you want.

3 Position the Place Gun cursor below the heading text on the left edge of the first column. Drag to the right and down until the pointer is on the right edge of the second column and the bottom edge of the new frame is about halfway down the page. This will make the text frame taller than needed, but that's okay.

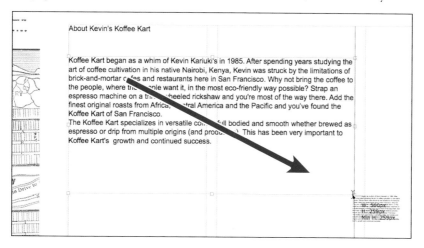

Unlike in Adobe InDesign, you can't drag a frame to make it smaller than the content inside of it. You can, however, make the text frame taller.

4 With the text frame selected, click the Transform panel tab on the right side of the workspace if it's not already showing. Change the Y value to **120** and press Enter or Return to accept it.

Note: If your screen resolution allows it, you may see the X, Y, W, H, and rotation options that you see in the Transform panel in the Control panel as well. You can make the transform edits in either location.

Instead of resizing or dragging a text frame using the Selection tool, you can be more precise by using the transform options in the Transform panel.

5 Choose File > Save Site.

6 Click the Preview mode link to preview the text.

7 Click the Design mode link to return to the ABOUT page.

Now that you have text on the page, you will begin to format it using the text formatting options available in Muse.

Copy and paste text from another program

You can also copy and paste text from your favorite application, such as your e-mail client or InDesign, although the formatting is lost when you paste the text in Muse. Much like when you place or type text directly on the page in Muse, pasted text is formatted according to the program defaults for text, which are: Arial, 14px, black color.

When you need to bring in a lot of text from InDesign, you can export it as a .txt file. To do that, select the text in InDesign with the Type tool, choose File > Export, and then choose Text Only from the Format menu to complete the export.

Formatting text

In this next section, you will learn a wide range of text formatting options available to you in Muse, from changing font size to adjusting paragraph spacing. You can find these formatting options in the Control panel (Window > Control) and Text panel (Window > Text).

The Text panel contains more formatting options than the Control panel, but sometimes the Control panel can be more convenient because it's always showing (by default).

Open the Text panel, by choosing Window > Text, and take a look at some of the formatting features available.

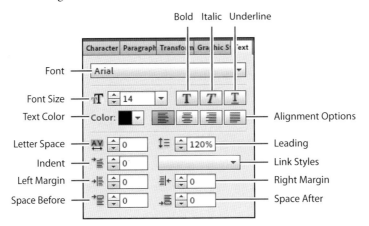

The first formatting you will address is the font size of the heading text.

Adjusting Font Size

In print work, most of us use the unit *points* to set the size of our text. In Muse, the font size unit used is *pixel.*

1   Double-click the header text "About Kevin's Koffee Kart" with the Selection tool to switch to the Text tool. Position the cursor over the text and click three times to select the text.

Note: Clicking text twice with the Text tool selects a word, clicking three times selects the paragraph, and clicking four times selects all of the text within a frame.

2   Select 24 from the Font Size menu in the Control panel.

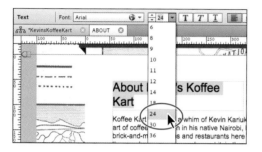

3   Select the Selection tool, and drag the right-middle bounding point to the right until the text fits.

4   With the Text tool selected, insert the cursor in the text frame of the text you placed below the heading text. Choose Edit > Select All.

5   In the Font Size menu in the Control panel, select the value 14 and type **22**. Press Enter or Return to accept the change.

▶ **Tip:** To change the font size by 1-pixel increments, you can also click the arrows to the left of the Font Size field in the Control panel or Text panel.

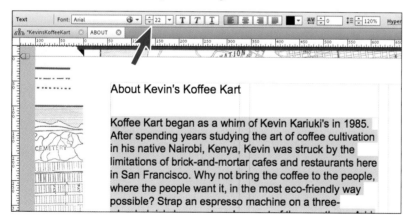

▶ **Tip:** If you have a text frame to which you would like to apply all the same text formatting, you can select the text frame rather than the text and edit the formatting using the Text panel.

6   Select the Selection tool, and notice that the text frame has gotten taller to fit the resized text.

You will also see a dotted line across the frame near the bottom of the text frame. This indicates a minimum height for the text frame. When you drag the frame shorter than the text and the dotted line appears, Muse inserts a style property called `min-height` in the code. This tells the browser that the frame must be at least that tall and can expand taller if the content dictates it.

7   With the Selection tool, drag the bottom-middle bounding point down until the dotted line disappears. You won't have to drag far.

▶ **Tip:** You can dynamically change the font size of selected text using keyboard shortcuts. To increase the font size in increments of 2 pixels, press Control+Shift+> (Windows), or Command+Shift+> (Mac OS). To reduce the font size, press Control+Shift+< (Windows), or Command+Shift+< (Mac OS).

Selecting a font

For years, web designers and developers had to rely strictly on "web safe" fonts, which generally came installed on Mac OS and Windows machines, for their web designs. The reason for using web safe fonts was because any font you used in your web pages needed to be installed on the machine of the visitor viewing your website in order for the text to render correctly.

Fortunately, times have changed! In fact, Muse supports three categories of fonts you can use:

* **Web fonts:** The newest category of font on the Web, these are fonts hosted by a company, sometimes for a fee. When a hosted font is viewed, your site visitor's browser gets the font from that company's server, so the font appears on your web page, regardless of whether that site visitor owns the specific font. Using Muse, you get access to hundreds of free fonts hosted by Adobe Typekit.

* **Web safe fonts:** Most systems or devices have these fonts installed, which increases the likelihood of them displaying correctly on your visitors' machines.

* **System fonts:** These fonts are those located on your machine. If you apply one of these to text on your pages, Muse converts that text to an image when your site is previewed, published, or exported.

Apply a web safe font

The first category of font you will use is a web safe font that you will apply to the placed text on the ABOUT page.

1   Double-click the placed text frame to switch to the Text tool. Insert the cursor in the text, and choose Edit > Select All.

2   Click the Font menu in the Control panel.

In the Font menu that appears, you will see the three font categories available: Web Fonts, Web Safe Fonts, and System Fonts.

3   In the menu, position the pointer over the Web Safe Fonts option. Position the pointer over the font Georgia in the list that appears.

A yellow tooltip appears. In the tooltip, you'll see the words "Alt Fonts:" and a listing of fonts. On the Web, if you choose a web safe font, just because it's web safe doesn't guarantee it will work, because visitors need to have the font (Georgia in this example) on their machines. The alt fonts are second, third, and so on choices for the browser, just in case Georgia isn't available. You don't have to worry about alt fonts, and you cannot change them in Muse. Just know that Muse selects fonts that are similar to your first choice font.

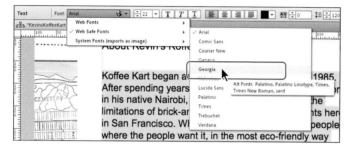

4   Click to select Georgia to apply that font to the text.

Apply a system font

The next category of font you will use is a system font. Applying this type of font converts the text into an image.

1   With the Text tool still selected, select the heading text "About Kevin's Koffee Kart."

2   Click the Font menu in the Control panel, and position the pointer over the System Fonts (Exports As Image) option. In the menu of fonts that appears, scroll down and choose News Gothic Std Bold. This may cause the text to wrap in the text frame. On Windows, you can choose News Gothic Std and click the Bold button in the Control panel.

After selecting the system font, you will see a small T with an image icon appear in the lower-right corner of the text frame. That icon indicates that the text will become an image when you publish the site.

3   Select the Selection tool in the Toolbox. If necessary, drag the right-middle bounding point of the frame to the right until the text fits horizontally.

Make the frame a little wider than the text in case you make size or font changes later that make the text larger in any way.

4   Drag the bottom-middle point of the text frame up until it's above the placed text frame, if necessary. That way they don't overlap.

5   Click the Preview mode link, and check out the fonts.

6   Position the pointer over the placed text in Preview mode, then click and drag to select it. Because you can select it like you can in Design mode means it is still text. Position the pointer over the text "About Kevin's Koffee Kart," click, and drag. You will see that it selects as a single object, which means that it is an image.

7   Click the Design mode link to return to the ABOUT page in Design mode.

Apply a web font

The next type of font that you will apply to text will be a web font. You will need an Internet connection to choose a web font the first time. Choosing a web font in Adobe Muse will download a local version of the font so that you can preview it in Muse when working on a site. Those fonts do not need to go with the site, because the code for your page will contain a link to the Typekit servers to view the font in the browser. Even if you decide to export the site content, and host the site elsewhere, you can still use the web fonts that are chosen within Muse.

1   With the Text tool selected, select the heading text "About Kevin's Koffee Kart."

2   Click the Font menu in the Control panel, and position the pointer over the Web Fonts option. Click Add Web Fonts in the menu that appears.

▷ **Tip:** If you are looking for a particular font, you can type the name of the font in the Filter By Name field in the upper-left corner of the Add Web Fonts dialog box to search for it.

3   In the Add Web Fonts dialog box, click the Sans Serif button in the Filter options.

Filtering allows you to see only specific font types, such as serif or sans serif. To stop filtering, click the Sans Serif button again.

Tip: You can add web fonts to the Fonts menu without selecting text. Choose File > Add/Remove Web Fonts to access the Add Web Fonts dialog box.

4   Click the Recommended For Headings button to the right of the Filter options.

5   Click to select the font Oswald, and click OK.

Note: Since the Typekit library may have changed since we wrote this lesson, the Oswald font may not be available. Feel free to choose another font if you like. Just know that any references to Oswald later in the lessons will be your font instead.

6   When the Web Fonts Notification dialog box appears, click OK.

This dialog box indicates that the font you've chosen is added to the Font menu. This font will appear in the Font menu no matter what site file is open, allowing you to apply it to any site.

Note: For each font you choose, the entire font family is down-loaded. This means that if there are any font styles such as bold or black, those font styles are downloaded as well.

7   With the header text still selected, click the Font menu in the Control panel, and position the pointer over the Web Fonts option. Choose Oswald Bold (or the font you selected) from the menu that appears.

Next, you will remove the Oswald font and add another.

8   With the header text still selected, click the Font menu in the Control panel, and position the pointer over the Web Fonts option. Choose Add Web Fonts.

9 In the Add Web Fonts dialog box, click the Show Selected Fonts button (the check mark) in the upper-right corner of the dialog box.

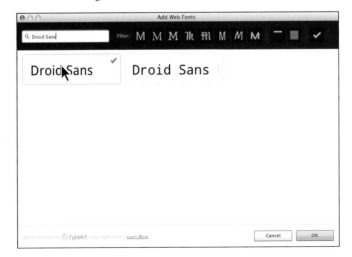

This shows a listing of all of the web fonts that you've selected in the past.

Note: Any font styles in a family, like Oswald Bold, that are applied to text when you remove them in the Add Web Fonts dialog box, will remain in the Web Fonts section of the Font list. Also, if you remove fonts that are used in a site file that is not currently open, when you open that site after removing the font, it will be downloaded again automatically.

10 Click Oswald (or the font you selected) to deselect it and remove that font family from the Web Fonts menu.

11 Deselect Show Selected Fonts (the check mark icon) to see all of the fonts again.

12 Type Droid Sans in the Filter By Name field in the upper-left corner of the dialog box. Click to select the Droid Sans font in the list (the first listed, without the bar to the right of the name). Click OK.

13 Click OK in the Web Fonts Notification dialog box.

14 With the header text still selected, click the Font menu in the Control panel, and position the pointer over the Web Fonts option. Choose Droid Sans Bold from the menu that appears.

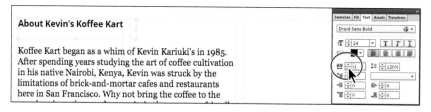

15 Click the Preview mode link, and check out the fonts. Return to Design mode, and choose Edit > Deselect All.

Changing alignment, leading, and letter spacing

With the main formatting complete, you can begin to fine-tune some of the text to better suit your design. As mentioned earlier, you can change the formatting options in either the Text panel or the Control panel, depending on what tool or content is selected in Muse and the resolution of your screen.

1 With the Selection tool, click to select the header text frame that contains the text "About Kevin's Koffee Kart," if it's not already selected.

2 Change the Letter Space option ( ) to **–1** in the Text panel on the right side of the workspace.

Letter spacing is the distance between characters (not just letters). When you select the entire text frame, Muse changes the spacing between all letters in the text frame. If you come from the print world, letter spacing is the web equivalent of tracking and kerning. Letter spacing uses pixel values rather than the typical print unit, points. On the Web, we typically use letter spacing for text like headlines, not entire stretches of body copy. Just keep in mind that every small kerning adjustment adds code to the HTML pages that Muse creates for you when you preview, publish, or export as HTML, which can ultimately increase download times for your pages.

3 Double-click the text frame to switch to the Text tool and insert the cursor between the apostrophe (') and "s" in Kevin's.

4 Press Control+= (Windows) or Command+= (Mac OS) a few times to zoom into the cursor position. (This is the shortcut for the View > Zoom In command.)

5 In the Text panel notice that the Letter Space is −1. Change the Letter Space to **−2**.

When you insert the cursor between characters, it controls the spacing between only those two characters. It also overrides the letter spacing for the two characters you set in the previous steps.

Note: You can enter a new value in the blank Letter Space field to apply a single letter-spacing value to the text.

6 With the cursor still in the text, choose Edit > Select All and look in the Text panel. The Letter Space value is blank. This means that there is more than one Letter Space value applied to the selected text.

7 Choose View > Fit Page In Window.

Now that the letter spacing is set, you will change the leading of the main text on the page. *Leading* refers to the distance between baselines of text (the space between lines of text).

8 Insert the cursor into the first paragraph of the text frame below the heading. Click three times to select the first paragraph (only).

In the Text panel, notice that the Leading value (⤒) is 120%. That means that the distance between the lines of text is 120% of the font size of the text.

9 Change the Leading value to **150%** in the Text panel.

You do not have to type the percent sign as Muse will assume that the unit is percent. You can also enter a value with px (for pixel), like 32px, instead of a percent, and Muse will keep it as a pixel value.

Note: If the panels are in the way, zoom out to see the third column.

10 Choose View > Fit Page In Window. With the Text tool, click and drag in the page's third column from the left to create a text frame for a caption. Make sure the frame is the width of that column. Its vertical position in the column doesn't matter right now.

11 Type **Photo by: Karen Koffee** in the text frame. Leave the cursor in the frame.

12 Press Control+= (Windows) or Command+= (Mac OS) a few times to zoom into the cursor position.

13 In the Text panel, click the Align Right button ( ) to align the text to the right in the text frame.

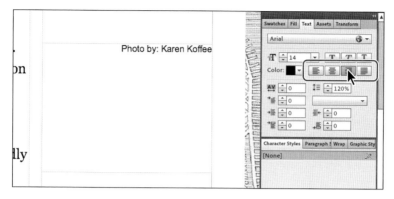

Muse offers 4 alignment options: Left, Center, Right, as well as Align Justify.

14 Choose View > Fit Page In Window.

15 Insert the cursor in the first paragraph of the main body text and click the Align Justify button ( ) in the Text panel.

About Kevin's Koffee Kart

Koffee Kart began as a whim of Kevin Kariuki's in 1985. After spending years studying the art of coffee cultivation in his native Nairobi, Kenya, Kevin was struck by the limitations of brick-and-mortar cafes and restaurants here in San Francisco. Why not bring the coffee to the people, where the people want it, in the most eco-friendly way possible? Strap an espresso machine on a three-wheeled rickshaw and you're most of the way there. Add the finest original roasts from Africa, Central America and the Pacific and you've found the Koffee Kart of San Francisco.
The Koffee Kart specializes in versatile coffee, full bodied and smooth whether brewed as espresso or drip from

You'll see that the Align Justify option justifies the entire paragraph (makes it look like a block of text), except for the last line of text in the paragraph.

16 Choose Edit > Undo Set Text Align. You could also have clicked the Align Left button in the Text panel.

17 Choose File > Save Site.

Adjusting paragraph indents, margins, and spacing

The text formatting options covered in this exercise reside in the Text panel only. You will create a quote in your text while utilizing these options.

1 Select the Selection tool, and choose File > Place. Navigate to the Lesson04 folder in the Lessons folder, select the text file named TextQuote.txt, and click Open (Windows) or Select (Mac OS).

2 Position the Place Gun in the third column, away from the caption text. Drag out a text frame that is the width (roughly) of the third column.

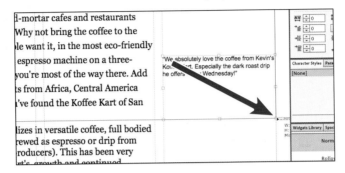

3 Double-click the text frame to switch to the Text tool. Choose Edit > Select All, then Edit > Copy to copy the text.

4 Insert the cursor in front of the paragraph that starts "The Koffee Kart specializes" and choose Edit > Paste. Press Enter or Return to add a paragraph return after the pasted text.

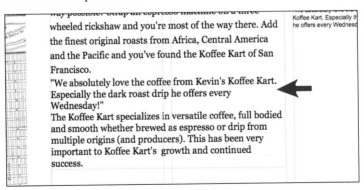

The text frame will grow to fit the new text.

5 Select the Selection tool; a dotted line indicating the minimum height may appear. Drag the bottom-middle bounding point of the text frame down a bit until dotted line disappears.

You can also tell by the measurement label that appears. When the H and Min H values are the same, then the dotted line no longer shows.

6 Select the text frame in the third column that you copied the quote from, and press Delete to remove it.

Now that the text is on the page, you will apply the formatting options to format the quote text.

Tip: You could also select the text frame and choose Edit > Clear.

7 Select the Text tool in the Toolbox, and select the quote text you pasted. Click the Italic button (T) in the Text panel.

If you come from a program like InDesign, you may be used to choosing a separate bold or italic font style. On the Web, assigning bold or italic is perfectly acceptable, and Muse has buttons in the Text panel for bolding, italicizing, and underlining text.

8 In the Text panel, change the Left Margin (→≣) to **40** and the Right Margin (≣←) to **40** as well. Change the Leading value to **150%** or whatever you think looks good.

9 Change the Space Before (↑≣) to **30** and the Space After (↓≣) to **30**.

Tip: The Left and Right Margin values can also be negative values. Using this negative value, you can pull the left and/or right side of a paragraph outside of the text frame in Muse to create some interesting type effects.

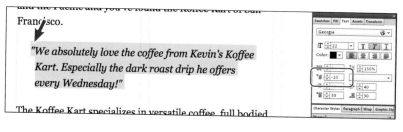

Tip: You can press the Tab key to move the cursor forward between fields or Shift+Tab to move the cursor backward through the fields in the panels.

The Left Margin, Right Margin, Space Before, and Space After values are pixel values. You can type in a % value like 10% in any off these four settings, and Muse will convert the value to pixels.

10 Change the Indent to **10** in the Text panel, and you'll see that only the first line of the quote is pushed in. Change the Indent to **−10** and you can achieve an outdent or hanging indent.

Changing the Indent to −10 moves the first line to the left of the left edge of the paragraph.

Tip: To learn more about pasting content into text, see the section "Create a Dotted Line" on page 128 of Lesson 5, "Working with Shapes and Color."

At this point, using the formatting you've learned so far, you can adjust the letter spacing between the quote mark (") and the text, and much more.

Keep in mind, however, that changing the font size of the first quote mark (") also changes the spacing of your paragraph. If you want a big first quote mark, you can create a separate text frame or even place an image to the left of the quote text or paste it into the text frame. (If you use a graphic, don't forget to delete the quote character in the text.)

Changing the color and case of text

The last bit of text formatting you'll learn about is changing the color of text and changing the case of text between lowercase and uppercase.

1   With the Text tool, select the header text "About Kevin's Koffee Kart."

Note: You will learn about creating and editing colors in Lesson 5, "Working with Shapes and Color."

2   Click the Color option in the Text panel (or Control panel) and change the RGB values to R: **110**, G: **51**, B: **41** to change the color of the heading text. You can press Return or Escape to save the change and close the Color Picker.

Note: If the text is wrapping in the text frame, change the width of the text frame with the Selection tool to fit the text horizontally.

3   Choose Edit > Change Case > UPPERCASE to capitalize all of the selected headline text.

Tip: You could also right-click (Windows) or Control-click (Mac OS) on the text and choose Change Case > UPPERCASE from the context menu.

4   Choose File > Save Site.

Now that you've explored the text formatting options in Muse, you'll learn how to work faster and with more consistency using paragraph and character styles.

Creating Type Styles

Using styles in Muse, you can quickly apply consistent formatting to text and make global changes across multiple pages in your site. After you create a style, you can update all of the text throughout your site that uses that particular style simply by editing the saved style. This is very similar to how styles in InDesign or Illustrator work. You can access Paragraph Styles in the Paragraph Styles panel (Window > Paragraph Styles) of Design mode.

When you publish your site for the world to see, Muse automatically converts your styles to CSS (Cascading Style Sheets) rules and applies them throughout your website.

Muse supports two types of styles:

- **Paragraph** styles retain text and paragraph attributes; apply them to an entire paragraph.

- **Character** styles retain text attributes only; apply them to selected text.

In addition, when you create a new site in Muse, a style named [None] appears by default in the Paragraph Styles panel. You can use this style to remove formatting from text to which you applied a paragraph style. As a best practice, apply text formatting using paragraph and character styles; doing so can cut down on your effort in Muse and also make a smaller site that has the potential to download faster on the Web.

Creating and applying paragraph styles

Paragraph styles apply formatting to an entire paragraph and encompass all of the formatting options found in the Text panel, including font size, alignments, indents, and more. Next, you will create a paragraph style to save the formatting for the heading text and another style for the main body text on the ABOUT page so that you can apply that formatting elsewhere easily. Remember, after you create a style, it appears in the Paragraph Styles panel no matter which page of the site is open.

1 Click the Paragraph Styles panel tab on the right side of the workspace.

Take a minute to familiarize yourself with the options in the Paragraph Styles panel. As you progress through this exercise, you will learn about each of these options.

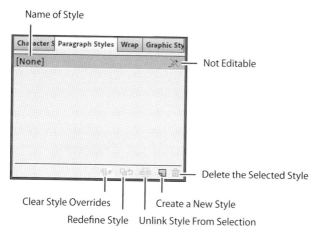

2 With the Text tool, click three times in the first paragraph that begins with "Koffee Kart began as a whim …" to select it.

Note: You do not have to select a paragraph to create a paragraph style. You can simply insert the cursor in the text, then click the Create A New Style button.

3 In the Paragraph Styles panel, click the Create A New Style button ( ) at the bottom of the panel.

Muse saves the formatting from the selected text as a paragraph style and adds it to the Paragraph Styles panel. By default, Muse names the new style Paragraph Style, but you can, and should, rename it.

4 In the Paragraph Styles panel, double-click the style named Paragraph Style to open the Style Options dialog box.

Note: The order of your settings may be different and that's okay.

5 Change the Style Name to **GeorgiaBody**.

In the Style Options dialog box, notice that the formatting options that were saved from the paragraph text appear. Also, you will see the Paragraph Tag menu. To learn more about the Paragraph Tag menu, see the "Paragraph_tags.pdf" file in the Lesson04 folder. Click OK.

When you create a new style from selected text, Muse does not automatically apply the style to that text; edits to the style would not affect the paragraph on which you originally based the style. To apply the new style to its paragraph of origin, you must apply the style after you make it. Double-clicking to name the style does that for you as well as lets you change the name to something that makes sense.

You can always tell which style is applied to text by selecting that text or inserting the cursor in it and looking in the Paragraph Styles panel where the applied style's name will be highlighted.

Note: The order of your settings in the tooltip may be different and that's okay.

6 Position the cursor over the new style in the list, now named GeorgiaBody.

A yellow tooltip appears, listing the style settings. This can help you to differentiate between styles with similar names.

7 With the Text tool selected, select the header text "ABOUT KEVIN'S KOFFEE KART." Repeat steps 3 to 5, naming this new style, **Heading**.

8 Insert the cursor into the paragraph that begins "The Koffee Kart specializes." In the Paragraph Styles panel, click the GeorgiaBody style to apply it to the text.

Note: If the resolution of your screen allows it, you may also see the Paragraph Style menu in the Control panel. This is another way to apply paragraph styles to your text.

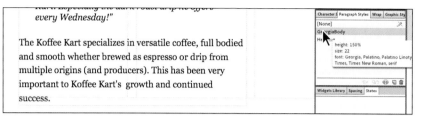

You can either simply insert the cursor in text or select the entire paragraph (or more) to apply paragraph styles.

After you create a paragraph style and begin working in your pages, you may change your mind later on and want to change the settings in the style. In Muse, when you change style settings, every paragraph that has that paragraph style applied will update.

Clearing overrides and editing a paragraph style

In Muse, changing a paragraph style setting is called *redefining* a style. To redefine a style, you edit the formatting for text that has the paragraph style applied. Then you redefine the style based on the changes. This makes the paragraph style match the new settings, and all other paragraphs with that style applied automatically update to match.

1 With the Text tool, select the heading text "ABOUT KEVIN'S KOFFEE KART." In the Control panel, change the Letter Space value to **0**.

Look in the Paragraph Styles panel. You can tell that the style named Heading is applied because it is highlighted, but you will also see a plus (+) to the right of the name. The plus indicates local formatting on the selected text. Local formatting means that there is formatting on the selected text that is different from the paragraph style applied to it.

Note: Changing the letter spacing may wrap the text in the frame. If that's the case, select the Selection tool and drag the frame's right-middle bounding point to the right until the text fits on one line.

2 Position the pointer over Heading+ in the Paragraph Styles panel. A yellow tooltip appears displaying the style settings, a dashed line (-----), and then kerning: 0. Settings listed below the dashed line indicate formatting on the selected text that is not a part of the applied paragraph style.

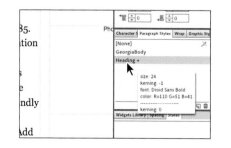

Note: Notice that the uppercase you applied is not listed in the tooltip. That's because uppercase cannot be saved in a paragraph style.

3 Click the Clear Style Overrides button (¶⁺) at the bottom of the Paragraph Styles panel to remove the letter spacing applied to the heading text.

▶ **Tip:** To clear the overrides on selected text, you can also right-click (Windows) or Control-click (Mac OS) the style name in the Paragraph Styles panel and choose Clear Overrides from the context menu.

This strips the formatting from the selected text, and reapplies the currently applied paragraph style. The plus (+) sign that was displayed to the right of the paragraph style's name disappears once you click the Clear Style Overrides button.

4 With the Text tool, select the entire first paragraph that starts with the text "Koffee Kart began as …" In the Control panel, change the Leading to **140%**. Also, click the Color option in the Control panel, and change the RGB values to: R: **110**, G: **97**, B: **97**.

▶ **Tip:** For any value in a field that you want to change, you can select the value in the field (like the 150% in the Leading field), press the up or down arrow to change the value. You can also press and hold the Shift key while pressing the up or down arrows to change the value in larger increments.

5 Press Enter or Return until the color options are hidden.

Once again, look in the Paragraph Styles panel and you will see a plus appear next to the style named GeorgiaBody. Instead of clearing the overrides (removing the extra formatting), you will change the style to match the first paragraph formatting (including the new leading value and color).

6 In the Paragraph Styles panel, position the pointer over the applied style named GeorgiaBody + and take a look at the overrides at the bottom of the yellow tooltip.

7 Click the Redefine Selected Style button (⌘↺) at the bottom of the panel.

▶ **Tip:** To redefine a style, instead of clicking the Redefine Selected Style button, you can right-click (Windows) or Control-click (Mac OS) the style name and choose Redefine Style.

Notice that the plus is gone from the right of the GeorgiaBody style name and that the bottom paragraph has updated to reflect the new formatting.

8 Choose File > Save Site and leave the first paragraph selected for the next section.

Deleting and duplicating a paragraph style

In Muse, you may wind up creating multiple paragraph styles that are very similar to each other. For instance, you may want to create two versions of the GeorgiaBody style, with only a difference in font size. In that case, instead of creating a whole new style to closely match another, you can duplicate an existing style and adjust the formatting as necessary.

1 In the Paragraph Styles panel, right-click (Windows) or Control-click (Mac OS) GeorgiaBody, the style applied to the selected text. Choose Duplicate Style from the context menu to create an exact copy of the style. Muse names it, not surprisingly, GeorgiaBody copy.

2 Right-click (Windows) or Control-click (Mac OS) the new style (GeorgiaBody copy) and choose Rename Style from the context menu. Change the name of the style to **GeorgiaBody small**, and press Enter or Return.

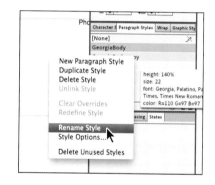

Renaming a style this way does not apply the new style to any selected text.

In order to change the style duplicate, you will redefine the style. First, you need to apply the style to some text.

3 Click GeorgiaBody small in the Paragraph Styles panel to apply it to the selected first paragraph. The paragraph will not change in appearance because the style is just a duplicate.

4 Change the Font Size in the Control panel to 20 by typing **20** and pressing Enter or Return.

5 Click the Redefine Selected Style button at the bottom of the Paragraph Styles panel to update the GeorgiaBody small style to match the selected text.

You will use the new GeorgiaBody small style in place of the GeorgiaBody style. To do this, you can simply apply the new style to selected text and keep the original GeorgiaBody style, or you can choose to delete the original GeorgiaBody style (if you no longer need it), and Muse allows you to choose a style to replace it with. You will do the latter.

6 Choose Edit > Deselect All in preparation for deleting the style.

7 In the Paragraph Styles panel, select the GeorgiaBody style. Click the Delete The Selected Style button (🗑) at the bottom of the panel.

► **Tip:** To delete a style, you can also right-click (Windows) or Control-click (Mac OS) the style name and choose Delete Style in the context menu.

► **Tip:** If you find yourself losing track of which of your many styles are actually in use in your site, Muse offers a quick solution. Right-click (Windows) or Control-click (Mac OS) a style name in the Paragraph Styles panel or the Character Styles panel, and choose Delete Unused Styles to delete all the styles that you are not using. Bear in mind, you will need to clean out the Paragraph Styles and Character Styles panels separately.

8   In the dialog box that appears, choose GeorgiaBody small and click Replace.

The GeorgiaBody style is now gone and the last paragraph has the GeorgiaBody small style applied. Notice the text now displaying in the specified smaller font.

9   Choose View > Hide Guides to temporarily hide the guides and get a better sense of what the text looks like on the page.

10 Choose View > Show Guides to show the guides again.

Unlinking a paragraph style

At times, you may want to strip the formatting from text and start over. Or, perhaps you want text to retain the formatting you originally applied to it with a paragraph style, regardless of changes you later make to that style. Both tasks are simple to accomplish in Muse.

1   With the Text tool selected, select the heading ABOUT KEVIN'S KOFFEE KART.

2   In the Paragraph Styles panel, select the [None] style to remove the formatting and replace it with default formatting.

3   Click the Heading style to reapply the style formatting.

4   With the Text tool, select the caption paragraph "Photo by: Karen Koffee."

The caption is formatted, but it doesn't have a paragraph style applied. You can easily strip the formatting from this sort of text as well, but you need to take a different route. In the Paragraph Styles panel, notice that the [None] style is already applied. That means that you cannot reapply that style to strip the formatting, but you can apply any other style, then click [None] again.

5   Select any other style in the Paragraph Styles panel to apply it to the text.

6   Select the [None] style to set the formatting back to default. Leave the text selected for the next steps.

⬤ **Note:** You may want to zoom in a bit to see all of the text.

7   Select the Heading style in the Paragraph Styles panel to apply the style to the caption paragraph.

Applying this style creates a starting point for formatting.

The last piece of working with paragraph styles involves unlinking a style from text. If you want to create a style similar to another style or apply a style, but don't want that text to update when the style updates, you can unlink the style from the text.

8   Click the Unlink Style From Selection button (⊕) at the bottom of the Paragraph Styles panel.

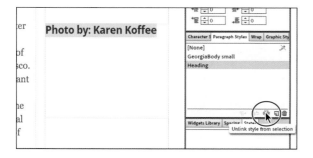

This applies the [None] style to the text, but leaves all of the Heading style formatting. You can now change the formatting of the selected text however you like and it will never update if the Heading style is redefined.

9   Change the Font Size to **12**, click the Italic button, click the Align Right button, and change the letter spacing to **0** in the Control panel. Notice that the caption text that you see may not appear to be italics.

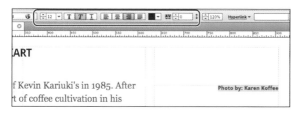

10 Choose View > Preview Mode. The Preview Problem dialog box may appear indicating that the web font you chose, Droid Sans Bold, does not have an italic style and it will be simulated. Click OK.

11 Choose View > Design Mode to return to the ABOUT page.

12 Choose File > Save Site.

Creating and applying a character style

Paragraph styles apply attributes to an entire paragraph, but you can apply character styles to selected text only. Character styles can include only the following formatting options: font, font size, color, styles (italic, bold, underline), and letter spacing. You access character styles from the Character Styles panel (Window > Character Styles).

Next, you will format the proper name "Koffee Kart" and apply that formatting throughout the page using a character style. Just know that once a character style is created, it appears in the Character Styles panel if any page in the site is open.

1   Click the Character Styles panel tab on the right side of the workspace.

Take a minute to familiarize yourself with the options in the Character Styles panel. They are the same as the Paragraph Styles panel.

Name of Style

Not Editable

Delete the Selected Style

Clear Style Overrides   Create a New Style
Redefine Style   Unlink Style From Selection

2   Choose View > Fit Page In Window.

3   With the Text tool, select the text "Koffee Kart" in the first paragraph.

4   Click the Italic button (*T*) in the Control panel.

5   Click the Text Color in the Control panel and choose the red color swatch (color square) that shows R=193 G=39 B=45 in the yellow tooltip when you position the pointer over it. See the figure for the correct red color.

6   With the text "Koffee Kart" still selected, click the Create A New Style button ( ) at the bottom of the Character Styles panel.

Position the pointer over the new style named Character Style, and you'll see the saved formatting appear in a yellow tooltip, just like in a paragraph style.

7   Double-click the new style named Character Style. In the Style Options dialog box, change the Style Name to **proper name** and click OK.

As with a paragraph style, by double-clicking to name the character style right away, you also apply it to the selected text from which the style was made.

▶ **Tip:** If your screen resolution allows it, you may also see the Character Style menu in the Control panel. This is another way you can apply a character style.

8   Select the first occurrence of Koffee Kart in the third paragraph.

9   Click the style named "proper name" in the Character Styles panel to apply that formatting to the text.

10 Click the Preview mode link to see the page in Preview mode.

11 Click the Design mode link to return to the page.

12 Choose File > Save Site.

Editing a character style

Editing a character style and the rest of the options in the Character Styles panel work identically to the Paragraph Styles panel.

1   With the Text tool, select the phrase "Koffee Kart" in the first paragraph.

2   Change the color of the text in the Control panel to a dark gray that appears as a swatch in the color options.

3   In the Character Styles panel, position the pointer over the applied style (proper name +) and take a look at the overrides at the bottom of the yellow tooltip.

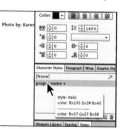

4 Click the Redefine Selected Style button (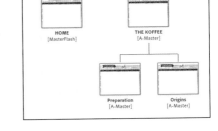) at the bottom of the panel.

Notice that the plus is gone from the right of the proper name style name and that the other Koffee Kart text has updated to reflect the new formatting.

5 Choose File > Save Site.

When working with Character Styles, you will find that a lot of the features like duplicating, deleting, unlinking, and more are identical in functionality to paragraph styles.

Now that you have your text formatted and your styles created, you will copy some content from another site.

Pasting text between Muse sites

In this section, you'll copy some text content from one page and paste it onto another. Copying and pasting text between pages in a site lets you keep the formatting. If you copy and paste text from one site to another site, the formatting is retained, and Muse copies any necessary text styles into the second site. This can be a great way to quickly duplicate styles from one site to another.

First, you need to add pages for this new content.

1 Click the Plan mode link with your site showing.

2 Position the pointer over the THE KOFFEE page thumbnail, and click the plus sign (+) beneath the thumbnail to create a new child page. Name the page **Preparation**.

3 Position the pointer over the new Preparation page thumbnail, and click the plus sign (+) to the right of the thumbnail to create a new sibling page. Name the page **Origins**.

Note: The two new pages you added will become a submenu in the menu. It will need to be formatted to look like the other submenu you formatted in Lesson 3. You will do that in Lesson 8, "Applying Effects, Graphic Styles, and Inserting HTML."

4 Double-click the Preparation thumbnail to open the page in Design mode.

5 Choose View > Fit Page In Window.

6 Choose File > Open Site. Navigate to the Lesson04 folder in the Lessons folder. Choose the file named CopyText.muse, and click Open (Windows) or Select (Mac OS). This is the site from which you're going to copy the content.

7 With the new site open in Plan mode, double-click the Preparation page thumbnail to open the page in Design mode.

8 Choose Edit > Select All, then Edit > Copy.

9 Choose File > Close Site to close the site file and the Preparation page.

You should now be back on the Preparation page you just created in your site.

10 Choose Edit > Paste In Place.

Pasting in place is a great way to paste content in the same relative location on a page as it was on the page you copied it from.

11 Open the Paragraph Styles panel, and notice the new style named StepBody small.

Note: You pasted images as well as text from the CopyText.muse site. When you copy and paste images between sites, the pasted images are linked to the same location as the original copied images. You will learn more about linking in Lesson 6, "Adding Images to Your Site."

Any styles associated with the copied text are brought into the site into which you are pasting the text. If you paste text with a style that has the same name as a style in the page that you are pasting the text into, the existing style overrides the new style you are pasting.

12 Choose File > Close Page to close the Preparation page and return to the ABOUT page.

13 Click the Preview link to preview the text changes on the ABOUT page, then click the Design mode link to return to Design mode.

14 Choose File > Save Site.

Rotating a text frame

As you've seen so far in this lesson, you can transform a text frame in multiple ways, including position and size. But you can also rotate a text frame. If you rotate text frames in Muse, the text in them is converted to an image when the site is previewed, published, or exported to HTML. It's really best to rotate only small pieces of text, because images can add to the download time of the pages in the browser.

You will rotate the caption text frame so that when you place an image in Lesson 6, "Adding Images to Your Site," you can position the text frame vertically to the right of the image.

1 Select the Selection tool in the Toolbox, and click to select the caption text frame.

2 Press Control+= (Windows) or Command+= (Mac OS) a few times to zoom into the caption text frame.

3 Position the pointer off any corner point on the frame, and you'll see a rotate symbol (↻) appear.

4 Click and drag in a clockwise fashion. As you drag, press and hold the Shift key. Drag until the frame is vertical on the page. Release the mouse button and then the Shift key.

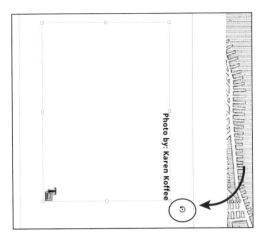

Muse shows a rotation value as you rotate in the Transform panel and allows you to change the rotation value numerically.

Also notice that after the text frame is rotated, the Rasterized Text Frame Indicator appears in the corner of the frame. It looks like a letter "T" with an image icon next to it. This indicates that the text frame will become an image when the site is published or exported.

▶ **Tip:** You could also avoid manually rotating with the Selection tool. Instead, simply select the object to be rotated and type the value in the Rotation Angle field in the Transform panel.

5 Open the Transform panel (Window > Transform), and you'll see the Rotation Angle (△) value. Make sure that the Rotation Angle is 270.

● **Note:** If you have a large enough screen resolution, you may see the Rotation Angle option in the Control panel as well.

Because you are going to place an image in a later lesson and align the caption text frame to it, leave it where it is for now.

6 With the Selection tool, drag the left edge (what used to be the bottom edge before rotation) to the left to close up the frame around the text, if necessary.

7 Choose File > Close Page.

8 Choose File > Save Site, and leave the site open in Plan mode for the next lesson.

In the next lesson, you will explore how to create and edit shapes as well as create and edit color in Muse.

Review questions

1   Name three ways that you can add text to your pages in Muse.

2   Explain the purpose of Smart Guides.

3   What are the three categories of fonts that can be used in Muse?

4   What is the difference between a character and paragraph style?

5   How can you bring paragraph and character styles from one site to another?

6   What happens to text when you rotate its frame?

Review answers

1   In Muse, you can type text directly into your pages after creating a text frame using the Text tool, you can paste text from almost any other application (the formatting will be lost), you can choose File > Place to place a .txt file, or you can copy text from another Muse site and paste the text into the site, retaining the formatting (and styles) of the text content.

2   Smart Guides are temporary snap-to guides and pop-ups that appear when you create or manipulate objects. They help you align, edit, and transform objects relative to other objects, page guides, or both by snap-aligning and sometimes displaying gap measurements to help evenly space multiple objects.

3   The three categories of fonts that can be used in Muse are: web safe fonts, web fonts, and system fonts.

4   Paragraph styles apply attributes to an entire paragraph, but character styles can be applied to selected text only. Character styles can include only the following formatting options: font, font size, color, styles (italic, bold, underline), and letter spacing.

5   The easiest way to bring paragraph and character styles from one site to another is to copy and paste text that has the desired styles applied from one site to another.

6   The text in the text frame is converted to an image when the site is previewed, published, or exported as HTML.

5 WORKING WITH SHAPES AND COLOR

Lesson overview

In this lesson, you'll add personality to your pages by adding shapes and color. Specifically, you'll learn how to

- Create and edit shapes
- Arrange content
- Create lines
- Apply background images to shapes
- Create 100% width content
- Create and edit color
- Work with swatches
- Work with gradients

This lesson takes approximately 30 minutes to complete. If you are starting from scratch in this lesson, use the method described in the "Jumpstart" section on page 5 of "Getting Started."

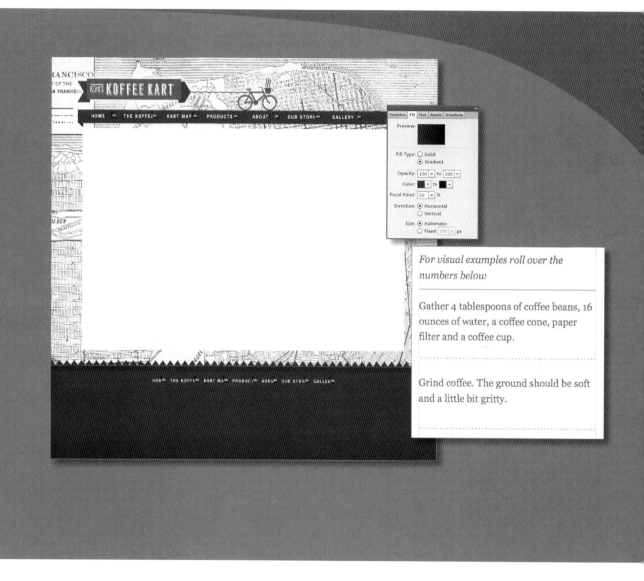

In this information-packed lesson, you'll spice up your website design and learn how to create different types of shapes, apply background images to frames, apply fills and strokes, create gradients, and more.

Working with shapes

● **Note:** If you have not already done so, copy the Lessons folder onto your hard disk, from the *Adobe Muse Classroom in a Book* CD. See "Copying the Classroom in a Book files" on page 3.

Muse comes with a single shape tool called the Rectangle tool, but don't be fooled by its name: You can create much more than boxes with it. In this section, you will use the Rectangle tool to create rectangles, lines, and circles, as well as learn other everyday formatting options. First, you'll prepare a page:

1 With your KevinsKoffeeKart site open in Plan mode, double-click the A-Master page to open that page in Design mode.

2 Choose View > Fit Page In Window, then press Control+- (Windows) or Command+- (Mac OS) twice to zoom out.

This shortcut is for the View > Zoom Out command.

● **Note:** The exercises in this lesson, like others in this book, require that you have the fonts supplied on the *Adobe Muse Classroom in a Book* disc installed on your machine. For more information on installing the necessary fonts, see "Fonts used in this book" on page 2.

3 Press and hold the spacebar to temporarily access the Hand tool. Click and drag up with the mouse until you see the footer area and below. Release the mouse and then the spacebar.

● **Note:** If you are starting from scratch using the Jumpstart method described in the "Jumpstart" section on page 5 of "Getting Started," your workspace may look different than the figures you see in this lesson.

Drawing with the Rectangle tool

In the footer of the A-Master page, you will first insert a rectangle to give the footer some color.

1 Select the Rectangle tool (▣) in the Toolbox.

▶ **Tip:** To see finer increments in the measurement label, you can zoom into the page before you draw the rectangle.

2 Below the footer page guide, and starting on the left edge of the page area, click and drag to the right and down to create a rectangle frame. When the measurement label that appears shows a height of approximately 200px and the right edge of the rectangle frame snaps to the right edge of the page area, release the mouse.

The measurement label shows the height and width of the rectangle you are drawing.

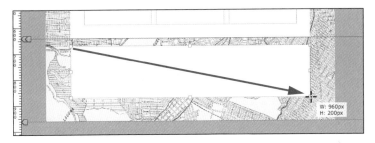

▶ **Tip:** If you hold down the Shift key before you begin drawing with the Rectangle tool, then release the mouse button followed by the Shift key, you can create a perfect square.

3 Click the Preview mode link and scroll down in Preview mode, if necessary, to see the rectangle frame in place.

By default, frames you draw have a white fill color and a black, 1-pixel stroke. You will learn all about how to change the color fill and stroke of this shape in the "Working with color" section on page 130.

4 Click the Design mode link to return to Design mode.

5 Click the Transform panel tab and make sure that the X value is **0** and the Y value is **685**.

The Transform panel also allows you to enter exact dimensions for width and height as well as rotation, if you want it to match the dimensions of another object, for instance.

● **Note:** In the Transform panel, the X value specifies where the left edge of the selected object is relative to the left edge of the page area. The Y value indicates where the top of the selected object is relative to the top of page guide. Changing the X and Y values of selected content positions the upper-left corner of the selected object to those coordinates.

6 Select the Selection tool in the Toolbox, and drag the bottom-middle bounding point of the frame down until it snaps to the bottom of browser guide. A red line will appear when the pointer touches the guide.

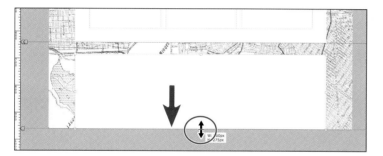

7 Choose File > Save Site.

Creating 100% width content

Content you place or create in Muse, like a rectangle frame, has a defined width and height. That means that it won't change size when displayed at different screen resolutions and it will center, by default, with the rest of the page content in the browser window.

You can, however, create shapes and text frames that stretch to fill the width of the browser window. This is called *100% width* content. A rectangle or text frame that you give 100% width characteristics resizes to fill the page no matter the screen resolution or browser window size.

1 With the frame still selected, drag the left bounding point to the left until it snaps to the edge of the page width. A vertical red line will appear to indicate that it has snapped.

2   Drag the right bounding point to the right until it snaps to the right edge of the page width and a vertical red line also appears.

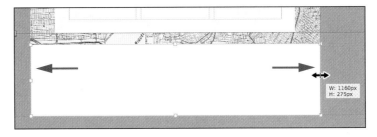

3   Click the Preview mode link, and scroll down to see the footer rectangle, if necessary.

On page 134, you will add color to the rectangle so that it better matches the design.

4   Click the Design mode link to return to Design mode.

● **Note:** You may see the submenus as well in the footer menu and that's okay.

5   With the rectangle frame selected, choose Object > Send To Back.

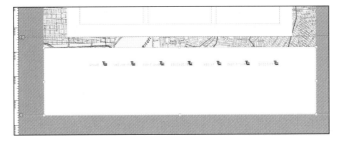

This step sends the rectangle to the bottom of the stack so it will now be behind the menu in the footer. Your menu may be showing the submenus, and that's okay.

6   With the Selection tool, click to select the footer menu. Click the blue circle with the white arrow in the upper-right corner of the menu. In the Options menu, choose Top Level Pages from the Menu Type menu, and choose Fit Width from the Item Size menu. This will make the menu smaller and will no longer show the submenus.

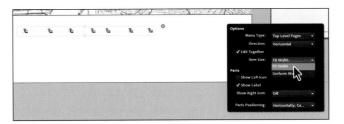

7 Drag the footer menu so that it is positioned approximately like in the figure, centering it against the page area.

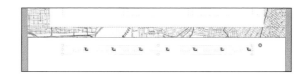

As you drag the menu, a center Smart Guide appears when the footer menu is aligned center with the page.

Like most design applications, Muse content has a stacking order on the page. This means that all of the content you add to your page is stacked one object on another, with the first object you create on the page being on the bottom of that stack. You can easily change the stacking order of content using menu commands.

About arranging objects

As you add more content to the page, you may need to send content behind or bring it in front of other content.

- To move an object to the top or bottom position on the page, select the object you want to move and choose Object > Bring To Front or Object > Send To Back.

- To move an object one step to the front or one to the back of a stack of objects, select the object you want to move, and choose Object > Bring Forward or Object > Send Backward.

Applying a background image to a frame

Text frames, image frames, and any empty frame you draw can all have background images applied to them to add to your designs. Background images in objects like these work just like the background image for the page area and the browser fill, showing behind the content in the frame and adding more design possibilities.

Next, you'll add a repeating triangle element to the footer.

1 Select the Rectangle tool, and draw a small rectangle in the middle of the footer area, below the menu bar.

2 Press Ctrl+= (Windows) or Command+= (Mac OS) several times to zoom into the frame.

3 In the Transform panel change Height to **16**.

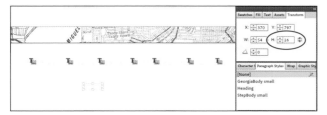

4 Select the Selection tool, and drag the rectangle from its center so that the left edge of the frame snaps to the left edge of the browser width and the bottom of the rectangle snaps to the top of the previous rectangle.

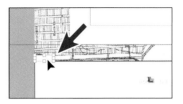

Note: You can insert .jpg .gif, .png, or .psd files in Muse as a background image. As you'll learn in Lesson 6, "Adding Images to Your Site," Muse automatically converts .psd files to a more compact format for the Web when you publish the site.

5 Click the Fill link in the Control panel and change the color to [None]. Click the Choose Background Image folder icon (▢) to select a background image. Navigate to the images folder in the Lessons folder, choose footer-zag.png, and click Open (Windows) or Select (Mac OS).

The brown triangle will appear in the frame. You inserted this image into the background so that you could repeat it easily in the frame, instead of placing that single image and pasting it numerous times.

6 Choose Tile Horizontally from the Fitting menu, and make sure that the lower-left point in the position indicator (▦) is selected. Click anywhere else on the page to close the Fill menu.

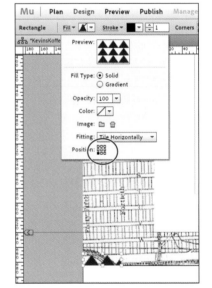

The brown triangle should now be repeating horizontally in the rectangle. The height of the frame also matches the height of the image for no other reason except to keep things neat.

7 Choose View > Fit Page In Window, then press Ctrl+- (Windows) or Command+- (Mac OS) several times until you see the edges of the page width.

8 Click and drag the right-middle bounding point of the frame to the right until it snaps to the edge of the browser width (until the red guide temporarily appears, indicating that the rectangle is set to display at 100% width).

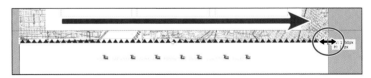

This will make the new frame 100% the width of the browser window as well as filled with repeating brown triangles. Don't worry about the black stroke around the frame; you will remove it later on page 136.

Creating a line

You can create a line in Muse by applying a stroke to a very thin rectangle or other shapes. The trick is to give the rectangle a really small height for a horizontal line or width to create a vertical line. In this next section, you'll add lines to the text on the preparation page in your site to help divide the content up visually. Lines can also be a great way to separate sidebars and other page areas from each other.

1   Click the Plan mode link to see the site map. Double-click the Preparation page thumbnail to open the page in Design mode. Make sure that you can see the top content on the page.

2   Select the Rectangle tool. Near the top of the page, but below the text "For visual examples roll over the numbers below," click and drag from the left edge of that column to create a frame that has a width of the column and a height of 10px.

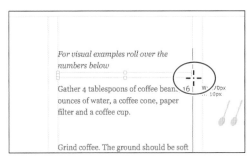

3   In the Transform panel, change Height to **1**. This will make the frame a single pixel tall.

4   Click the Fill color (▢▾) in the Control panel, and click one of the gray color swatches in the Color Picker panel that appears.

5   Change Stroke Weight in the Control panel to **0**, since drawn frames have a 1-pixel stroke (border) by default.

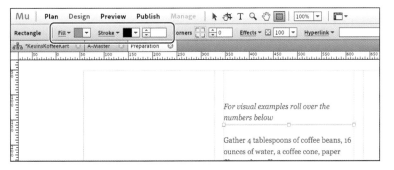

Later on page 135, you will learn all about working with strokes on objects.

Tip: Pressing the Shift key while pressing an arrow key moves the object 10 pixels each time.

6   With the Selection tool and the rectangle selected, press the down arrow key a few times to move the rectangle down on the page.

Pressing an arrow key once nudges the rectangle by 1 pixel. Try to visually center the rectangle between the two paragraphs of text.

For visual examples roll over the numbers below

Gather 4 tablespoons of coffee beans, 16 ounces of water, a coffee cone, paper filter and a coffee cup.

Creating a dotted line

Creating a dotted line combines two skills you've already learned: creating a line from a rectangle and inserting a background image into that rectangle to simulate the repeating dot in the dotted line.

1   On the Preparation page, select the Rectangle tool and create a rectangle at the top of the first column of the page that is the width of the first column and has a height of 20 pixels.

W: 270px
H: 20px
For visual examples roll over the numbers below

2   Click the Fill link in the Control panel and change the color to [None]. Click the Choose Background Image folder icon to select a background image. Navigate to the images folder in the Lessons folder, choose tile-dash.png, and click Select.

3   Choose Tile Horizontally from the Fitting menu, and make sure that the upper-left point in the position indicator (⠿) is selected.

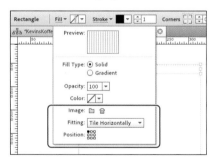

Created in Adobe Photoshop, the background image has a width of 5 pixels and a height of 2 pixels, and it contains a rectangle shape. It is repeating in the background to give the appearance of a dashed line. If you look in the frame on the page, you can see the image repeat.

4 Press the Escape key to hide the Fill options.

● **Note:** You can also click away from the Fill options to hide them.

5 Change Stroke Weight in the Control panel to **0**.

6 In the Transform panel, change Height to **2**, since the image is 2 pixels tall and the rectangle doesn't need to be any taller.

7 Select the Selection tool, and choose Edit > Cut.

8 Select the Text tool, and insert the cursor below the paragraph that starts with "Gather 4 tablespoons of coffee beans." Choose Edit > Paste.

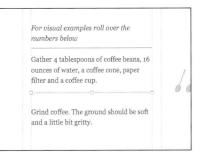

You can paste content like a frame or image into a text frame. This is called *inline content.* The advantage of pasting content into a text frame, instead of just placing it on top of the text frame, is that if the text size grows or shrinks in the browser or the frame moves, the inline content will move as well.

9 Select the Selection tool and with the dotted frame still selected, press the down arrow key on your keyboard to move the rectangle down.

When you press the arrow key, notice that the Y value in the Transform panel changes. You could also move the rectangle up or down by changing the Y value. The X value is dimmed, meaning you can't edit it because the shape is inline and can't go outside of the edges of the text frame that it's in.

10 Select the Text tool, insert the cursor between every two paragraphs below, and then choose Edit > Paste. You may need to scroll down the page.

Stop after you paste the rectangle between the last two paragraphs in the text frame; you don't need to continue into the next text frame.

If you need to adjust the Y position of any of the inline rectangles, you can click each rectangle frame one at a time with the Selection tool and press the arrow keys or change the Y value in the Transform panel. Although the position of the pasted frames may not be exactly the same in every browser, it will be very close. That is the nature of the Web, not Muse.

● **Note:** Selecting the inline rectangles you pasted may be a little challenging because they are very thin. Zooming in can help. The Smart Guides do show a highlight when you position the pointer over an object, indicating what would be selected if you were to click (View > Smart Guides).

11 Click the Preview mode link to preview the page and see your changes. Click the Design mode link to return to the Preparation page in Design mode.

12 Choose File > Save Site, then choose Edit > Deselect All.

Leave the Preparation page showing in Design mode. In the next section, you are going to begin to explore creating and editing color in more detail.

Working with color

Unlike print designs, which can use CMYK colors, Pantone color, or other color libraries, designs for the Web use only the RGB color model. All colors and images that you create must be in the RGB color mode. The good news is that when you save an image in .jpg, .gif, .png, or other web format using File > Save for Web & Devices (or File > Save For Web in CS6), Photoshop converts the colors to RGB mode automatically.

Web-safe colors

Ever heard of "web-safe" colors? Back when computers supported a maximum of 256 different colors, a list of 216 web-safe colors was created to ensure that all computers could display the colors correctly. That meant that you could design with only those 216 colors, to play it safe.

Today, web-safe colors are no longer necessary because most computers and devices can display millions of different colors.

In Muse, you can describe a color with individual red, green, and blue (R, G, and B) values or a single, six-character hexadecimal (hex for short) value. R, G, and B values range from 0 to 255. The values in a hex color value range from 0 to 9 and A to F. For example, the hex value AE1365 describes the same color as R: 174, G: 19, B: 101. The first two characters (AE) correlate to the red value (174), the second pair (13) to the green (19), and the third pair (65) to the blue (101).

Both the hex and RGB values tell the browser which color to display, in this case a dark magenta shade. You can think of RGB and hex values as two different numeric languages you can use to describe the same color; just like whether you say red or rojo, you're still describing the color of ketchup. Using either system of values you easily can transfer colors into Muse that you created in another application, such as Photoshop. Of course, in Muse, you also can simply create colors by eye using the Color Picker panel. Whichever method you use to specify a color, you can apply that color to a stroke and fill of a frame.

1   Click the Fill Color in the Control panel to see the Color Picker panel, and take a moment to familiarize yourself with the Color Picker's features:

Note: The colors you see in the Color Picker in the figure are the default colors, which are added automatically when you inserted the menu widget.

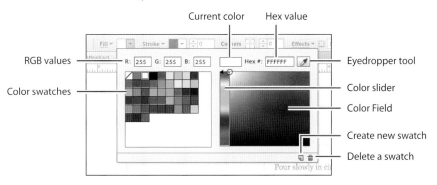

- **RGB values**: Specifies the values of the red, green, and blue channels of a color. Values range from 0 to 255.

- **Current Color**: Displays the color currently selected and described by the RGB and hex values.

- **Hex (hexadecimal) value**: Specifies the hexadecimal (or hex for short) value of the current color.

- **Eyedropper tool**: Enables you to select colors used on a page or in placed images; click the eyedropper on the desired color to sample it.

- **Color swatches**: Saved colors that you can apply, create, or delete in your site.

- **Color slider**: Enables you to select the hue or color to start from. You can then adjust the color's saturation and brightness in the Color Field.

- **Color Field**: Enables you to adjust the saturation and brightness of a color by dragging the circle. Saturation is shown horizontally and Brightness is shown vertically. Saturation, from left to right is less to more saturated, and Brightness from top to bottom is brighter to darker.

- **Create new swatch**: Saves a selected color in the list of color swatches.

- **Delete**: Deletes a selected color swatch in the list of color swatches.

For the remainder of the lesson, you'll experiment with color, learning how to create colors, apply them, and save them as swatches. You'll also work with color gradients to add some flair to your design.

Creating and applying a color fill

Muse offers many color options that help you easily create and save colors to reuse throughout your site. One of the most common applications is a color fill, which is color that appears inside of a shape or frame. To practice, you will create a color for a sidebar rectangle and then save that color so you can use it later. Before you begin, make sure the Preparation page is open in Design mode.

1 Select the Rectangle tool in the Toolbox. On the Preparation page, create a rectangle at the top of the first column on the left. Give it a height of 150px and the same width as the column (270px).

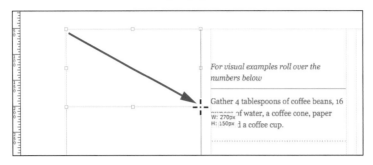

2 Click the Fill color option (▢▾) in the Control panel to show the Color Picker panel.

3 In the Color Picker panel, change the RGB values to R: **153**, G: **204**, and B: **204**.

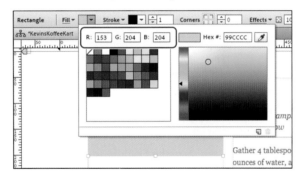

Notice the Hex value changes to 99CCCC.

● **Note:** If you want to match the exact color in the figure, you can change the RGB values to R: 165, G: 231, and B: 231. Editing the hue, saturation, and brightness will change the RGB color values of the selected color.

4 In the Color Field, drag the circle, indicating the selected color, up a little to increase the brightness of the color.

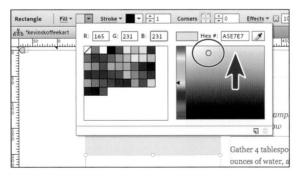

5 Press Escape to hide the Color Picker panel.

● **Note:** You can also click away from the Color Picker panel to hide it.

6 Change Stroke Weight in the Control panel to **0**.

7 Choose File > Save Site.

Sampling color

Sampling color is a great way to either reuse a color that wasn't saved or create a new color from a color in an image on the page. To change the large white rectangle in the footer to match the rectangle with the repeating triangle background, you will sample the brown color from the triangle image.

1 Click the A-Master page tab to see the master page in Design mode.

2 With the Selection tool, click to select the first, large white rectangle you created in the footer.

3 Click the Fill color (▢▾) in the Control panel to show the Color Picker panel.

4 In the Color Picker panel, click the Eyedropper tool (🖋).

5 Position the Eyedropper pointer over one of the brown triangles in the footer rectangle. When that brown color appears in the Current Color in the Color Picker panel, click to sample the color and leave the Color Picker panel open.

When you click Fill color in the Control panel, sampling with the Eyedropper tool automatically applies sampled color to the fill of a selected frame. If you didn't have content selected, the color would apply to the background of the page area.

Note: To ensure that you sampled the correct brown color, check the RGB color values and change them, if needed, to R: 90, G: 41, and B: 33.

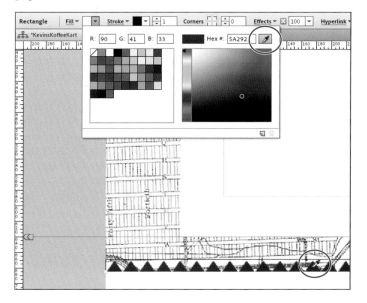

With a color created, you can now save the color as a swatch that you can later apply to the fill or stroke of selected content in this site only.

Saving and editing a swatch

Although you don't have to save the colors you create as swatches, saving a color can make your life easier later on if you want to reuse color or if you decide to use a consistent set of colors throughout your site. You can find saved swatches by clicking the Fill or Stroke colors in the Control panel or in the Swatches panel.

1   With the brown color still showing in the Color Picker panel, click the Create New Swatch button (⬚) at the bottom of the Color Picker panel.

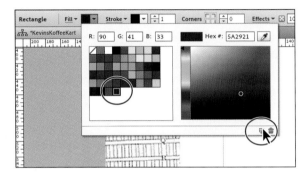

Creating a new swatch saves the current color into the swatch list at the end.

2   Position the pointer over the new swatch; a yellow tooltip appears showing the RGB color values of the new swatch.

By default, the tooltip displays the RGB color values, but you can change that via the Swatch Options settings. Many designers prefer the tooltips to indicate what a color is to be used for, such as a heading color, for instance.

3   Double-click the new brown swatch to open the Swatch Options dialog box.

4   Deselect Name With Color Value to add your own name. Change the Swatch name to **FooterBG**.

Adding the BG (background) to the color name is useful for later when you are trying to figure out where you used this color. Also notice that the Swatch Options dialog box shows the entire Color Picker set of options for editing the brown color or sampling another color.

> **Note:** Any changes that you make in the Swatch Options dialog box change the swatch as well as every object in your site to which you applied the color.

5   Click OK.

6 Position the pointer over the brown color swatch in the Color Picker to see the tooltip display FooterBG.

7 Press the Escape key to close the Color Picker panel, and choose File > Save

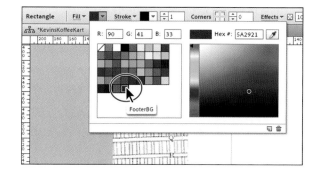

Site. Leave the brown-filled rectangle selected for the next section.

You can create and save as many colors as you need. Just remember that you don't have to save a color, but doing so can be very helpful, saving you time later on.

Creating and editing a color stroke

As in most other Adobe applications, color strokes, or borders, are very effective tools in Muse, much like fills. As you remember, Muse applies black, 1-pixel strokes to frames by default. You've already learned the basics of changing a stroke's weight, so this exercise focuses on customizing a stroke's color and saving that color as a swatch. You'll also tour the Stroke Options panel, which gives you even more control over a stroke's appearance.

1 In the Control panel, change the Stroke Weight to **10** to apply a 10-pixel stroke.

2 Click the Stroke color (■▾) in the Control panel to reveal the stroke Color Picker panel. Click the FooterBG color swatch to apply it to the stroke.

The stroke Color Picker panel is identical to the fill Color Picker panel you worked with in the previous few sections.

3 In the Color Field, drag the circle, indicating the selected color, up and to the left to make the brightness of the brown color brighter.

4 Click the Create New Swatch button (🗐) to save the color. Press Escape to hide the stroke Color Picker panel.

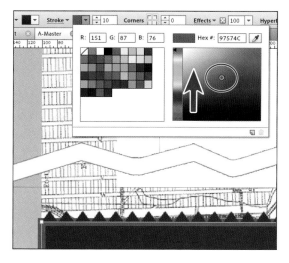

● **Note:** It's okay if the color you wind up with doesn't match the color in the example.

5 Click the Stroke link in the Control panel.

The Stroke Options panel that appears shows two main options: Stroke Alignment and Individual Stroke Weights. Stroke Alignment lets you align the stroke to the inside, outside, and the center of the edge of a frame. The Stroke Weight options allow you to change the stroke weight for each side of a frame independently, if you want.

6 Click the Align Stroke To Inside button (▣) and notice that the lighter brown stroke on the rectangle is now inside of the edges of the rectangle.

7 Change the Top Stroke Weight value to **0** and press Enter or Return.

All of the stroke weights will change because the Make All Settings The Same icon is selected (⚏).

8 Click the Make All Settings The Same icon off so that it looks like this (⚏). Now you can edit each of the Stroke Weight settings indepen- dently. Change the Top Stroke Weight to **15** and press Enter or Return. Press Escape to hide the Stroke Options panel, and leave the rectangle selected.

The same lighter brown stroke color should be applied to the stroke that now appears on only the top edge of the rectangle.

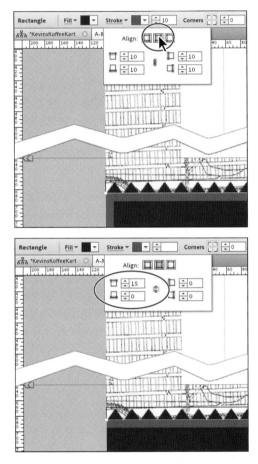

9 With the Selection tool, click the frame with the brown triangle background in the footer. Change the Stroke Weight in the Control panel to **0**.

10 Click the Preview mode link, and preview the page to see your changes. Click the Design mode link to return to the A-Master page in Design mode.

Duplicating and deleting a color swatch

Another place where you can create and edit color is the Swatches panel (Window > Swatches). The Swatches panel has a few more options than the Color Picker in the Control panel, and enables you to duplicate and delete colors.

1 Click the Swatches panel tab on the right side of the workspace to reveal the panel.

2 Click the triangle to the left of the text "Color Picker" in the Swatches panel several times to reveal and hide the Color Picker options.

You won't always need them, and hiding these makes seeing content in other panels easier. Make sure that the Color Picker options are showing before moving on.

3 Position the pointer over the FooterBG color swatch, in the top portion of the Swatches panel, right-click (Windows) or Control-click (Mac OS) and choose Duplicate Swatch from the context menu that appears.

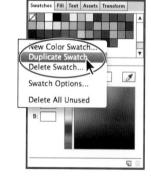

This creates an exact copy of the color and inserts the new color swatch at the end of the swatch list.

4 Position the pointer over the new swatch named FooterBG copy. Right-click (Windows) or Control-click (Mac OS), and choose Swatch Options from the context menu that appears.

● **Note:** Make sure that you don't double-click to edit the swatch. Although you can double-click a swatch to edit its properties, doing so will apply to the fill of whatever is selected on the page or, if nothing is selected, the fill will apply to the entire page area.

5 Change the name to **Footer Stroke** and change the RGB values to R: **67**, G: **30**, B: **24** in the Swatch Options dialog box. Click OK.

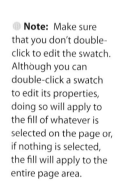

Now that you've duplicated a swatch and made changes to it, you will delete a swatch.

6 Position the pointer over the lighter brown swatch you made in the previous section. Right-click (Windows) or Control-click (Mac OS), and choose Delete Swatch from the context menu that appears.

7   Select Defined Swatch, and choose the Footer Stroke color from the menu in the Delete Swatch dialog box.

The Delete Swatch dialog box will appear only if the swatch you are deleting has been applied to content in your site. You can choose to replace the swatch with a defined swatch (a swatch you've saved previously) or an unnamed swatch. Choosing Unnamed Swatch deletes the swatch in the panel, but leaves the color applied to your content in the site. Click OK.

8   Choose File > Save Site.

9   Click the Preview mode link to see the changes in Preview mode. Click the Design mode link to return to the page in Design mode and leave the rectangle selected.

Working with gradients

You can also apply a color fill using a *gradient*, which is a blend from one color to another. Muse offers lots of options to help you make and apply gradients to the fill of all types of frames.

To add some depth to the footer rectangle, you'll fill it with a gradient.

1   With the Selection tool, click to select the large, brown rectangle in the footer, and then click the Fill panel tab to show the panel on the right side of the workspace.

The Fill panel shows the same options as clicking the Fill link in the Control panel, but because it's a panel, you can leave it showing all the time. You can create and edit gradients by clicking the Fill color in the Control panel as well.

2   Select Gradient in the Fill panel, and notice that the Fill panel options change.

For example, you can now specify two colors, rather than one for a solid fill. The gradient you're creating will eventually blend between the FooterBG color and the Footer Stroke color. By default, when you select Gradient, Muse applies the fill color of the selected object and black as the two colors that the gradient blends between.

3 Click the second Color option to select a new color. From the Color Picker, click to select the swatch named Red (to the right of the black color in the top row of the swatches).

▶ **Tip:** In the Color Picker, you can easily create and even save a new color while creating a gradient.

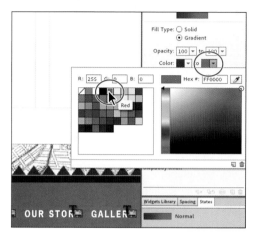

Later, you will change the red color to something more subtle, but for now red will help you to see the effect that the settings will have on the gradient.

4 Change the second opacity option from the left, for the Red color, to **50**.

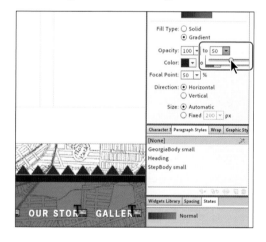

This adjusts the opacity to 50% for the Red color in the gradient, making it partially transparent or see-through.

5 Change the opacity back to **100**.

6 Select Vertical to change the Direction of the gradient.

This changes the direction of the gradient to top to bottom rather than side to side.

7 Click the arrow to the right of the Focal Point field and drag the slider left and right to see the effect on the gradient in the footer rectangle. Make sure that the value is 80 before moving on to the next step.

The Focal Point is where the transition between the colors occurs in the shape. For a vertical gradient, the closer the value to 0, the closer to the top of the shape the transition appears.

8 Select Fixed for the Size. Change the value to the right of the selection to 50 by selecting the value and typing **50**. Notice that the distance or blend between the two colors is much shorter. Try other values to see the effect. Make sure to select Automatic when you're ready to move on.

With the Automatic size option enabled, the Size setting of a gradient is automatically determined by the size of the object. By default, Muse sets each of the colors on opposite ends of the color fill to create a blend that stretches the width or height of the object, depending on the Direction setting you select. If you select Fixed, you can change the size or length of the gradient to achieve the desired effect.

9 Click the second Color option from the left (with Red applied), and select the Footer Stroke color swatch from the Color Picker.

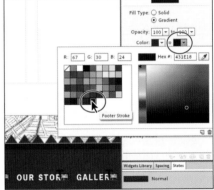

10 Press the Escape key to hide the Fill color options.

With the master content finished, that same content needs to be updated on the MasterFlash master page as well.

11 With the Selection tool, drag a selection marquee across the content in the footer to select it. Choose Edit > Copy.

12 Click the Plan mode link and double-click the MasterFlash page thumbnail to open the page in Design mode.

13 With the Selection tool, drag a selection marquee to select the existing menu widget in the footer and press Backspace or Delete to remove it.

14 Choose Edit > Paste In Place.

15 Choose File > Save Site, and close all open pages.

Now that you've explored the world of Muse color and shape creation, in the next lesson, "Adding Images To Your Site," you'll learn all about image types, placing images, copying and pasting content, and more. Leave the site file named KevinsKoffeeKart.muse open to be ready.

Review questions

1 What shape tools are available in Muse?

2 What content can be 100% width content?

3 From what content can you sample color?

4 What does hexadecimal refer to?

5 What happens when you delete a color swatch that is applied to content in your site?

6 Name two places where you can create a gradient.

Review answers

1 Muse currently offers the Rectangle tool. With this tool, you can create squares, rectangles, lines, circles, and more.

2 100% width content is content that stretches to fit the width of the browser window no matter how narrow or wide it is. You can apply the 100% width characteristics to a text frame or a frame you drew with the Rectangle tool.

3 You can sample color from almost any content, including frames that contain color, images, text, or background images.

4 Hexadecimal values, such as 330011, are one way that you can tell a browser exactly which RGB color you wish to use.

5 If the swatch you are deleting has been applied to content in your site, the Delete Swatch dialog box will appear. You can choose to replace the swatch with a defined swatch (a swatch you've saved previously) or an unnamed swatch. Choosing Unnamed Swatch deletes the swatch in the panel, but leaves the color applied to your content in the site.

6 You can create gradients by clicking the Fill link in the Control panel or in the Fill panel (Window > Fill).

6 ADDING IMAGES TO YOUR SITE

Lesson overview

In this lesson, you'll add images to your pages and learn to

- Place images

- Place Adobe Photoshop files

- Move, resize, rotate, and crop images

- Lock and group content

- Wrap text around an image

- Relink images

- Use the Edit Original command

- Fix missing and modified links

- Pin content

- Insert Flash files (.swf)

- Add alternative text and a title to images

 This lesson takes approximately 1 hour to complete. If you are starting from scratch in this lesson, use the method described in the "Jumpstart" section on page 5 of "Getting Started."

ABOUT KEVIN'S KOFFEE KART

 Koffee Kart began as a whim of Kevin Kariuki's in 1985. After spending years studying the art of coffee cultivation in his native Nairobi, Kenya, Kevin was struck by the limitations of brick-and-mortar cafes and restaurants here in San Francisco. Why not bring the coffee to the people, where the people want it, in the most eco-friendly way possible? Strap an espresso machine on a three-wheeled rickshaw and you're most of the way there. Add the finest original roasts from Africa, Central America and the Pacific and you've found the Koffee Kart of San Francisco.

Photo by: Karen Koffee

> *"We absolutely love the coffee from Kevin's Koffee Kart. Especially the dark roast drip he offers every Wednesday!"*

The *Koffee Kart* specializes in versatile coffee, full bodied and smooth whether brewed as espresso or drip from multiple origins (and producers). This has been v

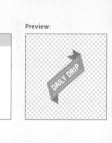

Muse allows you to place images you create and paste image content from other applications, such as Adobe Illustrator, Photoshop, and Fireworks. As you'll see throughout this lesson, images can be easily moved, scaled, rotated, pinned, and more to match your design concept.

Web-image basics

Images can enhance a website's visual interest, identity, and attitude. You simply need to choose the right image for the task. As you'll see, the key to the effective use of images is finding a balance of size and color to achieve the desired optimal quality. Whether you receive images from others or create your own in a program like Adobe Illustrator or Photoshop, you need to keep these considerations in mind. For example, although you can save images in a multitude of file formats, Muse allows you to place only .gif, .jpg, .png, and native Photoshop (.psd) files on your pages. In addition, Muse automatically converts placed Photoshop files (.psd) to .gif, .jpg, or .png files, because these formats are optimized for use on the Web and compatible with most browsers. Each format, however, has different capabilities and strengths. To understand which is best for your site design, take a closer look at some key factors.

Resolution

The resolution for images on the Web is 72ppi (pixels per inch). If you are used to working in print, then you are most likely used to 300ppi or something similar. The same resolutions that produce crisp images in print produce sluggish downloads on the Web where pixel loads add up fast. The 72ppi standard is a good compromise between image quality and file size. When you create your own images, make sure that you set the units to pixels and the resolution to 72ppi.

Color

When you create images in another application for later use in your website, do so in RGB color mode, which is the standard for monitors and other display devices. Print work, on the other hand, typically uses CMYK color mode. RGB images are smaller than CMYK in most cases, because they contain only three channels of color information (red, green, and blue) instead of four (cyan, magenta, yellow, and black). Again, smaller files mean a more efficient site and a better experience for visitors.

Image formats

When you create content for your site in Adobe Photoshop, Illustrator, Fireworks, or other programs, you will save most of that content in one of the three web-image formats: GIF, JPEG, PNG. The more you know about each format, the more easily you can decide which to use for what type of image.

GIF

Graphic Interchange Format, or GIF, was designed specifically for the Web. These files, which have the extension

.gif, are most useful for interface elements, buttons, graphical borders, and the like. When considering whether to use this format, remember that .gif files

- Support a maximum of 256 colors (8-bit palette)
- Use lossless compression (image data compression where no data is lost)
- Use a color space called Index
- Support index transparency, meaning you could use a program like Photoshop, for instance, to designate a background color behind a logo as transparent
- Support animation, meaning you could make an animated banner

JPEG

Named after the group that created the standard, the JPEG (Joint Photographic Experts Group) format is primarily intended for photo-quality images and uses the suffix .jpg. Most designers use .jpg files for images that must be displayed in higher quality on their websites. When considering whether to use this format, remember that .jpg files

Note: If you save an image for your site as a .jpg file in an image editing program, ensure that it is in the RGB color space not CMYK. In Photoshop and Illustrator, if you save an image as .jpg using the File > Save For Web & Devices command (File > Save For Web in CS6), the image is automatically converted to the RGB color mode.

- Support 16 million colors (24-bit color)
- Can be used for print and Web work because the format supports both the CMYK and RGB color spaces
- Use lossy compression, meaning that a .jpg file loses quality every time you save it, making a trade-off between image quality and file size
- Can compress image data greatly by discarding adjacent pixels of duplicate color, but too much compression can result in block-like "artifacts" that look unnatural.

PNG

Pronounced ping, the PNG, or Portable Network Graphic, format combines many features of .gif and .jpg files and then adds a few of its own into .png files. The format was originally designed to surpass the limitations of .gif files, and most designers now prefer it for images that require transparency, drop shadows, and the like. When considering whether to use this format, remember that .png files

- Support millions of colors (for RGB color, up to 48-bit color)
- Support alpha transparency (a drop shadow) and index transparency (a background color)
- Use lossless compression, meaning you do not lose any quality each time you save the .png file
- Include some features, such as alpha transparency, that are not fully supported in Internet Explorer 6 and other older browsers

Also keep in mind that Photoshop and Illustrator offer two versions of .png: 8 bit, which uses 8 bits of color or fewer per pixel, and 24 bit, which uses 24 bits of color per pixel.

Importing images

Muse offers several methods for getting images into your web designs, including placing and pasting. *Placing* an image into your Muse site using the Place command (File > Place) creates a link to the image file, which means that if you later update the image file, the instances of that file will be updated in Muse as well. *Pasting* image content into your pages embeds that content into the site, meaning changes to the original image file will not update the embedded image in Muse. To learn more about pasting content into Muse see the sidebar titled, "Copy and paste image content into Muse" on page 148.

Images in Muse, like text, live in rectangular frames, and are referred to as frames. The frame that contains an image can have a stroke, fill, or other formatting or transformations applied to it. Images that do not have transparency cover the fill color or background image, unless you make the frame larger than the image or make the image smaller than the frame (you'll learn how to do this on page 150).

If you move the frame on the page, the image moves as well. You can resize the frame and image together or separately to create some interesting effects. Unlike in Adobe InDesign, you cannot draw a rectangle first with the Rectangle tool and place the image inside that rectangle in Muse. However, you can use the Fill menu to add background images (tiled or not) as fills of a rectangle, image frame, or text frame.

Before you jump into placing images, gather your images into the same folder as your Muse site file to keep things neat. Often, designers create a dedicated subfolder named Images. You can place images (File > Place) from other locations, as well. As long as Muse can find the image files when you publish, Muse will collect copies into one folder when you publish or export the site.

Note: To learn more about web image best practices, see the "Web_images.pdf" file in the Lesson06 folder.

Note: If you have not already done so, copy the Lessons folder onto your hard disk, from the *Adobe Muse Classroom in a Book* disc. See "Copying the Classroom in a Book files" on page 3.

Note: For more information on adding strokes, fills, and background images to frames, see Lesson 5, "Working with Shapes and Colors."

About linked files

When you place images in Muse, you actually create a link from the page to the image. If you place a .gif, .jpg, or .png image, Muse links to the original image, wherever it lives, and collects all linked files into a single folder when the time comes to publish.

If you place a Photoshop document (.psd), Muse converts the file to the web format that best fits the content. As you work on the site, Muse preserves the link to the original .psd, and you can make any changes necessary in it, then update the image in Muse using the Assets panel (Window > Assets).

Placing an image

Whether you need to add interest to your pages selling products, call attention to a promotion, or showcase your latest employee of the month, images can help. In this exercise, you'll use the Place command (File > Place) to insert a JPEG image of the Koffee Kart's founder on the site's ABOUT page.

● **Note:** If you are starting from scratch in this lesson, use the method described in the "Jumpstart" section on page 5 of "Getting Started."

● **Note:** The exercises in this chapter, like others in this book, require that you have the fonts supplied on the Adobe Muse Classroom in a Book disc installed on your machine. For more information on installing the necessary fonts, see "Fonts used in this book" on page 2 of "Getting Started."

1 With the KevinsKoffeeKart site open and in Plan mode, double-click the ABOUT page to open it in Design mode.

2 Choose View > Fit Page In Window.

3 Choose File > Place. In the Import dialog box, navigate to the images folder in the Lessons folder. Select the image named MeetKevin.jpg, and click Open (Windows) or Select (Mac OS).

▶ **Tip:** To remove the selected image from the Place Gun and turn the pointer back into the Selection arrow, press the Escape key.

Move the pointer onto the page, and you now see the Place Gun with a handy thumbnail preview of the image that you are about to place. Remember, the upper-left corner of the image will align with the upper-left corner of the Place Gun when you click on the page to place the image.

4 Near the top of the third column, click and drag to place the image. Make the frame the width of the third column. Its vertical position in the column doesn't matter right now.

Notice that as you drag, you are sizing the image with the frame and an image thumbnail appears next to the pointer.

5 Choose Edit > Undo Place to remove the image from the page and reattach it to the Place Gun.

6 Position the pointer on the left edge of the third column toward the top. Click to place the image. Don't worry if it ends up on top of the rotated text caption from last lesson; you'll fix it later.

By simply clicking when placing, you create an image frame the same size as the image and place the image in the frame at 100% its original size.

● **Note:** In Muse, it's best to place images at 100% of their original size. When you enlarge an image, it can grow jagged on the edges and blurry, depending on the original resolution of the image. You are also adding to the file size of the images that are downloaded when visitors view the page.

7 Choose File > Save Site.

Copy and paste image content into Muse

If you want to copy and paste graphic content into a page in Muse from within the same site, from site to site, or from another program, consider a few things first:

- If you copy an image you placed on one page of your site and paste it to another page, the newly pasted image and the placed image both will link to the original image file on your hard drive. Changes to the original source file will change the copies on both pages.

- If you copy an image you placed on one site and paste it into another site, the placed image and pasted image both will link to the original image file saved in the original site's folder. Changes to the original source file will change the copies on both sites.

- If you copy and paste an image from Adobe Photoshop, Illustrator, Fireworks, or other program, Muse flattens the image content, removing any transparency and layer information, and embeds the image in the site. The pasted image does not link to an image file outside of Muse.

- You can paste a single slice of a Photoshop image into Muse. In Photoshop, create a slice with the Slice tool, select the slice, and choose Edit > Copy. In Muse, choose Edit > Paste to paste that content into your page; the resulting flattened image will contain all of the currently visible content in the Photoshop file.

- Pasted content is pasted at 100% of its original size and becomes a web image when you preview, publish, or export the site.

Placing a Photoshop file (.psd)

Placing a Photoshop file (.psd) in Muse comes with the same linking and updating benefits as placing a .jpg, .gif, or .png file, plus a few extras. If the Photoshop file has content in more than one layer, for example, and you place it in your site via File > Place, Muse gives you the choice of placing the composite image (all layers) or selected layers. This means that, for instance, you can create a complete page design in Photoshop with page-specific content on individual layers, then place only the layer you need for each page. Alternately, you could create multiple versions of a button or logo on separate layers, for instance, and place the version you like best.

When you publish or export the site, Muse converts the Photoshop content to a suitable format for the Web but does not publish or export the original .psd file. Don't let your imagination run too far, though, as for all other images that you place, you still need to consider file size, resolution, and color when creating Photoshop content.

To see how the Photoshop-specific options work, try placing a .psd file on the home page.

1   If you're still in Design mode, click the Plan mode link to access the page thumbnails. If you're already in Plan mode, simply double-click the HOME page thumbnail to open the home page in Design mode.

2   Choose View > Fit Page In Window.

3   Select the Zoom tool (🔍) in the Toolbox, and click twice on the upper-left corner of the page area below the header to zoom in.

4   Choose File > Place. In the Import dialog box, navigate to the images folder in the Lessons folder, then the image named DailyDrip.psd. Click Open (Windows) or Select (Mac OS).

    The Image Import Options (DailyDrip.psd) dialog opens. You can instruct Muse to place the composite image with all of the layers showing or only selected layers. Choose carefully: If you later want to turn on or off layers in the .psd in Muse, you must place the file again or relink it (more on that on page 160).

▶ **Tip:** You can place multiple images at once by selecting those images in the Import dialog box. When you click Open or Select, Muse shows the Place Gun with a number off the right edge of the image thumbnail indicating how many images are loaded in the Place Gun. You can press the right and left arrow keys to cycle between the images, stopping when you see the thumbnail of the image you are ready to place. You can then click to place each image. If you come to a thumbnail for an image in the Place Gun that you don't want to place, press the Escape key to remove it from the Place Gun.

5   Select Import Layer. Make sure that the banner text layer is selected. Select Clip To Layer Contents, and click OK.

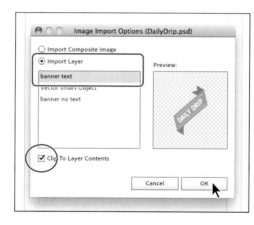

Suppose that you designed the entire web page in Photoshop, and you wanted to place a logo from one of the layers in the .psd into Muse. The logo is only a small part of the larger design. Selecting Clip To Layer Contents crops the placed image to the size of the selected layer content instead of making it the size of the entire design. The original .psd file remains unchanged. You can also select more than one layer in the Image Import Options dialog box if you select Import Layer. Simply Shift-click the layers or Ctrl (Windows)/Command (Mac OS) select noncontiguous layers and click OK.

Note: Layer groups in a layered Photoshop file are ignored when placing that image in Muse. In other words, you will not see the layer groups in the Import Options dialog box, and Muse treats the file as if there were none.

6 Position the Place Gun on the left edge of the page area, even with the top margin guide and click to place the image.

🔵 **Note:** After placing an image, Muse swaps to the Selection tool automatically, regardless of which tool was selected before.

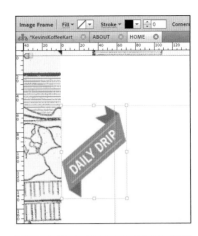

7 With the Selection tool, drag the image from its center to the left so that it hangs off the edge of the page area. See the figure for placement help.

8 Choose File > Save Site.

9 Click the Preview mode link to see the image, then click the Design mode link to return to the page.

10 Choose File > Close Page to return to the ABOUT page.

Moving, cropping, and resizing images

Getting images into your site design is only the first step. Unless you hit perfection on the first try, you may need to adjust the image's placement, size, rotation, or cropping. Using several tools and methods, you can transform only the rectangular frame of the image, only the image independently of the frame, or both frame and image together.

Transforming images with the Selection tool

You'll first focus on exploring image transformation using the Selection tool, which offers a lot of fast, powerful transformations without having to switch tools.

1 With the ABOUT page open in Design mode, click to select the MeetKevin.jpg image with the Selection tool.

2 Drag the image from its center until the top of the image is aligned with the top of the text that begins "Koffee Kart began as…"

A Smart Guide will appear across the top of the text and image when they are aligned. You will also see the aqua gap measurements showing 20px. The gap measurements show if another pair of objects has the same gap size—in this case it's the gap between all three columns. Make sure that the left edge of the image is still aligned with the left edge of the third column.

3 Click and drag the bottom-right point on the image frame down and to the right until the measurement label shows 120%.

With the Selection tool, if you drag a point on the frame to resize it, you also resize the image.

About resizing and cropping in Muse

The best practice for Web images is to place them at 100% without resizing in Muse. Figure out the size needed from your design, and adjust the image accordingly beforehand in an image-editing program like Photoshop.

If you must resize an image in Muse, know that resizing can make the image appear jaggy or blurry. If you place a .jpg, .gif, or .png file and resize it, the original image file remains unchanged, however. When you publish or export the site, Muse transforms a copy of that image.

In Muse, when you size an image larger than 100%, a warning icon appears in the Assets panel (Window > Assets). This warning icon indicates that you may need to link to a larger version of the image or scale the image down.

Also, when you open a site that contains at least one image that has been scaled larger than 100%, a dialog box appears.

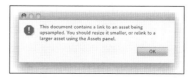

Note: You could also choose Edit > Undo Resize Item to return this image to its previous size.

4 Click and drag the bottom-right point on the image frame toward the center of the image until the measurement label shows 100%.

No matter how many times you resize an image, you can always get it back to 100%.

5 With the image selected, press and hold the Control (Windows) or Command (Mac OS) key, and drag the bottom-middle bounding point of the frame up to the bottom of Kevin's wrist in the image.

Note: Cropping an image in Muse does not crop the original image file.

Rather than resize the frame and image together, dragging while pressing Control (Command) lets you resize the frame only. In this case, you are cropping a part of the image so that it no longer shows. You could also make the frame larger than the image if you wanted a background color or background image applied to the frame to show.

6 Double-click the image with the Selection tool.

Notice that the once blue rectangle with eight bounding points turns into a brown rectangle with smaller points. Also notice that the pointer has changed from a black arrow to a hand when the pointer is positioned over the image. The lighter area of the image at the bottom is the part of the image that was cropped by the previous step. These indicators will help you resize the image within the frame and reposition it.

7 Click and drag the image from the center straight down just a bit.

You'll see that more of the bottom of the image looks lighter or semitransparent. By dragging an image after double-clicking it with the Selection tool, you are moving the image in the frame; you are not editing the frame. There is also a gap between the top frame edge and the top of the image. This is where a fill color or background image you applied to the frame will show.

8 Position the pointer over the image, and you will see the blue rectangle and the edge of the image in brown. Choose Edit > Undo Move Item.

9 Position the pointer over the bottom-right corner point of the image and the pointer changes to a double arrow. Drag down and to the right until the measurement label shows 140% to resize the image, not the frame.

Resizing an image this way automatically constrains the proportions of the image, not allowing you to distort it.

▶ **Tip:** If you position the pointer just off any of the corner bounding points, you will see the rotate arrow.

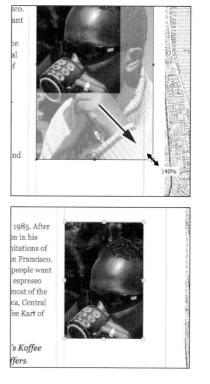

10 Press the Escape key to select the blue rectangle again.

You can see that the image is cropped within the frame and is now larger than it was.

⬤ **Note:** You can also click away from the image to deselect it, then click on it again to select the frame, not the image.

Using the Fitting commands

Another way to resize an image is to use the Fitting commands built into Muse. These commands allow you to fill a frame with an image or fit the image to the frame, while keeping the image in proportion.

1 Choose Object > Fitting > Fit Content Proportionally.

This command fits the entire image in the frame and centers it without cropping. Notice the gaps on the right and left of the image frame. Because the frame didn't have the same proportions as the image, Muse left a gap between the frame and image on two sides.

▶ **Tip:** You can also right-click (Windows) or Control-click (Mac OS) the rectangular image frame and choose a fitting command from the context menu that appears.

2 Choose Object > Fitting > Fill Frame Proportionally.

This command ensures that the image fills the frame and is centered, with no gaps, but will crop a portion of the image if the proportions of the frame don't match the image proportions.

Fit Content Proportionally

Fill Frame Proportionally

Using the Crop tool

Finally, you can crop or resize an image with the Crop tool. Found in the Toolbox, the Crop tool (✄) enables you to move, resize, and crop an image and its frame together or separately, much like the Selection tool methods discussed previously.

<table>
</table>

● **Note:** To change the image with the Crop tool, you do not need to first select the image because you can select it with the Crop tool.

1 Select the Crop tool in the Toolbox, and position the pointer over the image, away from the image center. Notice that the pointer changes from a crop icon (✄) to an arrow (▶) and the Content Grabber appears in the center of the image (the two circles).

2 When you see the arrow pointer over the image, drag the image from anywhere besides it center to another part of the page.

3 Choose Edit > Undo Move Item.

4 Position the pointer over the bottom-middle point of the image frame and when the pointer changes to double arrows, drag the point down to see more of the image. Don't go so far as to go beyond the image edge.

The Crop tool allows you to resize the frame without resizing the image.

5 Position the pointer over the Content Grabber in the center of the image. When the pointer changes to a hand, click and drag the image down to reveal more of the top of the image.

The Content Grabber is there to help you to select the image not the frame. The Smart Guides are also helping to align the image as you drag it.

6 Click the Content Grabber in the center of the image to select the image, not the frame.

Reveal more of the image   Drag the image down   Select the image

You can tell that the image (not the frame) is selected when you see the brown rectangle around the image. With the image selected, you could drag the image and reposition it within the frame, resize, or rotate it.

7 Press the Escape key to select the blue rectangular image frame and leave the image selected.

8 With the image selected, choose Object > Fitting > Fill Frame Proportionally.

9 Choose File > Save Site.

Locking and grouping content

As you work, Muse lets you lock and unlock content to prevent you from inadvertently selecting and editing it. You can also combine several objects into a group so that the objects are treated as a single unit. You can then move or transform a number of objects without affecting their attributes or relative positions.

1 Select the Selection tool.

2 With the MeetKevin.jpg image still selected, choose Object > Lock.

You cannot select locked content, which can be useful when you need to work on other content around the image.

3 Click to select the caption text frame that contains the text "Photo by: Karen Koffee."

4 Drag the text frame from its center to the right of the image so that you can see all of the text. Make the text frame fit tighter around the text by dragging the left, middle-bounding point to the left until the measurement label shows a height of approximately 20.

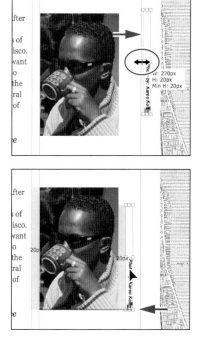

Note: The text frame may be underneath the image, making it hard to see and select. With the Selection tool, you can drag a selection marquee across the image and it will most likely select the text frame. Because the image is locked, it will not be selected.

5 Drag the text frame from its center until the last letter "e" in Koffee is aligned with the bottom of the image frame, then release the mouse button. A horizontal Smart Guide will show when the two are aligned. Press and hold the Shift key, then drag the frame to the left. When the aqua gap measurements read 20px, release the Shift key and then the mouse. Leave the text frame selected.

Pressing and holding the Shift key constrains the movement of content to 90 degrees.

6 Choose Object > Unlock All On Page.

7 Press and hold the Shift key and click to select the image. The text frame and image are now both selected.

The Shift key allows you to select multiple objects. If multiple objects are selected, holding the Shift key while clicking one of the objects allows you to deselect it.

8 Choose Object > Group to group the selected content.

A dotted box appears around the group. You now can move, rotate, and even resize the group of objects.

9 With the group still selected, click once more on the caption text frame to select only that frame.

> **Note:** To edit the objects within the group, you can also select the group and choose Object > Ungroup.

10 Press the left arrow key once to position the text frame one pixel closer to the image.

11 Press and hold the Shift key and press the left arrow once to position the text frame 10 pixels closer to the image.

12 Press the Escape key to select the entire group again.

13 Choose File > Save Site.

Rotating images

You can rotate all types of content in Muse using several methods. When it comes to images, you can rotate the frame and image together or just the image in the frame.

1 Choose File > Place. In the Import dialog box, navigate to the Lessons > Lesson06 > images folder. Select the image named OurFounder.png, and click Open (Windows) or Select (Mac OS).

2 Click just above the MeetKevin.jpg image to place the banner image at 100%.

3 Click the Transform panel (Window > Transform) tab to show the panel.

4 Position the pointer off the lower-right bounding point. When you see the rotate arrow (↻), click and drag clockwise. Watch the Rotation Angle in the Transform panel; when you see a value of 321, stop rotating.

▶ **Tip:** You can also rotate an image frame using the same method with the Crop tool.

Notice that the edges of the image look more jagged. The best practice in Muse is to rotate the image before placing it, but sometimes that can't be helped.

● **Note:** If your screen resolution allows it, you may see the X, Y, W, H, and rotation options in the Control panel as well as the Transform panel.

5 With the Selection tool, drag the image into position on top of the image of the MeetKevin.jpg image. See the figure for placement help.

6 Click to select the image frame and text frame group. Choose Object > Ungroup.

7 Click away from the image and text frame to deselect them.

8 Double-click the MeetKevin image frame to select the image inside.

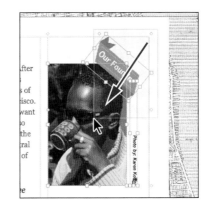

9 Position the pointer off any of the brown, image corner-bounding points. When you see the rotate arrow (↻), click and drag clockwise a bit. Release the mouse, and then press the Escape key to select the frame.

10 Choose Edit > Undo Rotate Item.

11 Position the pointer away from the content, and click to deselect the image. Drag a selection marquee across the content to select all three objects. Choose Object > Group.

12 Choose File > Save Site.

Wrapping text around content

Muse allows you to wrap text around frames that contain text, images, or nothing. This can be a great way to insert an image into a story, which is common on news sites, or a way to create a large first letter for text, called a drop cap. There are lots of uses for wrapping text around frames.

Wrapping text involves the Wrap panel (Window > Wrap) and requires that you paste the rectangle that the text will wrap around into the text. In this exercise, you'll place an image and wrap the story from the ABOUT page around it.

1   With the ABOUT page still open in Design mode, choose File > Place. In the Import dialog box, navigate to the images folder in the Lessons folder. Select the image named coffeebeans.jpg, and click Open (Windows) or Select (Mac OS).

2   Click to place the image anywhere on the page. Position doesn't matter.

3   Choose Edit > Cut.

● **Note:** Where you paste the rectangle matters. If you paste in the middle of a paragraph, then assign a left or right wrap, the top of the image aligns with the top of the line of text into which you pasted the image.

4   Select the Text tool and insert the cursor in front of the text that begins "Koffee Kart began as a whim..."

5   Choose Edit > Paste.

Muse pastes the image inline with the text. That means that it just flows with the text. If you tried to move the image with the Selection tool right now, you could only move it vertically because it is inline.

● **Note:** If you don't see the Wrap panel in the workspace, you can choose Window > Wrap to open it.

6   Click the Wrap panel tab to show the panel.

7   In the Wrap panel, click the Position Object To The Left button ( ).

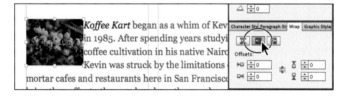

▶ **Tip:** Any objects that you paste into text to apply a wrap can have fills, strokes, and other effects applied.

The Wrap panel offers three options for positioning the image: inline, position left, and position right. The default position is inline, and that's what you see when you first paste the image into the text. Positioning the image to the right aligns it to the right and wraps the text around the left side of the image. Positioning the image to the left aligns it to the left and wraps the text around the right side of the image. You can try clicking each of the buttons to see what effect it has on the image and text, making sure that you click the Position Object To The Left button last.

Once you choose the correct image wrap option, you can also push the text away from the various edges of the image by using Offset in the Wrap panel.

8 In the Wrap panel, change Right Offset to **20**. Change Left Offset to **–50**. A negative value on the left allows you to move the image outside of the text frame, which can create some interesting effects. Change Left Offset to **0**. Leave the image selected for the next section.

▶ **Tip:** Try adding negative values to the other offsets. You can even get the text to appear over the image if you were to give the Right Offset a negative value.

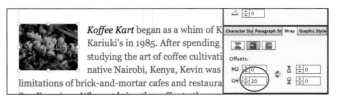

9 Choose File > Save Site.

10 Click the Preview mode link to see the image, then click the Design mode link to return to the ABOUT page.

Understanding the Assets panel

As you know, Muse links the images that you place (File > Place) on a page to their original image files. The Assets panel (Window > Assets) shows a listing of these files as well as all the other assets (.swf files and so on) used in your entire site, no matter which page is open in the Document window. The Assets panel also gives you menu commands with which you can ensure that the images are all linked properly.

1 Choose Window > Assets to show the panel.

2 With the Selection tool, click once on the group that contains the MeetKevin.jpg image to select the group, then click once more on the MeetKevin.jpg image to select only that image. In the Assets panel's list the selected image is now highlighted.

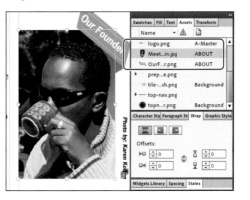

Clicking an image on a page selects that image in the Assets panel list. Assets listed in the Assets panel are listed alphabetically. You can click the column Name to sort them in descending, rather than ascending, order. Some assets listed have an arrow to the left of their name in the list. This indicates that there is more than one of that asset in the pages of the site. Clicking the arrow to the left of an asset expands the listing to detail every use

⬤ **Note:** If you attempt to select the image with the text wrap in the text frame by clicking with the Selection tool, you will select the text frame instead. Click once more on the image to select it. You can use the Selection Indicator to determine which element is selected: Text Frame means the text frame is selected, and Inline means that the image pasted in line with the text frame is selected.

Note: When you place an image on a master page, the Assets panel lists only the master page, not every instance. Other assets, such as PSD buttons and SWF files, also follow this same behavior.

of the image and the pages in the site where they appear. Muse calls an image on a page an *instance* of the original linked image file. As many times as a placed image appears in your site, every instance still links to the original image file. For example, if you placed the MeetKevin.jpg image on the HOME page as well as the ABOUT page, the expanded Assets panel would provide page details on both instances. Clicking an expanded arrow again closes the expanded listing and shows only the asset's name.

3   Position the pointer over the MeetKevin.jpg image name in the assets list, and Muse provides a yellow tooltip with the path to the image.

That tooltip tells you where the original image is located on your hard drive.

Note: The ArrowMenuDown.gif came from the menu widget you inserted in a previous lesson.

4   Scroll up in the Assets panel, and notice the image named ArrowMenuDown.gif. Position the pointer over the name in the list.

The icon to the right of that image (🖼) indicates that it is embedded in the Muse site, meaning it does not link to an original image file. If you paste content from another application, Muse embeds the content in your page.

The Assets panel not only lists the assets that are linked and embedded, but it also gives you a lot of functionality found in context menus—from editing images to relinking images and more.

Relinking images

After you place an image into Muse, circumstances sometimes may require you to replace that image (a different product becomes the monthly special, say) or link a different version of the original file to the instances on your pages (you recrop a photo to better highlight your office location). In the Assets panel, you can choose to relink an image, which replaces that image on a page.

On the ABOUT page, you are going to replace the coffeebeans.jpg image that you wrapped the text around.

Tip: If you place the same asset on multiple pages, you can easily relink every instance of the image throughout the site. For example, right-click (Windows) or Control-click (Mac OS) the parent listing (with the arrow to the left of it) in the Assets panel and choose Relink All Instances Of "image name."

1   With the Selection tool, click twice on the image that the text is wrapping around to select just the image. This also highlights the image in the Assets panel.

2   In the Assets panel, right-click (Windows) or Control-click (Mac OS) the coffeebeans.jpg listing, and choose Relink in the context menu that appears.

3 In the Relink dialog box, navigate to the images folder in the Lessons folder, then to coffeebeans2.jpg, and click Open (Windows) or Select (Mac OS).

The new image replaces the old image in the frame, fitting proportionally in the frame.

Koffee Kart began as a whim of Ke Kariuki's in 1985. After spending y studying the art of coffee cultivatio native Nairobi, Kenya, Kevin was s limitations of brick-and-mortar cafes and restauran San Francisco. Why not bring the coffee to the peop the people want it, in the most eco-friendly way poss an espresso machine on a three-wheeled rickshaw a most of the way there. Add the finest original roasts Africa, Central America and the Pacific and you've f Koffee Kart of San Francisco.

"We absolutely love the coffee from Kevin's Kart. Especially the dark roast drip he offe

Note: When you relink an image that is not the same dimensions, Muse fits the new image proportionally and centers it in the rectangle. That can lead to a small image being made much larger or vice versa. It's best to replace an image with an image of the same dimensions. You can also replace the image and scale the new image close to 100% using the Selection or Crop tools.

4 Choose File > Save Site.

Editing original

From within Muse, you can open a placed image in an image-editing program like Photoshop, make changes, save the file, and come back to Muse to see it updated in your design. This is called the Edit Original command and is only available for placed assets that are linked.

Note: To perform this exercise, you need Adobe Photoshop on your machine. If you do not have Photoshop, you can relink the DailyDrip.psd image in the Assets panel to DailyDrip-final.psd in the images folder within the Lessons folder. If you relink the image, make sure to select Import Layer and select the layer called banner text. Also, choose Clip To Layer Contents in the Image Import Options (DailyDrip-final.psd) dialog box.

Note: Using Edit Original can be helpful for .psd, .gif, and .png file formats, but you need to be careful with .jpg images. Every time you save a .jpg file, it's further compressed and the image quality may begin to suffer eventually.

1 Choose View > Fit Page In Window.

2 With the Selection tool, right-click (Windows) or Control-click (Mac OS) the OurFounder.png image, and choose Edit Original from the context menu that appears.

3 With the image open in Photoshop, notice in the Layers panel (Window > Layers) that there is only one layer.

If you wanted to change the layers in the image import options, you would need to place the image again in Muse.

Note: The program that the images open in is based on your Operating System file association settings. If you can't get it to open in an image-editing program, you can always go to your image-editing application (preferably Photoshop for this exercise) and open the file directly. You will need to update the modified link in Muse, and will learn about that in the next section.

4 Choose Image > Adjustments > Brightness/Contrast.

5 Drag the Brightness slider to the left until the Brightness value is **−30**. Click OK.

6 Choose File > Save, then click OK in the PNG Options dialog box.

7 Choose File > Close to close the OurFounder.png file, then close Photoshop if you like (you don't have to), returning to Muse.

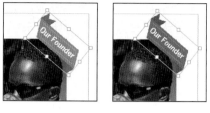

Before   After

Note: The Edit Original command is not available for embedded content that was pasted from another program like Photoshop.

The image should automatically update on the page. If you find the image hasn't updated, you could always go to the image name in the Muse Assets panel, right-click (Windows) or Control-click (Mac OS) and choose Update Asset. The Assets panel displays a triangle icon with an exclamation point next to the asset's name in this case.

8 Choose File > Save Site.

Fixing broken and modified links

The link between the original file and the instances you place in your site is extremely important, because if an image you placed moves from its original location, Muse will consider that linked file to be missing and you will need to fix the link before publishing or exporting. Likewise, if an image that you placed in your site is opened, edited, and saved outside of Muse in a program like Photoshop, that image needs to be updated in Muse to show the changes.

You can fix missing and modified links easily in Muse, as you'll see in this exercise.

Note: If the warning dialog box you see indicates more than one modified image, fix all of them in the Assets panel.

1 Choose File > Open Site. In the Open dialog box, navigate to the Lesson06 folder in the Lessons folder. Select the Muse site named FixLinks.muse, and click Select.

When you open a site that has missing and modified links, a warning dialog box appears. Clicking OK instructs Muse to update any modified assets in the site. You then need to go to the Assets panel to fix the missing links. Clicking Cancel opens the site but does not fix a thing. Be careful with clicking OK, because you may not know what has been modified.

Note: If the site you are opening has a missing asset only, the dialog box that appears will offer an OK button only, because you need to fix the missing link(s) in the Assets panel.

2 Click Cancel in the warning dialog box.

3 In Plan mode, double-click the HOME page thumbnail to open the page in Design mode. Choose View > Fit Page In Window.

4 With the Assets panel showing (Window > Assets), scroll down in the panel until you see a red stop sign to the right of the DailyDrip.png listing.

5 Right-click (Windows) or Control-click (Mac OS) the name and choose Relink from the context menu that appears.

6 In the Relink dialog box, navigate to the images folder in the Lessons folder. Select the image named DailyDrip.png, and click Select.

If the image had changed in dimensions, it would be fit proportionally in the frame.

7 In the Assets panel, right-click (Windows) or Control-click (Mac OS) the image name, cloud-1.png, and choose Update Asset from the context menu that appears.

Update Asset forces Muse to go look at the image again and update what you see on the page to match the changes made in the linked cloud-1.png image.

8 Choose File > Close Site. You don't need to save this site.

Pinning content

You've invested a lot of time learning how to reposition content on a page and can now easily move an image in relation to the other elements (images, text, and media) that also exist on the page. But how do you make something always stay visible when you scroll in the browser window? If a page is long (contains a lot of vertical content), visitors no longer can see content from the top of the page when they scroll down. What if you wanted a Twitter follow button, menu, or just an image to always be visible as the rest of the content scrolls. You need to *pin* the content. The Control panel makes pinning content easy. You simply set the pinned content, such as an image, to a specific location in relation to the edge of the browser window. It always stays in one spot regardless of other scrolling page elements.

The pinned element will move to maintain its pinned position in relation to the browser if the visitor resizes the browser window, but the pinned element will not move if the visitor scrolls the page content horizontally or vertically.

Next, you will pin a cloud image.

1 Back in the KevinsKoffeeKart site, click the Plan mode link, and when in Plan mode, double-click the HOME page thumbnail to open that page in Design mode.

2 Choose View > Fit Page In Window.

3 Choose File > Place. In the Import dialog box, navigate to the images folder in the Lessons folder and then to the image named cloud.png. Click Open (Windows) or Select (Mac OS).

4 Click to place the image just off the right side of the page, so you can see part of the cloud on top of the background image. The exact position right now doesn't matter.

5   In the Control panel, click the top-right position of the six possible options in the Pin tool located in the Control panel.

6   Choose View > Smart Guides to turn off the Smart Guides and snapping to other content and page elements.

7   With the Selection tool, drag the cloud so that the right edge of the frame is a bit to the left of the page width. See figure for placement help.

8   Choose View > Smart Guides to turn them back on.

9   Click the Preview mode link and decrease and increase the width of the Preview window by dragging the bottom-right resize handle.

You'll notice that the cloud image moves horizontally as you resize the width of the browser window and stays stuck to the right edge of the Preview window. Later, if you add more content to the home page to make it longer, the image will still stay put and remain visible—even if the visitor scrolls down to see the bottom of a lengthy page.

10 Click the Design mode link and choose File > Close Page to close the HOME page and return to the ABOUT page.

11 Choose File > Save Site.

Inserting Flash files

Muse allows you to place published Flash files or .swf files in your pages. The Flash content you add to your Muse site can be created in any number of programs, including Adobe InDesign. Using the File > Place command, you can place .swf files in your site just like you do images.

1   Click the Plan mode link, and then double-click the MasterFlash thumbnail to open the page. Scroll up in the Document window so that you see the entire header area.

2   Choose File > Place. In the Import dialog box that appears, navigate to the Lessons folder and in the images folder, select the logo.swf file. Click Open (Windows) or Select (Mac OS) to choose the file, and close the Import dialog box.

3   Position the Place Gun above the page area on the left side of the header, and click to place.

You will see a frame appear with a Flash icon in the upper-left corner, indicating that .swf content is in that frame. Leave the frame selected on the page.

You learned earlier that by dragging, you can size content as you place it. In the case of Flash files, however, you're better off placing the file at 100%. Be especially wary of resizing the file if it contains raster images, for instance. Resizing may distort certain content and it may become pixellated-looking. Because the .swf file is in a frame, you can resize it or move it to a different location on the page later.

4   With the Transform panel showing and the SWF file selected, change the X value to **–350**. Change the Y value to **–185** to move the frame into position vertically.

A positive value for X moves content to the right, and a negative value moves it to the left. For the Y value, a positive value moves content down the page and a negative value moves it up.

5   Choose Object > Send To Back to send the SWF file behind the menu.

6   Click the Assets panel tab in the panel dock on the right side of the workspace.

When you place .swf content, Muse treats it like a placed image. The pages that contain the content link to the original file. That means that you can edit and replace the .swf file outside of Muse and update its content in Muse easily using the Assets panel.

.SWF content and associated files

When you publish your site to either Adobe hosting or by exporting the files to HTML, Muse creates the web pages and collects copies of the linked content, which is listed in the Assets panel, into a single folder. When you place a .swf file, the .muse site file links to the original .swf file that you placed, so Muse will collect it when the site is published or exported to HTML. If the .swf file requires external files to run, such as XML, ActionScript, or images, Muse will not collect those files when you publish or export the site. You will need to gather those files yourself and upload them to the host separately.

7   Choose File > Save Site and File > Close Page to return to the ABOUT page.

Adding alternative text and a title to images

In Muse, you can add information such as alternative text and a title to your images. Alternative text is useful for several reasons, including for SEO purposes (depending on the search engine), for accessibility (to be read aloud by screen readers), and to show when an image link is broken. Alternative text is intended to state the purpose of the image, but in addition to a sentence that describes the picture's function you can include some relevant targeted keywords. Likewise, a title is a way to provide additional information about the image to search engines and visitors. Keep titles relevant, short, and descriptive. The image title actually appears as a tooltip in some browsers when a visitor hovers the cursor over the image.

You'll find fields for adding alternative text and a title in the Image Properties dialog box in Muse. Setting alternative text or a title is typically done on an image-by-image basis. If you have an image appearing multiple times throughout your site, it's best to add alternative text and a title based on the context of the image.

1 On the ABOUT page, with the Selection tool, click the coffeebeans2.jpg image (the one with text wrapped around it) twice to select the image, not the text frame.

▶ **Tip:** You can also edit the title or alternative text for an image by right-clicking (Windows) or Control-clicking (Mac OS) the image file name in the Assets panel and choosing either Add Title or Add Alternative Text from the context menu that appears.

2 Right-click (Windows) or Control-click (Mac OS) the image, and choose Add Title from the context menu that appears.

The Image Properties dialog box appears. In this dialog box you can add both a title and alternative text if you choose.

3 In the Image Properties dialog box, enter **San Francisco coffee supplier to the Bay Area** in the Title field.

4 In the Alternative Text field, enter **Koffee Kart gourmet coffee beans** and click OK.

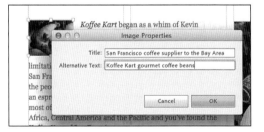

5 Choose File > Save Site, and leave the ABOUT page open for the next Lesson.

In the Lesson 7, "Working with Links and Buttons," you'll learn how to add links to other pages within your site and other sites, create e-mail links, add interactive buttons, create linking in a long page, and much more.

Review questions

1 Which image file formats can you place into Muse?

2 Briefly describe the significance of an image link.

3 What options are available when placing a layered Photoshop file?

4 Where must an image or other rectangular frame be placed in order to wrap text around it?

5 What is meant by pinning content?

6 What are alternative text and an image title used for on the Web?

Review answers

1 You can place .jpg, .gif, .png, and .psd (Photoshop) files by choosing File > Place in Muse.

2 When you place (File > Place) an image, Muse creates an image link between the instance of the image on the page and that image's original file. If you later update the original file, Muse updates all instances of that image in your website as well.

3 When you place layered Photoshop files, the Image Import Options dialog box allows you to place a composite image (all visible layers showing) or selected layers. You can also crop the placed image to the bounds of the layer content.

4 To wrap text around content like an image, you must either cut or copy the image from its original location, insert the cursor in the text, and paste the image in the text frame. Then you can use the Wrap panel to set the wrapping options.

5 Pinned content is set to a specific location in relation to the edge of the browser window. It stays in one spot regardless of other scrolling page elements.

6 Alternative text is useful for several reasons, including for SEO purposes (depending on the search engine), for accessibility (to be read aloud by screen readers), and to appear when image links are broken. Adding a title to an image is a way to provide additional information about the image to search engines and visitors. Both alternative text and image titles should be relevant and descriptive.

7 WORKING WITH LINKS AND BUTTONS

Lesson overview

In this lesson, you'll work with adding links and buttons to your pages and learn to

- Create different types of links
- Edit link properties
- Style links
- Add links to images
- Create and link to anchors
- Create a button in Muse
- Work with states
- Place an Adobe Photoshop button

This lesson takes approximately 45 minutes to complete. If you are starting from scratch in this lesson, use the method described in the "Jumpstart" section on page 5 of "Getting Started."

ABOUT KEVIN'S KOFFEE KART

Koffee Kart began as a whim of Kevin Kariuki's in 1985. After spending years studying the art of coffee cultivation in his native Nairobi, Kenya, Kevin was struck by the limitations of brick-and-mortar cafes and restaurants here in San Francisco. Why not bring the coffee to the people, where the people want it, in the most eco-friendly way possible? Strap an espresso machine on a three-wheeled rickshaw and you're most of the way there. Add the finest original roasts from Africa, Central America and the Pacific and you've found the Koffee Kart of San Francisco.

"We absolutely love the coffee from Kevin's Koffee Kart. Especially the dark roast drip he offers every Wednesday!"

Our Founder

Photo by: Karen Koffee

kevin@kevinskoffeekart.com

follow us on

Create an Anchor...

Create an anchor

FrenchPress

Cancel   OK

The Kof...

follow us on

follow us on

Site Properties

Layout   Hyperlinks

[Default Link Style]
email links

	T	T	T
Normal:			☐
Hover:			☑
Visited:			☑
Active:			☑

Cancel   OK

Whether you need to link a website, link to a part of the same page, or create interactive buttons in Muse or Photoshop, Muse can help, enabling you to create and edit many types of links with ease, flexibility, and some great design features.

Working with Links

Note: The exercises in this lesson, like others in this book, require that you have the fonts supplied on the *Adobe Muse Classroom in a Book* disc installed on your machine. For more information on installing the necessary fonts, see "Fonts used in this book" on page 2 of "Getting Started."

A hyperlink, also called a link, takes your users to a resource on the Web or within your site. The resource can be anything that a computer can store and display: a web page, an image, a movie, a sound file, and more. With Muse, you can create three types of links: internal, external, and e-mail links.

The simplest hyperlink is an *internal link*, which takes the visitor to another part of the same page in Muse, another page in your site, or to other content, like a PDF, stored in the same site folder. An *external link* takes the visitor to a document or resource on another website or another Web host. An e-mail link is a link to an e-mail address that, when clicked, launches the visitor's default e-mail program and creates a new e-mail to be sent to the e-mail address you enter in the link in Muse.

Creating an internal link

Muse makes it easy to add different types of hyperlinks to your content. In this section, you'll link text on the ABOUT page to other pages in your Muse site.

Note: If you have not already done so, copy the Lessons folder onto your hard disk from the *Adobe Muse Classroom in a Book* disc. See "Copying the Classroom in a Book files" on page 3.

Note: If you are starting from scratch using the Jumpstart method described in the "Jumpstart" section on page 5 of "Getting Started," your workspace may look different than the figures you see in this Lesson.

1 With your site open, and the ABOUT page open as well, choose View > Fit Page In Window.

2 Select the Text tool, and insert the cursor at the bottom of the main story (you may need to scroll down) after the text "This has been very important to Koffee Kart's growth and continued success." Press Enter or Return.

3 Type **Learn more about our story and all of the exciting things coming to Kevin's Koffee Kart!**

4 With the cursor in the text, click the Text panel tab (Window > Text), and change the Space Before setting (⁺▤) to **16**.

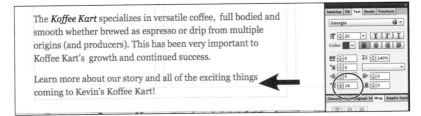

5 Select the phrase "our story," click the arrow to the right of the Hyperlink field in the Control panel, and choose OUR STORY.

Note: You can't add a text link to selected text that has been rotated or that uses a System Font because it will be rasterized when the site is published or exported. You can, however, add a link to a rotated text frame or font by selecting the text frame, not the text, and applying the link to it.

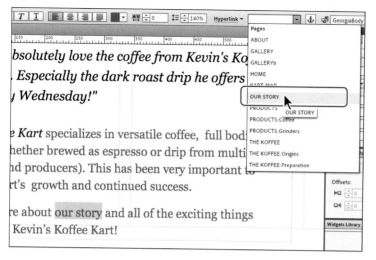

The Hyperlink field menu lists all of the pages in the site, except for the master pages—even pages that are not included in the navigation, like GALLERYb.

6 Click in the "our story" text on the page to see the default blue and underline formatting applied. Later, you will change the appearance of the links you create.

Note: Notice the Hyperlink field menu is dimmed. To change a link on text, you need to select all of the text that is linked.

7 Select the Selection tool, and drag the bottom-middle bounding point of that same text frame down until the Min H (minimum height) value matches the H (height) value in the measurement label and the dotted line disappears.

8 Click the Preview mode link to see the links (you may need to scroll down on the page). Click the link to go to the OUR STORY page.

By default, when you create a text link, the new page or website replaces the existing page in the same browser window or tab.

9 Click the Design mode link to return to the ABOUT page.

Creating an external link

Besides linking to pages within your site, you can also link to other websites. These links are called external links.

1 Select the Text tool, and select the first instance of the words "San Francisco" in the first paragraph.

Note: Muse adds the http:// to the website URL, so you don't have to type that.

2   Insert the cursor in the Hyperlink field, type **maps.google.com**, and then press Enter or Return.

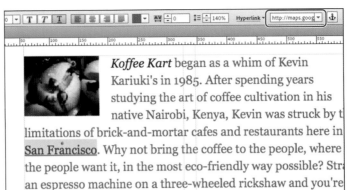

Koffee Kart began as a whim of Kevin Kariuki's in 1985. After spending years studying the art of coffee cultivation in his native Nairobi, Kenya, Kevin was struck by t limitations of brick-and-mortar cafes and restaurants here in San Francisco. Why not bring the coffee to the people, where the people want it, in the most eco-friendly way possible? Str an espresso machine on a three-wheeled rickshaw and you're

At any time later, you can select the "San Francisco" text and edit the hyperlink.

3   Click the Preview mode link to see the links on the ABOUT page. Click the San Francisco link to go to maps.google.com.

By default, the linked website (maps.google.com) replaces the original page in the Muse Preview window. In Muse, there is no back button, so once you click to view an external link, you need to click the Design mode link to return to the original page.

4   Click the Design mode link to return to the ABOUT page.

Creating an e-mail link

You create an e-mail link exactly as you do an external link, only instead of providing a website address, you type an e-mail address.

1   With the Text tool, click and drag to create a text frame below the image of Kevin on the right side of the page. Make sure that the left edge of the text frame aligns with the left edge of the third column and that it's as wide as the column. Type **kevin@kevinskoffeekart.com**.

2   Click the Paragraph Styles panel tab to show the panel. With the cursor in the e-mail address, click the style named "StepBody small."

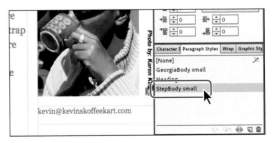

3   Select the address kevin@ kevinskoffeekart.com, and choose Edit > Copy.

4 Insert the cursor in the Hyperlink field in the Control panel, and choose Edit > Paste. Press Enter or Return. You could have typed the e-mail address into the field, but this is faster.

5 Click the Preview mode link to see the email link you just created (you may need to scroll down). Click the kevin@kevinskoffeekart.com link to open the default e-mail application on your machine.

> **Tip:** If you want to add more e-mail addresses, type a comma (,) after kevin@kevinskoffeekart. com and add another. After every e-mail address (except the last one), type a comma.

Note: The text on the page doesn't have to be the actual e-mail address. You may see phrases like "E-mail us" or "Contact us" instead.

Note: If you don't have an e-mail application installed on your machine, the link will do nothing. If you have an e-mail application installed, but it's not set up, you may be asked to set it up when the link is clicked. If the e-mail application is installed and configured, a new message window will appear with the e-mail address automatically entered in the To field.

6 Click the Design mode link to return to the ABOUT page.

7 Choose File > Save Site.

Editing link properties

By default, links you create open the linked page or site in the same window or tab, replacing the page you're linking from. You can change this setting to make external links open in another browser window or tab so that your site remains open for visitors to return to.

1 With the Text tool, select the linked text "San Francisco" in the first paragraph.

2 Click the word "Hyperlink" in the Control panel to see the Hyperlink options.

3 Select Open The Link In A New Window Or Tab.

This option opens the linked page or website in a new window or tab.

4 In the Title field, type **map location of Kevin's Kart in San Francisco.**

A link title can be beneficial in several ways. It shows as a tooltip in some browsers when the cursor is over the text link on the page, it can be read aloud by screen readers, and it can give more information to search engines, among other things. The title text provides information about where the link will send the user, and can contain keywords and other relevant information.

5 Press the Escape key to hide the Hyperlink options.

6 Choose File > Save Site.

Styling your text links

When you create text links, you'll likely want to change their appearance to better match your design and to differentiate the various types of links with unique styling. For instance, in the Koffee Kart site, the links in the footer will need to be white, or a lighter color, to be readable on the brown, but links in the page area will need to be a darker color to be readable. Of course, all of your links should still give the appearance of being a link and clickable. In this section, you'll edit the default appearance of the links, called Link Styles, and create styling for different types of links.

1 Click the word "Hyperlink" in the Control panel, and then click the Edit Link Styles button in the Hyperlink options to open the Site Properties dialog box. These are the same site properties you can access by choosing File > Site Properties.

Every site in Muse has default formatting for the text links. That default style is called [Default Link Style] and is listed in the Site Properties dialog box. You can change the appearance of the default link style and all text links in your site will change to match. Link styles also have four states: normal, hover, visited, and active. See the sidebar "About link states" to learn more about states. For each state, you can change the color, add bold or italic, and remove or keep the underline.

2 Click the Normal color, and in the Color Picker that appears, click to select the red color swatch with the values R: 193, G: 39, B: 45. Click away from the Color Picker panel to hide it and return to the Site Properties dialog box.

3 Select the box in the Underline column once until the box is blank. This will remove the under-line for all of your links.

Note: When you click several times on one of the boxes in either the Bold, Italic, or Underline columns, you will see that there are three selection options: a check mark, a blank box, and a box with a filled box inside. A check mark indicates that the formatting is applied to the link; for instance, a check mark in the Underline column tells the browser to underline the link and write that in the code. A blank box tells Muse to write the code for underline, but set it at the default of no underline. A box with a filled box inside tells Muse not to write anything in the code for underline—leaving the formatting at default (no underline).

4 Change the color for Hover to the Footer Stroke color (you can try another color if you like), and leave the rest of the options for Hover at default.

5 Change the color for Visited to a lighter version of the FooterBG color, and leave the rest of the options at default.

6 Leave the Active options at the their defaults. You can always experiment later. Leave the dialog box open for the next steps.

About link states

On the Web, text links have four states: link, visited, hover, and active. You can create different styling for each state of a link. These states are similar to the functionality of the states found in States panel in Muse.

- **Normal:** This is the first state that visitors will see. When a page is opened and the text links appear, the normal state is what a link looks like when a visitor hasn't interacted with it yet.

- **Hover:** When a visitor positions the cursor over a link on your web page, you can change the appearance of the link.

- **Visited:** After a visitor clicks a text link, then returns to the same page, you can change the appearance of the link to indicate that the link has been clicked previously.

- **Active:** The active state can change the appearance of the link between the times the visitor presses the mouse button and releases it.

7 Click the New Link Style button (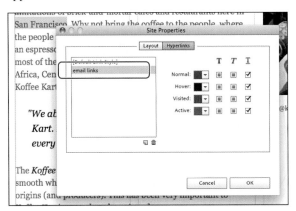) at the bottom of the Site Properties dialog box.

Muse creates a new link style in the Site Properties dialog box that is an exact copy of the default link style. The default link style applies to every link by default, but you can apply your new style to text links that you want to look and behave differently. This new link style will be available for use on every page within the current site only.

8 Double-click to select the new style named "[Default Link Style] copy," and rename it **email links**.

Note: Later, you can change the appearance of the link styles or create more in the Site Properties dialog box. There is also a Delete button to remove any link styles that you don't want to keep. You can use these link styles throughout your site.

9 Leave the settings for the four states at default, except for the Normal state. In the Normal state, select the box in the Underline column until a check mark appears to add an underline. Click OK.

Tip: You can also apply link styles in the Text panel (Window > Text).

10 With the Text tool, select the kevin@kevinskoffeekart.com text, click the word "Hyperlink" in the Control panel and select the style named "email links" from the Text Link Style menu.

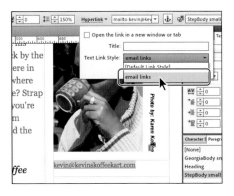

Note: If you see the visited link appearance on some of the links when you test the page, it's because your browser has those links cached (you've visited them before). You can clear the browser's cache.

11 Choose File > Preview Site In Browser. After the Home page loads, click ABOUT in the top menu widget to open the ABOUT page. Interact with the links by hovering the cursor over one, and notice the change. Click and hold down, without releasing the mouse button; in most major browsers the active state formatting will show. Click the San Francisco link, and notice that the maps.google.com page opens in a new window or a new tab. Return to the original window or tab to see the ABOUT page and the visited link style displayed.

12 Close the browser and return to Muse.

Adding links to images

To add a link to an image, you follow the same steps as for creating a text link. Instead of selecting text, however, you select an image. Most sites have a link on the company logo to the home page of the site, and that's exactly what you are going to add here.

1   Click the Plan mode link, and double-click the A-Master page thumbnail.

2   With the Selection tool, select the Kevin's Koffee Kart logo image in the header on the A-Master page. Drag the image so that the bottom of the bicycle wheels align with the top edge of the brown in the menu, and the left edge of the logo aligns with the left edge of the menu.

3   With the logo selected, choose HOME from the Pages section of the Hyperlink options menu to the right of the word Hyperlink in the Control panel.

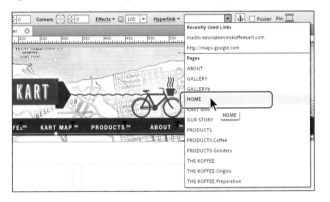

▶ **Tip:** Notice the Recently Used Links at the top of the Hyperlink menu. External or e-mail links that you type in are listed here so that if you want to reuse them in this site, you can just select them in the menu.

4   Click the Preview mode link, and click on the logo to navigate to the HOME page.

5   Click the Design mode link to return to the A-Master page, then choose File > Close Page.

6   Choose File > Save Site.

Working with anchors

Long pages with a lot of vertical content to scroll through can be cumbersome for visitors to navigate. You can alleviate this issue in Muse by creating internal links that make the page jump to a specified section when a visitor clicks the link. The commonly used Back to Top link, which quickly scrolls to the top of the page when clicked, is a good example of this type of internal link.

To link to a part of a page, you need to insert an anchor at the desired spot and then link to that anchor. The anchors are invisible to visitors, but allow you to create internal links to different parts of a page.

Creating anchors

The first step toward aiding visitors in scrolling long pages is to insert the anchors to which you will later link.

1 Click the Plan mode link, and open the Preparation page by double-clicking its thumbnail. After the page opens, make sure that the page is scrolled all the way to the top.

▶ Tip: You can also choose Object > Insert Link Anchor to insert an anchor.

2 Click the Anchor button (⚓) in the Control panel. The pointer will change to a Place Gun. Position the Place Gun at the very top of the page, below the ruler, toward the left edge of header. Click to insert an anchor and open the Create An Anchor dialog box.

3 In the Create An Anchor dialog box, change the name to **top** and click OK.

◉ Note: You can name anchors anything you want, just keep it simple. Anchor names cannot start with a number, and Muse will warn you if you use an illegal character.

You should now see the anchor icon on the page with the word "top" to the right. With the Selection tool you can move the anchor, or you can select it and press Delete to remove it. If you need to rename the anchor, right-click (Windows) or Control-click (Mac OS) the anchor icon and choose Rename Anchor from the context menu that appears.

4 Click the Anchor button in the Control panel twice.

▶ Tip: You can also copy and paste an anchor on the page when it's selected, or press Alt (Windows)/ Option (Mac OS) while you drag the anchor with the Selection tool to create a copy, and then rename it.

Move the Place Gun cursor in the page, and you'll see the anchor icon with (2) to its right (⚓ (2)). Clicking the Anchor button twice loads two anchors into the Place Gun that you can then place.

5 Scroll down the page until you see the text "French Press" in red.

6 Position the Place Gun on the left edge of the first column and above French Press. (See the figure for placement help.) Click to place another anchor.

◉ Note: When you click a link that is linked to an anchor farther down the page, the page will scroll so that the anchor is at the top of the browser window. For example, if the anchor is aligned with the "French Press" text, the page will scroll so that French Press is at the very top of the browser window.

7 In the Create An Anchor dialog box, change the name to **FrenchPress**, and click OK.

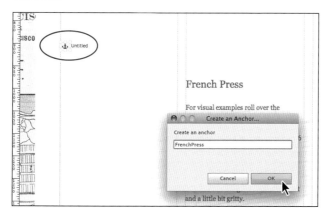

8 Scroll down the page until you see the word "Espresso" in red, position the Place Gun on the left edge of the first column and above Espresso," and click to place another anchor.

9 In the Create An Anchor dialog box, change the name to **Espresso**, and click OK.

Linking to an anchor

Now that the anchors are in place, you can create links to the anchors.

1 Scroll back to the top of the Preparation page.

2 Select the Text tool, and create a text frame on top of the aqua rectangle at the top of the first column. Type **DRIP COFFEE**. Select the text, and click the Heading style in the Paragraph Styles panel to apply the style. In the Control panel, click the Font menu and choose the New Gothic Std Bold font from the System Fonts (Exports As Image) menu.

3 Select the Selection tool, and position and size the text frame like in the figure.

4 Press and hold Shift+Alt (Windows) or Shift+Option (Mac OS) and drag the text frame straight down to create a copy. Release the mouse button and then the keys. See the figure for how far to drag the frame.

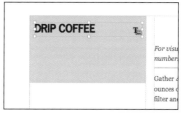

5 Create one more copy for a total of three text frames. When dragging the last one down, you will see the gap measurements to help you space the frames evenly. Once again, release the mouse button and then the keys. If your gap measurement doesn't match the figure exactly, that's okay.

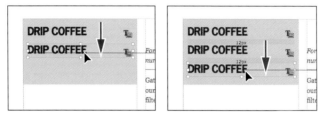

Create the first copy   Create the second copy

You are going to apply the link to the text frame, but not by selecting the text like you did earlier. Applying the link to a text frame will not change the appearance of the text in the frame. That's why you are creating three separate text frames, because each text frame will link to a different anchor.

6 Using the Text tool, change the middle text frame's text to **FRENCH PRESS** and the text in bottom text frame to **ESPRESSO**.

7 Change the text color of FRENCH PRESS to a red color and the ESPRESSO text color to black in the Control panel.

8 Select the Selection tool, and click the text frame that contains the phrase "DRIP COFFEE."

Note: Notice that the link has been applied to the text frame and the text inside hasn't changed in appearance. The text doesn't change because the font applied to the text is a system font, so although it is editable text, the text frame will be rendered as an image (not text content) when the site is previewed, published, or exported as HTML.

9 Click the arrow to the right of the Hyperlink field in the Control panel. In the menu that appears, you'll see a new category called Anchors. You may need to scroll down in the menu because anchors appear last in the list. Choose Preparation:top.

10 Select the text frame that contains the phrase "FRENCH PRESS," and choose Preparation:FrenchPress by clicking the arrow to the right of the Hyperlink field in the Control panel.

▶ **Tip:** The reason why the link appears as Preparation:FrenchPress in this example, and not just FrenchPress, is to indicate that the anchor is on the page named Preparation. This sort of naming scheme helps if you plan to link between pages. If you open another page and create a link to this same anchor, for example, Muse will open the Preparation page first, then scroll down to the anchor named FrenchPress when the link is clicked.

11 Select the text frame that contains ESPRESSO, and choose Preparation:Espresso by clicking the arrow to the right of the Hyperlink field in the Control panel.

12 With the Selection tool, drag a marquee selection across the aqua-filled frame and the three text frames. Choose Object > Group.

▶ **Tip:** You can hide the Rasterized Text Frame indicators by choosing View > Hide Rasterized Text Frame Indicators.

13 Click the top-middle position of the six possible options in the Pin tool (⬚) located in the Control panel.

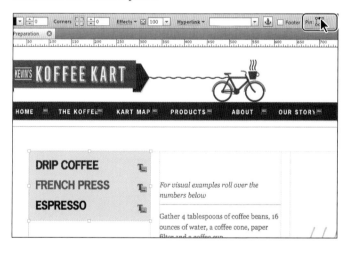

This pins the entire group to the center of the browser window horizontally (which will be the horizontal center of the page) and the same position down, relative to the top of the browser window.

14 Click the Preview mode link and click the FRENCH PRESS link, then click the DROP COFFEE link to return to the top of the page.

Notice that the page slides down smoothly. Also notice that group of three links is pinned in place and floating above the other content.

15 Click the Design mode link to return to the Preparation page and choose File > Close Page.

Working with buttons

On the Web, designers use buttons as well as links to link to other content, other pages, or other websites. A button is usually styled to look more three-dimensional so it resembles a physical button that you can press. Buttons tend to appear on a web page less frequently than text links. Site designers use them primarily to encourage users to do something or as a call to action on a website, giving them action names like Buy, SignUp, Search, or View My Portfolio.

Creating a button in Muse

You can create a button out of almost any object in your design—text frames, image frames, and rectangle shapes. Muse lets you change the appearance of the button object with states, a background color and image, strokes, effects like drop shadows, rounded corners, and much more.

In this section, you'll create a button from a text frame, using the States panel and adding a link to it. This button will refresh a Google map that you will add in a Lesson 8, "Applying Effects, Graphic Styles, and Inserting HTML."

1   Click the Plan mode link and double-click the KART MAP page thumbnail to open the page in Design mode.

2   Choose View > Fit Page In Window.

3   Select the Text tool. Click and drag to create a text frame starting in the upper-left corner of the first column guides, stretching all the way to the right edge of the third column across the page. Make sure that it has a height of approximately 50px.

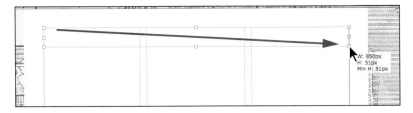

Note: Don't worry if the frame isn't positioned to match the figure exactly. In Lesson 8, you will move it into its final position.

4   Type **CLICK TO GET DIRECTIONS!**

5   Select the text. In the Control panel, change Font to the Web Safe font **Geneva**, set Font Size to **34**, click the Bold button, and change the color to white.

6 Select the Selection tool, and Muse selects the text frame. Click the Fill link in the Control panel, and click the Choose Background Image folder icon to select a background image for the text frame. Navigate to the images folder in the Lessons folder, and choose the image named MapFindUs.png. Click Open (Windows) or Select (Mac OS). Make sure that Original Size is chosen in the Fitting menu and that the upper-left corner (⊞) is selected for the Position option.

The entire background image will not show in the text frame, but you will see the text again.

7 With the Selection tool, drag the right-middle bounding point of the text frame to the right until you see the entire background image. Stop when you see a width of approximately 915px. Drag the bottom-middle bounding point down until you see the entire banner image in the background. Make the frame a little taller than the image, approximately 60px.

8 Click the Spacing panel tab (Window > Spacing) on the right side of the workspace to reveal the panel. Change the left padding to **40** and the top padding to **3**.

As you saw in Lesson 3, "Working with Master Pages," the Spacing panel allows you to add padding inside the frame. In this case, padding pushes the text in from the edge of the text frame.

9 Click the Preview mode link and check out the new button you've started. Click the Design mode link to return to the page in Design mode, leaving the text frame selected.

10 Choose File > Save Site.

Using the States panel to add button states

Muse allows you to add states to your button. As you've learned previously, states are useful for indicating a change in appearance when visitors interact with the button. You don't have to add states to a button, but as you'll see, sometimes it can be good to indicate that something will happen when the button is clicked.

1 Click the States panel tab (Window > States) on the right side of the workspace.

2 With the text frame still selected, click the Rollover state in the States panel.

Note: You need to have the frame selected, not the text, in order to edit the states using the States panel.

3 In the Text panel, change the color of the text to the FooterBG swatch.

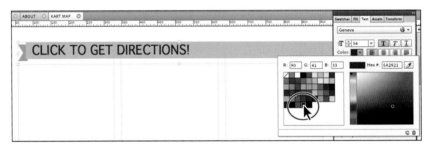

This is a really simple rollover option, but you could have instead replaced the background image, added an underline to the text, almost any number of changes to the text frame or text.

Look in the States panel, and you will see that the Mouse Down state looks the same as the Rollover state. You could change the appearance of the Mouse Down or Active (Normal) state if you like, but in this case it's not necessary.

4 Click the Normal state again in the States panel to see the white text.

5 Click the Preview mode link to preview the button. Position the pointer over anywhere in the text frame, and you will see the rollover state change.

6 Click the Design mode link to return to the KART MAP page in Design mode.

7 Choose File > Save Site.

Adding a link to a button

Adding a link to a button typically involves selecting the button (frame), not the contents, before adding the link.

1 With the text frame still selected, click the arrow to the right of the Hyperlink field in the Control panel. Choose KART MAP from the menu.

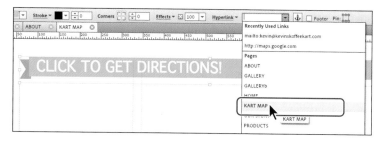

It may seem odd to be linking to the same page that you are on, but this will be a placeholder link until you insert a Google map into the page in the next lesson.

2 Click the Preview mode link to preview the button. Position the pointer over the text frame, and the rollover state may not change because it is linking to the same page that it's on. Don't worry, you will change the link at the end of Lesson 8, and the rollover will work again.

3 Click the Design mode link to return to the KART MAP page in Design mode.

4 Choose File > Save Site, then File > Close Page to close the KART MAP page.

Setting up a button in Photoshop

Although you can create buttons in Muse, you also have the option of creating a button in a program like Photoshop, which gives you even greater design flexibility. Using the File > Place Photoshop Button command, you can then place the layered .psd file on you page. If you name the layers in Photoshop the same as the typical states found in the States panel—Normal, Rollover, Down, and Active— Muse automatically assigns the content on those named layers to the state with the same name in the States panel.

Note: When naming the layers in Photoshop to match a Muse state name like Normal, the names are not case-sensitive. For example, in Photoshop you could name a layer normal, Normal, NORMAL, or any combination of upper- and lowercase. Muse still would recognize it and assign it to the Normal state.

In this exercise, you will open Photoshop and explore a button that is set up using best practices for placement in Muse.

1 Open Adobe Photoshop.

2 Choose File > Open. In the Open dialog box, navigate to the images folder in the Lessons folder. Select the image named twitter_button.psd, and click Open.

Note: For this exercise, you need to have Photoshop installed on your machine. If you do not, you can skip to the next section, "Placing your Photoshop button."

3 Open the Layers panel (Window > Layers) and you'll see two layers named normal and rollover.

Remember, when you place a Photoshop button (.psd file) in Muse, you can select a single layer for each state that you want the button to have. For any states in Muse that you don't care to use, don't include a layer with the name of that state in the Photoshop file. Also, ensure that any layers you want to show in Muse have content on them.

Looking at the Layers panel in Photoshop, you will see that the layers in the Photoshop button file (.psd) are each Smart Objects and have a unique layer thumbnail (⊞). Smart Objects are layers that can contain image data from raster or vector images, such as Adobe Photoshop or Adobe Illustrator files.

Because the layers in a group in your .psd file will show up in the Photoshop Import Options but the groupings themselves are ignored, you're better off creating Smart Objects from your layers with multiple layers of content in each Smart Object layer.

4 Close Photoshop and return to Muse.

Placing your Photoshop button

With the Photoshop button created, you can now place it in Muse using the File > Place Photoshop Button command.

1 With the ABOUT page showing in Design mode, choose View > Fit Page In Window. If the ABOUT page is not open, in Plan mode, double-click the ABOUT page thumbnail to open it in Design mode.

Note: Placing a Photoshop button creates a link to the original .psd file and adds it to the list in the Assets panel. As with other assets listed in the panel, you can relink the button to another Photoshop file, embed the link, and more.

2 Choose File > Place Photoshop Button. Navigate to the images folder in the Lessons folder, and select the image named twitter-button.psd. Click Open (Windows) or Select (Mac OS).

In the Photoshop Import Options dialog box, Muse assigns layers in the Photoshop file to a state of the same name, if those layers are present. For each state of the button in Muse, you can choose a different layer in the Photoshop file. Notice that the Normal state has the layer named normal selected and the

Rollover state has the layer named rollover selected automatically. The Mouse Down and Active states have nothing selected because the Photoshop file contained no layers named mouse down or active.

▶ **Tip:** You don't have to name the Photoshop layers the same as the states. You can name them whatever you like and simply choose them from the menus in the Photoshop Import Options dialog box.

3 Click the Normal State menu, and you can see the Photoshop layers in the file listed as well as the Composite option.

◗ **Note:** Any layers in the Photoshop file that are empty will not show in the state menus in the Photoshop Import Options dialog box.

Selecting the Composite option for the Normal state would show all of the layer content visible in Photoshop when the file was last saved.

4 Click OK.

5 Click to place the button just below the e-mail link kevin@kevinskoffeeKart.com on the page.

6 Click the Rollover state in the States panel; notice that Muse is using the rollover layer from Photoshop as the rollover state. Muse also uses it as the Down state for this button, while the normal layer from Photoshop is used as the Active (Normal) state.

You can select each state and add different effects like a drop shadow or even rounded corners. When you publish or export the site, Muse will save the states as separate images.

▶ **Tip:** With the button frame selected, if you click the Fill link in the Control panel, you will see that the layers in the Photoshop file become background images in the states of the button. This is similar to how you created the button on the KART MAP page.

Edit the Photoshop button

Just as you can do with other assets listed in the Assets panel, you can edit a button's original file (in this case, edit the .psd file in Photoshop) and update it in Muse. With the button selected on the page, you can open the Assets panel (Window > Assets), right-click the name of the .psd file, and choose Edit Original in the context menu that appears. Edit the image in Photoshop, save it, and return to Muse to see the updates. This allows you to edit each of the layers in the Photoshop file.

If you delete a layer in Photoshop that is named after a state in Muse, the corresponding state will revert to the Normal state content. On the flip side, if you add a layer to the Photoshop button file that is named after a Muse state, when you save the Photoshop file and return to Muse, the new layer will become the contents for the corresponding state.

Adding a link to your Photoshop button

With the Photoshop button on the page, you need to add some sort of interactivity to it. In this case, you will add a link to the Twitter page for Kevin Koffee.

1   With the image frame still selected, insert the cursor in the Hyperlink field in the Control panel. Type **twitter.com/kevinkoffeekart/**. Press Enter or Return to accept it. Muse adds the "http://" automatically.

2   Click the Preview mode link to preview the button. Position the pointer over the text frame to see the rollover state change. Click to see twitter.com.

3   Click the Design mode link to return to the ABOUT page in Design mode.

4   Choose File > Save Site, then File > Close Page to close the ABOUT page and return to Plan mode with no pages open.

Review questions

1 Name and describe the three generic types of links.

2 Briefly describe what a link title can be used for.

3 What is an anchor used for?

4 How can you apply a link to text wihout changing the appearance of that text?

5 What is the benefit of placing a .psd using File > Place Photoshop Button?

Review answers

1 The three generic types of links that you can create in Muse are: internal, external, and e-mail. Internal links take the user to another part of the same document or to another page or document in the site. An external hyperlink is designed to take the user to another website, or web host. An e-mail link is intended to launch the visitor's default e-mail software and compose an e-mail.

2 A link title shows as a tooltip in some browsers when the cursor is over the text link on the page; it can be read aloud by screen readers, and it can give more information to search engines, among other things.

3 An anchor allows you to link to a part of a page. The anchor is invisible to site visitors, but it gives a link a place to scroll to.

4 If you select the text frame and not the text, then apply a link, the appearance of the text within the frame isn't changed.

5 Placing a layered Photoshop file using the Place Photoshop Button command opens the Photoshop Import Options dialog box. In this dialog box you can apply layers in the Photoshop file to states in the button.

8 APPLYING EFFECTS, GRAPHIC STYLES, AND INSERTING HTML

Lesson overview

In this lesson, you'll add more design creativity to your site with effects, opacity changes, embedded HTML, and more. Specifically, you'll learn to

- Round the corners of frames
- Apply such effects as drop shadows, glows, and bevels
- Make opacity (transparency) changes
- Save and apply graphic styles
- Embed and edit HTML from other sites

 This lesson takes approximately 30 minutes to complete. If you are starting from scratch in this lesson, use the method described in the "Jumpstart" section on page 5 of "Getting Started."

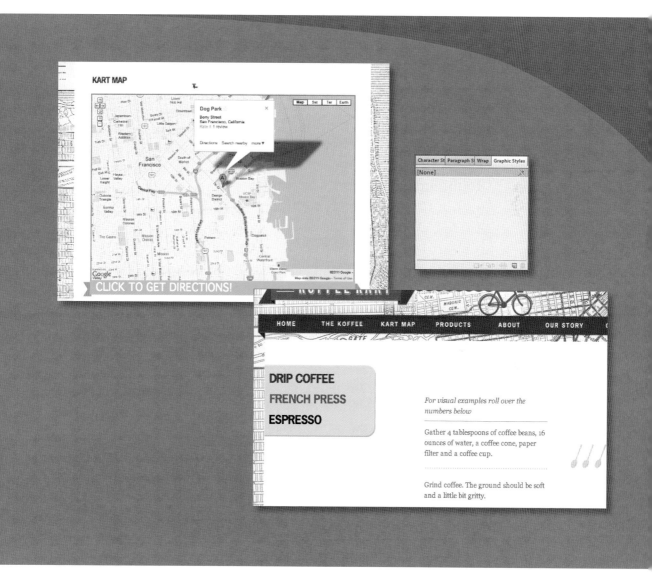

Muse has a lot of great options to add punch to your web designs, including drop shadows and other effects, rounded corners, embedding HTML like a Google map, saving object formatting as graphic styles, and much more.

Working with rounded corners, effects, and opacity

● **Note:** If you have not already done so, copy the Lessons folder onto your hard disk, from the *Adobe Muse Classroom in a Book* disc. See "Copying the Classroom in a Book files" on page 3.

In Muse, there are many formatting options that can help you to add some real design flair to the content on your pages, aid in readability, keep up with today's design trends, and more. Those formatting options include Effects, which encompass drop shadows, bevels, and glows, rounded corners, and opacity (transparency) changes. All of these options are easily applied to content from the Control panel. You'll experiment with all of these formatting options in the exercises that follow, starting with rounded corners.

● **Note:** The exercises in this lesson, like others in this book, require that you have the fonts supplied on the *Muse Classroom in a Book* disc installed on your machine. For more information on installing the necessary fonts, see "Fonts used in this book" on page 2.

Rounding the corners of a frame

You can round the corners on a text frame, image frame, or rectangle. In addition, you can round each corner individually or round all of a frame's corners at once. Either way, you can easily adjust your initial rounding settings, as you'll see in this section.

1 In Plan mode with the KevinsKoffeeKart site open, double-click the Preparation page thumbnail to open the page in Design mode.

2 With the Selection tool, click to select the aqua rectangle with the three links in it. Notice that the Selection Indicator in the Control panel shows Group. Click once more in the aqua color above the DRIP COFFEE text frame to select the aqua rectangle.

3 Press Control+= (Windows) or Command+= (Mac OS) several times to zoom into the rectangle.

4 Change the Corner Radius to **10** in the Control panel.

Changing the Corner Radius changes all four corners of the shape to a radius of 10 pixels. The larger the radius, the more rounded the corner will become.

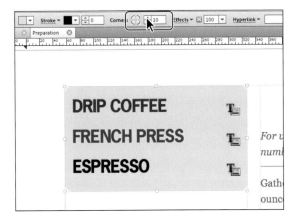

5 Click the Preview mode link to see the rounded corners. Click the Design mode link to return to the page.

6 Click the upper-left Enable/Disable button (⌐) in the Control panel (to the right of the Corners text link). Click the lower-left Enable/Disable button (⌐) in the Control panel as well.

You can turn on and off the corner radius for each corner of a selected frame to give you much more creative control.

7 Change the Corner Radius value to **20**.

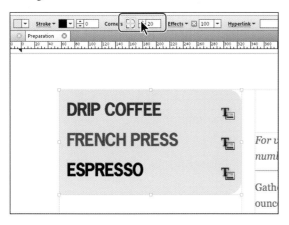

● **Note:** To remove the rounded corners, you could change the Rounded Corners value to 0 or click the Enable/Disable buttons until they all show a square corner.

8 Press the Escape key to select the group. With the Selection tool, drag the right-middle bounding point to the left until the width of the group is approximately 240px in the measurement label.

9 With the group selected, set the X value to **0** in the Control panel, if your screen resolution allows it, or open the Transform panel and set the X value to **0**.

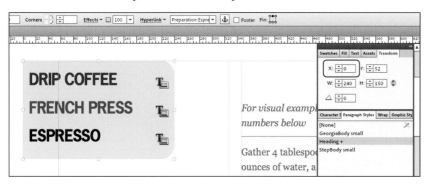

Setting the X value to 0 aligns the left edge of the group with the left edge of the page area.

10 Choose File > Save Site and leave the Preparation page open.

Applying a Shadow effect

The first type of effect that you will explore is the Shadow effect (sometimes referred to as drop shadows). Drop shadows on the Web can add depth to your design content, so that it takes on a more 3D appearance. You can add drop shadows to a text frame, image frame, or rectangle.

1 Click the Plan mode link, and double-click the HOME page thumbnail to open the home page in Design mode.

2 Click to select the DAILY DRIP image with the Selection tool, then press Control+= (Windows) or Command+= (Mac OS) several times to zoom into the image.

Note: You can apply a shadow to only rasterized text or to the frame that the text is in if it's filled with a color. You cannot apply shadows to frames filled with a background image nor to ordinary, non-rasterized text.

3 Click the Effects link in the Control panel to reveal the Effects options. Making sure that Shadow category is chosen at the top of the options, select On.

The effect options that appear contain three types of effects: Shadow, Bevel, and Glow as well as the specific options for each effect.

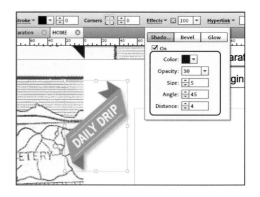

4 Click the Color in the Shadow options, and select the Footer Stroke color swatch to change the color of the drop shadow. Click back in the Shadow options menu to hide the Color Picker.

5 Change the rest of the shadow options to the following:

- Opacity: **30**

- Size: **5** (specifies the "thickness" of the shadow)

- Angle: **45** (moves the drop shadow around the rectangle; use the default)

- Distance: **4** (specifies the distance between the drop shadow and rectangle)

Note: Notice that the drop shadow follows the contour of the image, not the edges of the image frame. If you were to apply a color fill to the same image frame, the drop shadow would follow the contour of the color fill. If you were to apply a background image to the image frame, the drop shadow would follow the contours of the background image or image in the frame.

Try adjusting the settings to see the effect it has on the shadow. Be sure to return to the settings in step 5 when you are ready to continue. Click away from the Effects options to hide them.

6   Choose File > Save Site, then choose File > Close Page to return to the Preparation page.

Applying a Bevel effect

The Bevel effect adds a beveling to the edge of an object, such as an image or frame filled with color. You can apply the Bevel effect to give objects a more realistic, three-dimensional look.

1   On the Preparation page, with the group of objects still selected, click once more to select just the aqua rectangle.

2   Click the Effects link in the Control panel to reveal the Effects options. Click the Bevel category at the top of the options, select On, then change the Bevel options to

   • Opacity: **20**

   • Size: **0**

   • Angle: **60**

   • Distance: **3** (specifies the distance between the border of the rectangle and the faded edge of the bevel)

Try adjusting the settings to see the effect on the bevel, but be sure to return to the settings in step 2 when you are ready to continue. Click away from the Effects options to hide them.

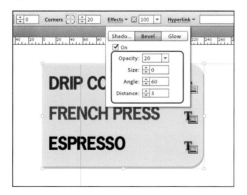

3   Click the Preview mode link to preview the bevel effect. Click the Design mode link to return to the Preparation page, then choose File > Close Page.

4   Choose File > Save Site.

Applying a Glow effect

The Glow effect causes a glow to emanate from under the object, but you can also apply a glow to the inside of an object. You can apply a glow to a rectangle, image frame, or rasterized text. In this exercise, you'll insert a new image into the footer and apply a Glow effect to it on the A-Master page.

1 In Plan mode, double-click the A-Master page thumbnail to open the master page in Design mode.

2 Choose View > Fit Page In Window.

3 Choose File > Place. In the Import dialog box, navigate to the images folder in the Lessons folder. Select the image named coffeecup.png and click Open (Windows) or Select (Mac OS).

4 Click to place the image at 100% on the right side of the page, above the footer. Zoom in a bit, and scroll the page so that you see the footer area. Drag the coffee cup image down to insert it into the footer area below the footer guide.

Like you've seen before, the footer guide will simply move down because the new image isn't a footer item by default.

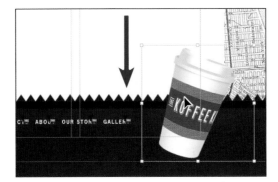

▶ **Tip:** You could also right-click (Windows) or Control-click (Mac OS) the coffee cup image and choose Footer Item from the context menu that appears, or you could choose Object > Footer Item.

5 With the image selected, select Footer in the Control panel to assign the coffee cup image to the footer. Drag the image to approximately match the position you see in the figure, making sure that the top edge of the coffee cup is below the footer guide.

6 Click the Effects link in the Control panel to reveal the effect options. Click the Glow category at the top of the options, then select On.

Notice the glow outside the edges of the image.

7 Select Inner Glow to apply the glow to the inside edges of the coffee cup image.

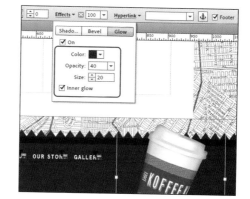

8 Click the Fill color, and select the FooterBG color swatch to change the color of the glow. Click back in the Glow options menu to hide the Color Picker.

9 Change the rest of the Glow options to

- Opacity: **40**

- Size: **20**

Try adjusting the settings to see the effect on the glow, but be sure to return to the settings in steps 7 to 9 when you are ready to continue. Click away from the Effects options to hide them.

Tip: You can apply multiple effects to a single object. For instance, you could also add a drop shadow to the coffee cup image to give it a more realistic, three-dimensional look.

10 Choose Rasterized Text Frame Indicators from the View Options menu above the Control panel. This disables the rasterized text frame indicators and lets you look at the footer without the indicators showing in the menu. Choose Rasterized Text Frame Indicators from the View Options menu to select and show them again.

Tip: The View Options menu to the right of the Tools panel is another way to turn on and off guides, grids, indicators, and other hidden elements.

11 With the coffee cup image still selected, choose Edit > Copy. Click the Plan mode link, and double-click the MasterFlash page thumbnail to open the page.

12 Choose Edit > Paste In Place, then File > Close Page.

The coffee cup image should paste in the same position on the page and be a footer item.

13 With the A-Master page showing in Design mode, click the Preview mode link to preview the glow effect (you may need to scroll down). Click the Design mode link to return to the A-Master page.

14 Choose Edit > Deselect All, if necessary.

15 Choose File > Save Site, leave the A-Master page open.

Adjusting opacity

Another great feature for adding design interest to your pages is the ability to change the opacity (transparency) of content. You can use opacity changes to aid in readability when placing text on an image, for instance.

In this exercise, you'll place text on an image and insert a rectangle frame between the image and the text for readability.

1 Click the Plan mode link, then double-click the PRODUCTS page thumbnail to open the page in Design mode. Choose View > Fit Page In Window.

2 Choose File > Place. In the Import dialog box, navigate to the images folder in the Lessons folder. Select the image named Origins.jpg, and click Open (Windows) or Select (Mac OS).

3 Click to place the upper-left corner of the image in the upper-left corner of the page area.

Red Smart Guides will appear on the left and top edges of the page area if the image is snapped to the page edge.

Note: If your screen resolution allows it, you may see the X, Y, W, H, and rotation options that you see in the Transform panel in the Control panel as well.

4 Open the Transform panel (Window > Transform). Hold down the Control (Windows) or Command (Mac OS) key and drag the bottom-middle bounding point of the image frame up until the Height setting in the Transform panel shows 150.

5   Select the Rectangle tool in the Toolbox, and draw a frame on top of the new image that stretches from the left edge of the page area to the right edge of the page area and has a height of approximately 70px. Don't worry about its exact vertical position right now, as you will change it later.

6   Change the Fill color of the frame to the red color swatch with the values R: **193**, G: **39**, B: **45**. Change Stroke Weight to **0** in the Control panel as well.

7   Change the Opacity setting to **60** in the Control panel.

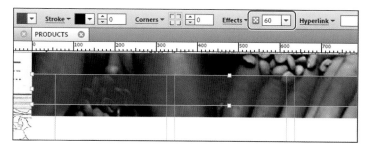

▶ **Tip:** To change the opacity, click Opacity in the Control panel and then adjust the drop-down slider or type the value directly in the Opacity field.

Opacity changes the transparency of the selected object. If the rectangle you drew had a background image, stroke, and so on, the opacity adjustment would apply to the frame and all of its contents.

8   Select the Text tool, and draw a text frame whose left edge aligns with the left edge of the first column guides, on top of the red-filled frame. Type **OUR PRODUCTS**. Don't worry about the vertical position of the text frame.

9   Select the text and change the Font to **News Gothic Std Medium** in the System Fonts section of the Fonts menu, the Font Size to **36**, and the text color to **White**.

Note: If you are on Windows, choose News Gothic Std for the font.

10 Select the Selection tool, and position the red rectangle and the text frame like you see in the figure.

11 Click the Preview mode link to preview the changes. Click the Design mode link to return to the PRODUCTS page.

12 Choose File > Save Site, then choose File > Close Page to close the page and return to the A-Master page in Design mode.

Working with graphic styles

Just as you use paragraph and character styles to quickly format text, you can use graphic styles to quickly format graphics and frames. Object styles include settings for stroke, fill color, effects, wrap, and more, but do not contain text formatting. If you work in Adobe InDesign, you're probably familiar with Object styles. Object styles in InDesign are very similar in basic functionality to Graphic styles in Muse.

In Muse, graphic styles are used for formatting submenus, image frames, and tooltips, as well as much more.

1 Click the Graphic Styles panel tab on the right side of the workspace.

Take a minute to familiarize yourself with the options in the Graphic Styles panel. As you progress through this exercise, you will learn about each of these options.

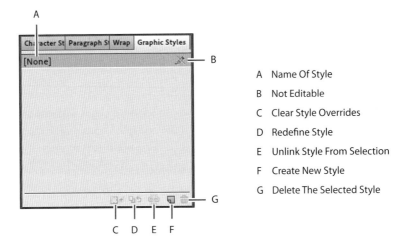

A   Name Of Style

B   Not Editable

C   Clear Style Overrides

D   Redefine Style

E   Unlink Style From Selection

F   Create New Style

G   Delete The Selected Style

Creating and applying a graphic style

In Lesson 3, "Working with Master Pages," when you inserted the menu widget, you styled the submenu for the PRODUCTS parent page. Later, you added several sub-pages to THE KOFFEE page. Unfortunately, the new submenu that was created had the default styling. To style the new submenu, you will create a graphic style.

1 On the A-Master page, choose View > Fit Page In Window, and then scroll to the top of the page so that you can see the menu.

2 With the Selection tool, click twice on the PRODUCTS menu item to show the submenu, if necessary. Click the Coffee submenu item twice to select it. The words "Menu Item" should appear in the Selection Indicator on the left end of the Control panel.

3 With the Graphic Styles panel showing, click the Create A New Style button (![icon]) at the bottom of the panel to create a new graphic style based on the submenu item formatting.

Note: The submenus you see may look different than those in the figure and that's okay—as long as the Normal state is selected in the States panel.

4 Double-click the new graphic style named Style. Change the Style Name to **Submenu**, and notice all of the formatting that was captured in the Style Setting area of the Style Options dialog box. Click OK.

Next, you will create a paragraph style to make sure that the text in both submenus has the same formatting (remember, graphic styles do not contain text formatting). Then you will apply the graphic style.

5 With the PRODUCTS submenu showing already and the Coffee submenu item selected, click on the Coffee menu item to select the text frame.

6 In the Paragraph Styles panel, click the Create A New Style button (![icon]) at the bottom of the panel. Double-click the new style named Paragraph Style, and change the name to Submenu in the Style Options dialog box. Click OK.

7 Click THE KOFFEE menu item until the submenu appears. Click the Preparation submenu item twice to select it. The words "Menu Item" will appear on the left end of the Control panel.

8 Click the Submenu graphic style in the Graphic Styles panel to apply the formatting to both submenu items.

Graphic styles cannot contain formatting like sizes of objects (width and height), text formatting, and more, so this submenu won't look exactly like the other submenu.

Note: Be careful not to click a graphic style in the Graphic Styles panel with nothing selected. The graphic style will actually apply to the page area. If you accidentally do this, you can select the graphic style named [None] to remove the formatting.

Finish the submenu formatting

Because graphic styles don't capture text formatting, sizes, and more, you will need to finish formatting the submenus using text styles and other options.

1 With the Preparation menu item still selected, change the Height in the Transform panel or Control panel to **30**. Select the Origins submenu item, and change its Height to **30** as well.

2 Click the Preparation submenu item twice to select the text frame. The words "Text Frame" appear in the Control panel.

3 Click the Submenu paragraph style in the Paragraph Styles panel to apply it to the text for both submenu items. This occurs because the Edit Together option is selected in the Menu options for the menu widget.

4 Press the Escape key to select the Preparation menu item.

5 In the States panel, select Rollover and click the Reset To Default button (🗑) at the bottom of the panel.

6 Change the text color in the Text panel to the orange color with the tooltip that shows R=251 B=176 G=59.

7   Select the Active (Normal) state in the States panel, and click the Reset To Default button to match the appearance of the Normal state.

8   Change the text color in the Text panel to the orange color with the tooltip that shows R=251 B=176 G=59.

9   Click the Origins submenu item to select it. The words "Menu Item" will appear in the Control panel.

10 Repeat steps 2 through 8 for the Origins submenu item and text. When you are finished applying the formatting to the Origins submenu item, make sure that Normal is selected in the States panel before you move on.

11 Click the Preview mode link, and position the pointer over the PRODUCTS and THE KOFFEE menu items to see the submenus. Click the Design link to return to the A-Master page in Design mode.

12 Choose File > Save Site.

Clearing overrides and editing a graphic style

In Muse, updating a graphic style is accomplished by *redefining* that style. To redefine a style, you edit the formatting for an object on the page that has that graphic style applied. Then you redefine the style based on the changes. This makes the graphic style match the new settings, and all other objects with that style applied automatically update to match.

1   On the A-Master page, choose Edit > Deselect All, if necessary.

2   With the Selection tool, click twice on the PRODUCTS menu item to show the submenu, if necessary. Click twice on the Coffee submenu item to select it.

3   Change the Fill color in the Control panel to Black.

4 In the Graphic Styles panel, notice that the Submenu style has a plus (+) to the right of the name. Position the pointer over the Submenu style name. In the tooltip that appears, below the dotted line, you will see the local formatting options (formatting that is applied to the selected content that is different from the graphic style).

Note: The styling options you see may be in a different order than in the figure and that's okay.

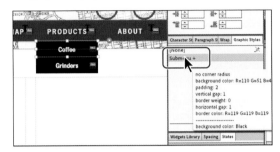

5 Click the Clear Style Overrides button ( ) at the bottom of the Graphic Styles panel to remove the fill color override.

Next you will redefine the graphic style formatting.

6 With the Coffee submenu item still selected, change the Fill color in the Control panel to Footer Stroke.

7 In the Graphic Styles panel, the Submenu style has a plus (+) to the right of the name again. This time you will redefine the style.

8 Click the Redefine Style button ( ) at the bottom of the panel.

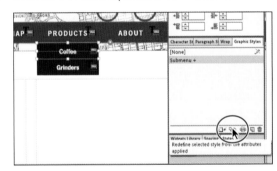

9 Click the Preview mode link, and position the pointer over the PRODUCTS and THE KOFFEE menu items to see the submenus. Click the Design link to return to the A-Master page in Design mode.

The last step is to copy this menu to the MasterFlash master page so that the menus are the same.

10 Choose Edit > Deselect All. Click to select the menu with the Selection tool, and choose Edit > Copy.

11 Click the Plan mode link, and double-click the MasterFlash thumbnail to open the page in Design mode.

12 With the Selection tool, click to select the menu in the header. Press Delete or Backspace to remove it.

13 Choose Edit > Paste In Place to paste the menu onto the MasterFlash page.

14 Choose File > Save Site and File > Close Page to close the MasterFlash master page. Choose File > Close Page to close the A-Master page as well and return to Plan mode.

Graphic style extras

Graphic styles have many of the same options that paragraph and character styles have, including deleting, duplicating, and unlinking. To access most of these options, in the Graphic Styles panel, you can right-click (Windows) or Control-click (Mac OS) a style name and make a selection in the context menu that appears.

Deleting a graphic style removes it from the list. If it is applied to content in your site, a dialog box will appear asking you to replace the graphic style with another.

Duplicating a graphic style makes an exact copy of the style.

Unlinking a graphic style from selected content is useful if you want to create a style similar to another style or apply a style, but don't want the formatting of that content to change when the graphic style updates. You can unlink selected content from a graphic style by clicking the Unlink Style From Selection button (⊛) at the bottom of the Graphic Styles panel or choosing it from the context menu as explained above.

Embedding HTML

In Muse, you can incorporate source code content generated by a number of different websites such as a map from Google, a YouTube video, Flickr content, or an Adobe FormsCentral form. You simply copy and paste the code from those sites and then embed that HTML into your pages. Embedding HTML into a Muse page is like putting a window inside a page on your site that displays the content of a third-party site.

Embedded HTML is a great way to add complex information (such as maps, contact forms, weather forecasts) as well as rich media (like videos, slideshows, and audio files) quickly and easily to your Muse site.

Although embedding HTML has limitless uses, in this section, you will focus on one: inserting a Google map. For ideas on inserting video from YouTube, adding a contact form, adding a bullet list, and more, see the sidebar at the end of this section titled "More embedding HTML examples."

Adding a Google map

To practice embedding HTML content into your pages, in this exercise you will insert a Google map that shows the location of Kevin's Koffee Kart.

1   In Plan mode, double-click the KART MAP page thumbnail to open the page in Design mode.

2   Choose View > Fit Page In Window.

3   Choose File > Preview Page In Browser. In the browser window that opens, type **maps.google.com** in the navigation bar to visit the page.

4   Type **Dog Park, Berry Street, San Francisco, CA** in the search field toward the top of the maps.google.com page. Click the Search Maps button.

5   Click the Link button (∞) on the left side of the maps.google.com page. In the options box that appears, click the text link "Customize and preview embedded map."

Your browser opens a new page where you can customize the size of the map before you copy the code to embed the map into Muse.

6   Toward the top of the new Google Maps page, select Custom under the Map Size options, then change Width to **850** and Height to **600**.

7 At the bottom of the page, select all of the code, and then copy it by pressing Control+C (Windows) or Command+C (Mac OS) or by choosing copy from the menu. Close the browser window with the map options, but leave the maps.google.com page open.

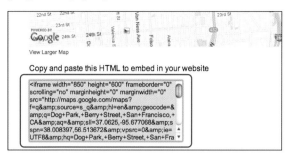

8 Return to Muse, and choose Object > Insert HTML. In the HTML Code dialog box, delete the sentence "Insert your HTML here." With the cursor in the dialog box right-click (Windows) or Control-click (Mac OS) in the HTML Code dialog box, then choose Paste from the context menu that appears. Click OK. A map appears.

Tip: You can also paste HTML code directly into the page. Muse detects HTML source tags and will automatically paste the code as HTML into the page.

9 With the Selection tool, drag the map from the upper-left corner to align with the left edge of the first column and a little down from the top margin guide. See the figure for placement help.

Notice that when you position the pointer over the map frame, that an icon (⬚) appears off the upper-left corner of the frame. This icon indicates that the content in the frame contains embedded HTML.

When you insert HTML into Muse, the live content will appear in Design mode in most cases, but it won't be interactive until you preview the page. Also, Muse places the HTML content into a frame that is the width of a single column. The width of the frame has no bearing on the HTML content.

10 Choose Object > Send To Back.

11 With the map frame selected, open the Transform panel and change the width to **850** and the height to **600**.

You don't have to do this, but you will apply a stroke to the frame and want it to show around the edges of the map.

> **Note:** You can apply certain formatting options like fill and stroke, as well as background images to the frame that the HTML is in, but other options like rounded corners will not work properly, and you cannot apply effects.

12 Change Stroke Weight to **3** and the stroke color to a medium gray in the Control panel.

13 With the Selection tool, drag the CLICK TO GET DIRECTIONS! button down to cover the bottom of the map, directly over the View Larger Map link to cover it up. You will remove that link later.

14 Select the Text tool, draw a frame at the top of the first column, and type **KART MAP**. Open the Paragraph Styles panel (Window > Paragraph Styles), and click the Heading style to apply it.

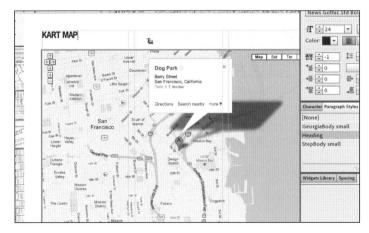

15 Click the Preview mode link to see the map, and try interacting with the map. Click the Design mode link to return to the KART MAP page.

More embedding HTML examples

Embedding HTML has the added benefit of enabling you to use a third-party's site as a hosting service and uploading interface. For example, if you create a free account with YouTube, you can create your own YouTube channel and upload the video content from your site. YouTube includes a web page that simplifies the upload process and hosts the video files on their site. When you want to update your site, simply add more videos to your YouTube channel, copy the embed code, and then paste it into a page to add new videos to your Muse site.

Adding YouTube video to pages in Muse is just one example of the many uses for embedding HTML code into your Muse pages. To learn how to insert some of the most widely used social media, video, and other features into your pages, check out the PDF named AppA_MuseCIB.pdf on the *Adobe Muse Classroom in a Book* disc.

In that PDF, you will explore other options for embedding HTML code, including

- Adding Google driving directions
- Inserting a Twitter feed
- Inserting a numbered or bulleted list
- Adding video from YouTube

Editing the embedded HTML

After you embed the HTML content, you can either delete the frame to delete the HTML content, or you can edit the HTML if you want to make changes or replace it.

1   With the Selection tool, right-click (Windows) or Control-click (Mac OS) the map frame. Choose HTML... from the context menu that appears.

In the HTML Code dialog box, you can edit the code directly, or you can return to maps.google.com and repeat the process for getting the code, changing the size of the map in the process.

2   In the beginning of the code, find the line `height="600"` and change it to `height="580"` instead. Also, to remove that link you covered up on the bottom of the map, find the `</iframe>` tag. Delete all of the code after that tag, starting with `<br/><small>`, to the end of the code. Click OK.

Tip: You can also right-click (Windows) or Control-click (Mac OS) in the HTML Code dialog box and choose commands like Select All or Paste from the context menu that appears.

After a few seconds, the map should update to show the new height. You may need to move the blue button up to cover the bottom of the map.

3 Return to the maps.google.com browser window, and click the Link button. In the link options that are still showing, click the text link below Short URL and copy the text.

For a last enhancement, you are getting a link from maps.google.com to apply to the blue button so visitors can go directly to maps.google.com if they like.

4 Return to Muse. With the Selection tool, select the blue CLICK TO GET DIRECTIONS! button. In the Hyperlinks field, select KART MAP and paste the link you copied from maps.google.com. Press Enter or Return.

5 Click the Preview mode link to see the map, and click the blue button to visit maps.google.com. Click the Design mode link to return to the KART MAP page.

6 Choose File > Save Site and close all open pages.

In Lesson 9, "Working with Widgets," you'll see how to add some really cool interactive features to your pages, such as lightboxes and slideshows, tabbed panel systems, and sliding panels.

Review questions

1 Name the three main effects that you can apply to content in your pages.

2 Where are the options for applying effects found?

3 What is a graphic style used for?

4 Briefly explain how to update a graphic style.

5 How can you embed HTML content in your pages?

Review answers

1 The three main effects that you can apply to content in Muse are shadows, bevels, and glows.

2 You can apply effects to selected content by clicking the Effects link in the Control panel, selecting the desired effects, and setting the options in the options box that appears.

3 Just as you use paragraph and character styles to quickly format text, you can use graphic styles to quickly format graphics and frames. Graphic styles include settings for stroke, fill color, effects, wrap, and more.

4 In Muse, updating a graphic style is accomplished by redefining that style. To redefine a style, you edit the formatting for the object on the page that has a graphic style applied. Then you redefine the style based on the changes. This makes the graphic style match the new settings, and all other objects with that style applied automatically update to match.

5 You can insert HTML source code generated by a third-party website by copying the source code from the original website, choosing Object > Insert HTML, pasting the code into the dialog box that appears, then clicking OK.

9 WORKING WITH WIDGETS

Lesson overview

In this lesson, you'll add widgets to your pages that allow visitors to show and hide content by clicking, using a range of animations like fading and sliding. Specifically, you'll learn how to

- Insert and edit a Lightbox Display composition widget

- Insert and edit a Blank slideshow widget

 This lesson takes approximately 30 minutes to complete. If you are starting from scratch in this lesson, use the method described in the "Jumpstart" section on page 5 of "Getting Started."

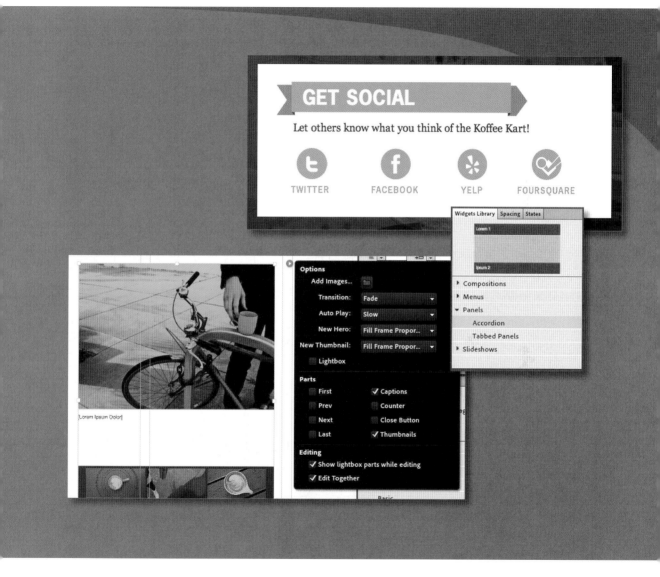

Muse provides an easy way to add powerful interactivity to your pages in the form of widgets. In this lesson, you'll explore various widget types, such as compositions and slideshows, and see how easily you can customize them.

About widgets

● **Note:** If you have not already done so, copy the Lessons folder onto your hard disk, from the *Adobe Muse Classroom in a Book* CD. See "Copying the Classroom in a Book files" on page 3.

On the Web these days, you see all sorts of cool, interactive content like slideshows that cycle through larger images, and much more. You may have even heard of jQuery or Adobe Spry, the behind-the-scenes technologies that power these advanced features. Muse provides much of the same interactive functionality in the form of widgets. *Widgets* are reusable building blocks of interactivity and behavior that are completely customizable and that you can simply drag onto your pages—all the power without the programming.

Muse groups widgets into four categories in the Widgets Library panel (Window > Widgets Library): Compositions, Menus, Panels, and Slideshows. Each provides an easy way of adding interactivity to your web pages.

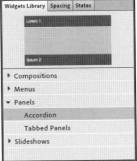

● **Note:** See Lesson 3, "Working with Master Pages," for more information on working with menus.

● **Note:** The exercises in this lesson, like others in this book, require that you have the fonts supplied on the *Adobe Muse Classroom in a Book* disc installed on your machine. For more information on installing the necessary fonts, see "Fonts used in this book" on page 2 of "Getting Started."

Although each category has specific controls, the overall procedure of adding a widget to your page is the same for all types:

1 Open the Widgets Library panel.

2 Drag the desired widget onto your page.

3 Edit the widget (change its options, format the widget, and style the appearance).

4 Add content to the widget.

To better match your design process, you can even change the order of steps 3 and 4.

More widget examples

In this lesson, you will insert two widgets. To learn about the other widgets in each category, check out the PDF named AppB_MuseCIB.pdf on the *Adobe Muse Classroom in a Book* disc.

Inserting a composition widget

The Widgets Library panel offers five composition widgets: Blank, Featured News, Lightbox Display, Presentation, and Tooltip. Each has the same options available, but has different options set, so that you can customize the widget's action. All five widgets, however, are comprised of at least one small container (the *trigger*) that displays content in a larger content area (the *target*) in response to visitor interaction.

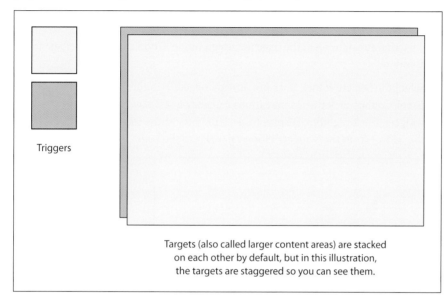

Triggers

Targets (also called larger content areas) are stacked
on each other by default, but in this illustration,
the targets are staggered so you can see them.

Note: The Tooltip Composition widget has the targets set to be staggered by default.

Composition widgets can have trigger content that is different from the target content, and they're not limited to displaying images. You could list a recipe that contains a trigger in the text. When the visitor clicks the trigger phrase "cube the potatoes," for example, an image with text and even a video could appear in the larger content area, providing hints on uniformly cubing potatoes.

In composition widgets, you can move the larger content areas independently of each other. You can stack them on one another, so only one at a time is seen as in an image slideshow (the default), or you can scatter them around the page so that you can see more than one at a time, like in a tooltip that displays content next to the cursor on a page.

In this section, you will insert and edit the Lightbox Display composition widget, which will give you a feel for working with a composition widget.

Inserting a Lightbox Display composition widget

A Lightbox Display widget dims the rest of the page while the content area element display is active. Like other composition widgets, it can show and hide text, images, and more. Using a Lightbox Display widget can be a great way to show other content without forcing the visitor to go to another page or to reload the same page.

In this section, you will insert a Lightbox Display widget to show social media links that visitors can click to see Kevin's Twitter content, Facebook page, and more.

● **Note:** If you are starting from scratch using the Jumpstart method described in the "Jumpstart" section on page 5 of "Getting Started," your workspace may look different than the figures you see in this lesson.

1   In Plan mode with the KevinsKoffeeKart site open, double-click the A-Master page thumbnail to open the page in Design mode. Choose View > Fit Page In Window.

2   Select the Selection tool, if it's not already selected. In the Widgets Library panel, double-click the Compositions category to display that category's widgets. Click Lightbox Display to see a preview at the top of the panel. Drag the widget from the Widgets Library panel into the page.

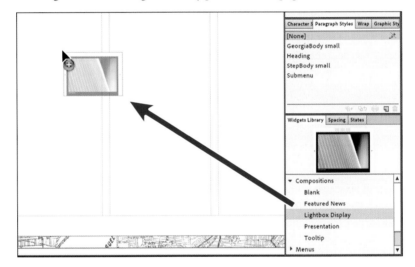

▶ **Tip:** You can also insert a composition widget by choosing Object > Insert Composition > [specific widget you need].

3 Drag the Lightbox Display widget down the page a bit until it overlaps the footer.

You may need to scroll down to see, but notice how the footer doesn't move down to accommodate the larger content area of the widget (the black rectangle with the image in it). The footer doesn't need to move because the content area is hidden when the page displays in the browser; it appears only when you click one of the small gray trigger rectangles.

4 Drag the lightbox up until it mostly fits in the page area and leave the widget selected. The word "Widget" appears in the Selection Indicator on the left end of the Control panel to tell you that the widget is selected.

> **Note:** The selected widget has eight points around the widget container, which in Muse usually means that you can resize something, but that's not the case for Composition or Slideshow widgets. Here, they have no function.

5 Click the Preview mode link to test the widget. Notice that the larger content area that contains the big images is hidden to start. Click one of the gray trigger rectangles to show the lightbox content area. Also, notice that when you position the pointer over each of the three triggers, they change to a darker gray color.

When the content area appears with the larger image and the rest of the page is dimmed, you can click the arrows left or right to show the previous or next images. Also notice the caption beneath each image, both images and captions are only placeholders at the moment. You can change or hide these later, like most everything in the widget.

6 Click the Design mode link to return to the A-Master page.

7 Choose File > Save Site.

Editing composition widget options

After inserting any widget, you can edit its options, which allow you to turn on and off widget features, as well as customize the widget's actions. All composition widgets offer the same group of options for you to edit, but each has them set slightly differently to suit the widget's specific purpose. These settings are simply a starting point, however. You can further customize a composition widget's function as well as its content and appearance to suit your needs.

Next, you will edit the options for the Lightbox Display widget.

Note: To learn more about each Composition widget option, check out the PDF named AppB_MuseCIB.pdf on the *Adobe Muse Classroom in a Book* disc.

1 Choose Edit > Deselect All, then click the widget to select it. You may need to zoom out for the next steps. Click the editing options icon (white arrow in the blue circle) and make the following changes in the widget Options menu that appears:

- Position: **Lightbox** (the default setting)

- Event: **On Click** (the default setting)

- Transition: **Fading** (the default setting)

- Speed: **Medium**

- Auto Play: **None** (the default setting)

- Triggers On Top: **Deselected** (the default setting)

- Hide All Initially: **Selected**

- Prev and Next: **Deselected** (this removes the arrows from the lightbox)

- Close Button: **Deselected** (the default setting)

- Show Lightbox Parts While Editing: **Selected** (the default setting)

- Show All in Design Mode: **Deselected** (the default setting)

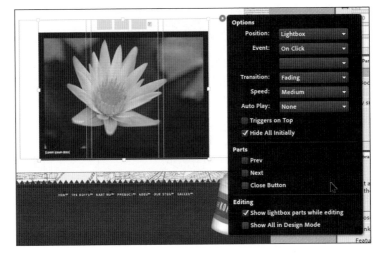

2 Press the Escape key to hide the widget Options menu, and choose File > Save Site.

▶ **Tip:** The Prev (previous) and Next buttons are each embedded images in their own container. If you chose to keep them showing in the options for the widget, you can add text, replace the image, or add another type of content to the container using design features in Muse.

Adding or deleting a trigger

When you drag a Lightbox Display widget onto your page, it includes three triggers (the small gray boxes) that when clicked, show one of three large target areas. Each gray trigger container can contain text, images, and more. The larger target areas are stacked on top of each other by default, so it looks like there's only one.

Next, you will add and remove triggers. When you add or remove a trigger, its associated target area is also added or removed (along with the content in it).

1   With the Selection tool, click the small, gray trigger rectangles, one at a time, to see each associated target area and its content.

    In Design mode, the widgets will work, but with limited functionality.

2   Click the plus (+) icon that appears to the right of the trigger elements to add another trigger and blank target area.

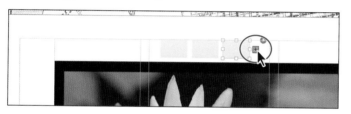

▶ **Tip:** You can also position the pointer over any of the triggers, right-click (Windows) or Control-click (Mac OS) on the trigger, and choose Insert Element to add another trigger and target.

3   Click the newly added trigger to select it (if it's not already selected), and press Delete or Backspace to remove the trigger and the associated content area.

4   Click twice on the third trigger from the left to select it. Position the pointer over the selected trigger, right-click (Windows) or Control-click (Mac OS), and choose Delete Element.

Two small triggers remain.

5 Using either of the previous methods, delete the trigger on the right, leaving one trigger and one target area.

Each trigger and target area can contain content and have formatting applied. In the following sections, you will edit the trigger and target areas. If you had more than one trigger and target area, you would repeat the steps for each, even creating graphic styles and text styles to make it easier to ensure consistent design formatting.

Editing a trigger

The triggers in a Composition widget can contain backgrounds, text, images, effects, and more. Each trigger is a container that can contain other content. In addition, triggers can show interaction by changing the appearance of the different states in the States panel.

You are going to insert a Photoshop button into the trigger so that it will change appearance when the visitor interacts with it.

1 Choose File > Place Photoshop Button. Navigate to the images folder in the Lessons folder and select the image file named btn_share.psd. Click Open (Windows) or Select (Mac OS). Click OK in the Photoshop Import Options (btn_share.psd) dialog box.

2 Position the Place Gun over the small, gray trigger at the top of the widget and the edges will show a blue highlight. Click to insert the button into the trigger rectangle.

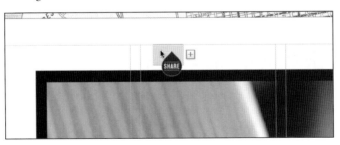

As you remember from placing a Photoshop button during Lesson 7, layers in the Photoshop file become states in the button in Muse if they are present and named properly in the .psd. Notice also that the trigger container grows to fit the button. The trigger container will grow to fit any content changes you make going forward. You can add text, images, and more to the trigger container, for instance, by either dragging that content into the trigger container or drawing a text frame in the container.

3   With the Selection tool, click three times on the Share button image to select it.

    With the image selected, you will see Rectangle in the Selection Indicator on the left end of the Control panel.

4   Press the Right Arrow key several times to move the image in the trigger container until it's roughly in the center horizontally.

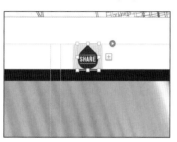

The trigger container (gray box) is the link area that the visitor will click.

Note: You could also select the trigger container (not the image) and resize it to match the content inside (in this case the Photoshop button).

5   Press the Escape key to select the trigger container, not the button image. Open the States panel (Window > States).

    Each state in a trigger has a background color and no stroke. You can select each state, like you've done before, and edit the appearance of the trigger. With each trigger, you could simply add a text frame and leave it at that, insert a background image that changes with each state, and more.

6   With the Normal state selected in the States panel, click the Fill color in the Control panel and choose [None] from the Color Picker.

7   Click the Rollover state, and click the Reset To Default button (🗑) at the bottom of the States panel.

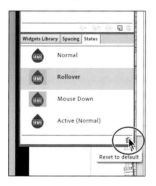

8 Zoom out by choosing View > Zoom Out several times, if necessary, so that you can see the entire header area.

9 With the Selection tool, drag the trigger up into the right end of the header, above the page area. See the figure for placement help.

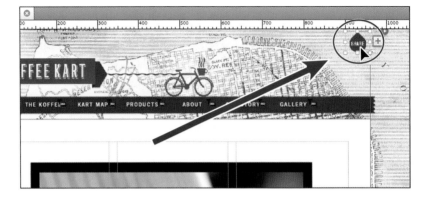

10 Click the Preview mode link to test the widget. Click the Design mode link to return to the page.

11 Choose File > Save Site and leave the page open.

Adding content to a target area

Now that the trigger is complete, you can focus on the larger content area for that trigger. The content area is where the main content appears. You can add text, images, or any other type of content using Muse's design features by drawing frames or rectangles within the bounds of the content area or dragging content into area.

● **Note:** When you click away from content in the page area, you deselect that content but wind up selecting the page. Be careful when making changes at that point, because it would affect the page.

1 Click away from the widget on the page to deselect it. Click twice on the larger content area to select it.

The word "Container" appears in the Selection Indicator on the left end of the Control panel. The black rectangle is selected behind the default image. That rectangle covers or dims the web page and displays the target content (the image and text) in a spotlight (also called a lightbox) drawing the user's focus to the displayed content. When you edited the widget options, if you had selected an option other than Lightbox for Position, the black rectangle wouldn't show.

2 Click the Fill link in the Control panel, and change Opacity to **30**. Press Return and then press the Escape key to hide the Fill options.

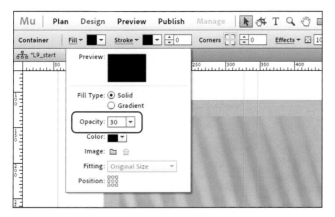

▶ **Tip:** You could change the fill of the container to include a different color, a gradient, or even a background image. Just make sure that the background isn't too busy and that the lightbox content is readable.

3 Click the Preview mode link, click the Share image in the trigger to test the widget, and notice that the rectangle behind the target content is more transparent. Click the Design mode link to return to the page.

4 Click the larger content area once more to select the container within.

This selects another container that by default contains an image and a text frame.

5 Click once more on the text frame that contains [Lorum Ipsum…], and press Delete or Backspace to delete it.

6 Click four times on the large image until Image Frame shows in the Selection Indicator on the left end of the Control panel, and press Delete or Backspace to delete the image as well.

This removes the container that the image and text were in. You can create, paste, place, or drag other content into that area, however, and Muse will create a new content container for the trigger.

7 Choose File > Open Site. In the Lesson09 folder in the Lessons folder, select the Muse file named Lightbox.muse. Click Open (Windows) or Select (Mac OS). In Plan mode, double-click the Home page thumbnail to open the page in Design mode.

8 Choose Edit > Select All, then Edit > Copy.

9 Close the Lightbox.muse site by choosing File > Close Site.

10 Back in the A-Master page, choose Edit > Paste. With the Selection tool, drag the group into the larger content area. When the container shows a blue highlight around the edge, release. Position the group like you see in the figure.

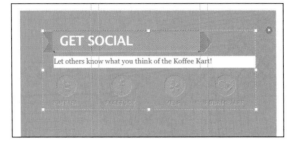

At this point, you could click again on the group you pasted to edit content within that group if necessary. You could also create more content in the larger content area or drag other content in as well.

11 Press the Escape key once to select the container that holds the group.

12 Click the Fill Color in the Control panel, and change the fill color of the container to white in the Color Picker. Press the Escape key to hide the Color Picker.

13 With the Selection tool, drag the bottom, middle point of the container up to a height of approximately 265px.

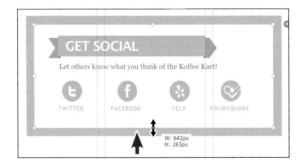

14 Choose View > Fit Page In Window. Drag the container so that it is approximately centered horizontally and vertically in the page area. You can tell when it is centered horizontally because a vertical red Smart Guide appears in the middle. You can tell when it's centered vertically in the page area when the gap measurements show the same values on top and bottom.

Note: Your gap measurements may not be the same as in the figure and that's okay.

15 With the container selected, click the editing options icon (white arrow in the blue circle). When the Widget Options menu appears, deselect Show Lightbox Parts While Editing. Because this widget is on a master page, you need to hide the larger content area so that it doesn't show on each page with the master applied in Design mode. Press the Escape key to hide the widget Options menu.

16 Click the Preview mode link to test the widget by clicking the SHARE button. Click the Design mode link to return to the page.

17 Click the SHARE button in the header to select the widget. Choose Edit > Copy. Click the Plan mode link, and double-click the MasterFlash thumbnail to open the master page in Design mode. Choose Edit > Paste In Place to paste the entire widget onto the MasterFlash page.

18 Close all open pages and return to Plan mode. Choose File > Save Site.

Working with slideshows

Slideshow widgets are a great way to add robust image slideshows to your pages and are what you typically see on the Web these days.

Muse offers four slideshow widgets: Basic, Blank, Lightbox, and Thumbnails. Each has different options set to create a specialized configuration, but all have the same options available. You can explore each slideshow configuration to discover which works best for your project.

Slideshow widgets are different from composition widgets because they can contain only images and they have a caption, first and last buttons, as well as thumbnails that can be shown or hidden for each larger image. The larger content areas must be stacked, showing one at a time (unlike composition widgets).

In this section, you will insert a Blank slideshow widget.

Adding a Thumbnails slideshow widget

In the next section, you'll insert a Blank Slideshow widget, which represents one type of simple slideshow. To learn how to insert and edit a Thumbnails slideshow widget, check out the section "Adding a Thumbnails slideshow widget" in the PDF named AppB_MuseCIB.pdf on the *Adobe Muse Classroom in a Book* disc.

Adding a Blank slideshow widget

A Blank slideshow widget is one of the simplest slideshows and contains only one larger content area (target area) without any triggers showing. By default, there is a previous and next arrow that allows the visitor to cycle between the images.

1 In Plan mode, double-click the HOME page thumbnail to open that page in Design mode. Choose View > Fit Page In Window.

▶ **Tip:** You can also insert a Slideshow widget by choosing Object > Insert Slideshow > [specific widget you need].

2 In the Widgets Library panel, double-click the Slideshows category to show the slideshow widgets. Drag the Blank slideshow widget into the middle of the page. Leave the widget selected; you'll reposition it later in the lesson.

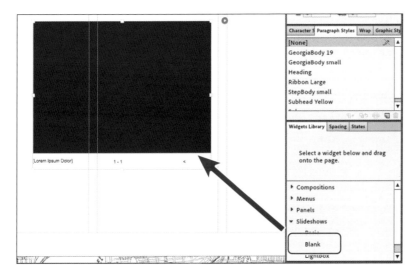

3 Choose File > Save Site.

Edit slideshow widget options

After inserting any widget, you can edit the widget options specific to the slideshow widgets. Next, you will edit the options for the Blank slideshow widget.

1 With the widget still selected, click the editing options icon (white arrow in the blue circle). In the widget Options menu that appears, set New Hero to Fill Frame Proportionally.

The Hero is the image in the larger content area.

By setting this first, images you add to the slideshow will fill the larger content area, ensuring that there are no gaps and that a portion of the image is cropped. If the image frame is resized later, the image will always fill the frame proportionally.

2 Still in the widget Options menu, click the Add Images folder icon. Open the Lessons > images > _widgets folder. Click the image named KoffeeKart_HP_Hero_01.jpg, press and hold down the Shift key, and click the image named

KoffeeKart_HP_Hero_04.jpg, to select four images. Click Open (Windows) or Select (Mac OS). The images are loaded into the slideshow and you see only one on the page.

3 Continuing in the widget Options menu, ensure the following options are set accordingly:

- Transition: **Fade** (the default setting)
- Auto Play: **Slow**
- New Hero: **Fill Frame Proportionally** (you set this previously)
- New Thumbnail: **Fill Frame Proportionally** (the default setting)

  There are no thumbnails showing in the Blank Slideshow widget by default, so this won't have any bearing right now.

- Lightbox: **Deselected** (the default setting)

  Selecting the Lightbox option would hide the larger content areas initially, as with the composition Lightbox widget.

- Prev, Next, and Counter: **Deselected**
- Captions: **Selected** (the default setting)
- **Thumbnails: Selected**

  You will hide the thumbnails later, but will use them to show each image and change its caption.

- Editing options: **Both selected** (the default setting)

This will hide all of the slideshow parts except for the larger content areas and the captions.

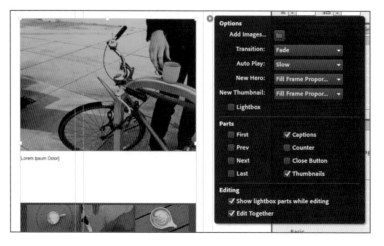

4 Press the Escape key to hide the widget options.

Editing the appearance of the Blank slideshow widget

Slideshow widgets can have all sorts of formatting options applied to the triggers and the larger content areas (targets), just like the other widgets. In this section, you will resize the larger images, then edit and style the captions.

1 With the Selection tool, drag the entire widget into the upper-left corner of the page area until it snaps. Choose Object > Send To Back to arrange it behind the content already on the page.

Note: Currently, in Muse content associated with the footer is always behind content in the page area.

2 Click once more on the large image (the content area) to select the image frame. With the Selection tool, drag the lower-right bounding point down and to the right until it snaps into the lower-right corner of the page area. You may need to zoom out.

The image now covers the page area and the measurement label shows 100%. Each image will fill the image frame automatically, without distorting. When the images were created in a program like Photoshop, they were sized to match the page area (960 pixels wide by 640 pixels in height).

Note: You can change the formatting of the image frame, including background fill, stroke, rounded corners, effects, and more.

▶ **Tip:** You can also change the dimensions of the image frame using the Transform panel, or if your screen resolution allows it, the Width and Height options in the Control panel.

3 With the Selection tool, click to select the caption. Drag it so that it snaps into the upper-left corner of the first column. Click and drag the right-middle bounding point to snap to the right edge of the second column.

4 Click the green image thumbnail to show the larger image and caption.

5 Click to select the caption text frame. In the Text panel, change the font to the web safe font Lucida Sans, the font size to **34**, and the color to white.

6 Select the Text tool, and change the text to **Get FREE pastry on Tuesday with coffee purchase**.

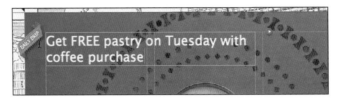

7 Click the second blue thumbnail to show the larger content area caption. Change the caption to **Start each day with great coffee**.

8 Click the third yellow/orange thumbnail to show the larger content area caption. Change the caption to **Coffee is Art**.

9 Click the fourth blue thumbnail (with the bike) to show the larger content area caption. Change the caption to **Kevin's commute**.

▶ **Tip:** If you want to edit the larger images or the captions, you need to show either the Prev and Next arrows or the thumbnails, use them to cycle through the images, then hide them again.

10 With the caption still selected, click the editing options icon (white arrow in the blue circle) and deselect Thumbnails to hide them.

11 Click the Preview mode link to test the widget. Click the Design mode link to return to the page.

12 Choose File > Save Site, then File > Close Page.

Congratulations! You've finished your site and are now ready to publish the site content. Of course, you can always go back and practice adding and modifying content. In the next lesson, you will learn about publishing content to Adobe Business Catalyst and exporting site content to HTML.

Review questions

1 What are Muse widgets?

2 What are the four types of widgets available in Muse?

3 Describe what a trigger and target are in a Muse widget.

4 What is a Lightbox?

5 Name the major difference between composition and slideshow widgets.

Review answers

1 Widgets are reusable building blocks of interactivity and behavior that allow visitors to click or hover (or auto-run) to show and hide content. They are completely customizable. Widgets provide an easy way of adding interactivity to your web page.

2 The four types of widgets available in Muse are: composition, menu, panel, and slideshow. Each of these categories offers multiple widgets, each customized for a specific purpose.

3 Widgets are comprised of at least one small container (the trigger) that displays content in a larger container (the target) in response to user interaction. Triggers can be hidden in certain widgets to have an auto-play widget.

4 A widget with Lightbox selected in the widget options dims the rest of the page while the element being displayed is active.

5 Slideshow widgets are different from composition widgets because they can contain only images, and they have a caption and first and last buttons, as well as thumbnails that can be shown or hidden for each larger image. The larger content areas must be stacked, showing one at a time (unlike composition widgets).

10 PUBLISHING AND EXPORTING YOUR SITE

Lesson overview

In this lesson, you'll learn how to

- Exclude pages from export

- Publish your site to Adobe Business Catalyst

- Publish changes

- Convert your temporary site to a paid site

- Export your site as HTML

 This lesson takes approximately 30 minutes to complete. If you are starting from scratch in this lesson, use the method described in the "Jumpstart" section on page 5 of "Getting Started."

Muse offers two methods for publishing site content: Either publish directly from Muse to an Adobe Business Catalyst account, or use the File > Export As HTML command to create a local copy of all the files for your website, which you can then FTP up to the hosting provider of your choice.

Understanding Muse publishing

Note: If you have not already done so, copy the Lessons folder onto your hard disk, from the *Adobe Muse Classroom in a Book* CD. See "Copying the Classroom in a Book files" on page 3.

After you've finished designing your site, the next step is to publish the site or export it as HTML using the File > Export As HTML command. If you want to publish the site for the world to see, you can publish directly to Business Catalyst hosting from within Muse. If you plan on using your own hosting provider or want to hand the site content off to someone else, you can export the site as HTML.

Using either method will generate HTML files, CSS, scripting, images, and other content necessary to make the site work in a browser. All of the .psd files in your Muse site will also be converted, at this point, to the best web format, depending on the image content.

Excluding pages from export

Note: The exercises in this lesson, like others in this book, require that you have the fonts supplied on the *Adobe Muse Classroom in a Book* disc installed on your machine. For more information on installing the necessary fonts, see "Fonts used in this book" on page 2.

When you publish your site or export as HTML, Muse exports all of the pages in your site map, even those that you've excluded from the navigation (such as the example project's GALLERYb). If you are experimenting with a design, have a page containing an old product, or have an outdated sale page, you may not wish to export that page. To hold back pages that aren't necessary, you can exclude them from export, specifying them either from Plan or Design mode. If you stop a page from exporting, none of the assets unique to that page export either. Assets, such as images, common to the excluded page and necessary pages do export.

Although clearing your site map of extraneous pages as you work is the best practice, excluding pages at the end of the process is simple.

Note: If you are using the Jumpstart file (L10_start_mac.muse or L10_start_win.muse), you will see that the Appendix B exercises were fully explored and match the examples in Appendix B (AppB_MuseCIB.pdf).

1   With the KevinsKoffeeKart site open and in Plan mode, right-click (Windows) or Control-click (Mac OS) the GALLERYb page thumbnail and choose Export Page to deselect the option.

Note: You need to be careful when choosing which pages not to export. Suppose you choose to not export the KART MAP page that appears in the menu. The text "KART MAP" will still appear in the menu when the site is exported, but the page will not be present, so the link will not work.

When a check mark appears to the left of the Export Page command, then the page will export when you either publish or use the File > Export As HTML command.

Note: The thumbnails you see in the figure may not match what you see, and that's okay.

2   Choose File > Save Site.

Publishing your site

Using Muse, you can create and publish an unlimited number of temporary sites. This is very convenient because you can upload in-progress sites to share with your clients. As you work with your client through the design and approval process, you can choose either to update the existing temporary site or to publish new temporary sites to compare several iterations. Some clients prefer to visit links to preview several different designs at once, so they can view them side by side during the approval process.

Each temporary site you create is active for 30 days. However, if a temporary site you are designing expires, you can extend it by simply opening the .muse file and publishing the site again. Using this strategy, you can keep working on a site and incorporating client feedback until the site design is deemed complete. Then you can upgrade and launch it.

After designing a site (even if it is not completely ready for primetime), you can publish it as a temporary site. Some web designers prefer to review the live sites in a browser this way, before showing their clients. All temporary sites are created using the site name of your choosing, followed by the Business Catalyst domain name. A temporary site's URL will look something like http://my_site.businesscatalyst.com.

The publishing process itself is very easy and intuitive.

1   Click the Publish link in the upper-left corner of the Application window or choose File > Publish.

Note: If you previously created a Business Catalyst account and used the same login e-mail to create your Adobe ID, the system will detect that the e-mail address you entered matches a record in the Business Catalyst database. When you log in via Publish or Manage from Muse for the first time using your Business Catalyst account information, you'll see a dialog box that appears only once and that merges your Business Catalyst account with your Muse account when you enter your password.

Note: The site's URL field in the Options section automatically removes any special characters and spaces that you enter in the Site Name field. It creates a suggested URL that will be used to access the live temporary site. You can edit the contents of the URL field to change the automatically generated URL, if desired.

2   In Publish dialog box, enter a site name. When you publish this site as a temporary site for testing, this name will be a part of the initial URL. So, if you typed "KevinsKart" for instance, the URL for the temporary site would be kevinskart.businesscatalyst.com. Leave the Publish dialog box open.

The Starting Address is used only when you are testing your site. This will be the temporary address at which you can view the site in a browser or send to your clients for reviewing the site. You can change the address to something permanent later if you upgrade the site to a paid site. Business Catalyst checks the starting address to determine if it's valid (it works) and if it's available. If the name is not available, the field will update with an alternate suggestion. You do not have to use that suggestion, if you prefer to change the site name to another name that is not yet taken. Remember, this is just a URL for testing purposes.

Note: If your client lives in a different country, you can choose the Data Center closest to your client's location. The site will load and perform best in the location that corresponds with the Data Center you select. So if your client is viewing the site in Australia, you can choose the Australia Data Center option to ensure that the site looks best to them, even if you are located in the United States.

3   Click the Options to reveal more options. Leave New Site selected in the Publish To menu, notice the URL that your testing site will have, and leave the Data Center at the default Automatic (this is where you want the site hosted). Click OK, and the temporary site will be created on the Business Catalyst servers.

Muse now generates the site files (HTML files, CSS, scripting, images, and other content that is necessary to make the site work in a browser) and uploads them to the server. Muse also converts the .psd files in your site to the best web format, depending on the image content. This may take a little while.

When Muse completes its work, and the temporary site is published, the site will open in the default browser on your machine.

4 Close the browser and return to Muse, if necessary. The New Site Created dialog box appears. Click OK to close it.

Now that the site has been published, you can share the domain name (kevinskart.businesscatalyst.com) with your clients for review by simply e-mailing them the domain name.

Note: If you are working on a shared workstation with another person, you can change the publish account associated with Muse. Choose Adobe Muse > Preferences (Mac OS) or Edit > Preferences (Windows), and select Switch Accounts from the Publish With Account Menu. This will allow you to enter the username and password for an existing Business Catalyst account. Using this strategy, you can each use your own individual preferences. Whenever you sign in to Muse on the computer, your preferences will be preserved.

Making and uploading edits

After you upload your testing site, you can make changes to your site in Muse, and then upload any changes you make to the Business Catalyst host. In this section, you will explore some of the publishing options available, then you will make a change to a page in your site and publish the changed page and content.

The first option for publishing that you will explore is how to retrieve the domain name for your site if you've forgotten it.

Note: To view a site domain name in the browser using this method, you will need to have published the site, which you did in the previous section.

1   Click the Publish link in the upper-left corner of the Application window. The Publish dialog box opens and lists the name of the site. Click the name to open the default browser and view the site.

2   Close the browser, and return to Muse. Click Cancel in the Publish dialog box to close it.

    This is an easy way to help you to remember the site domain name.

3   In Plan mode, double-click the ABOUT page thumbnail to open that page in Design mode. Choose View > Fit Page In Window.

    You're going to make a change to a page, then publish that changed content.

4   Select the Text tool, select the entire quote that begins with "We absolutely love the coffee," and change the text color to the FooterBG color swatch in the Control panel. Click away to close the Color Picker.

5   Choose File > Save Site.

Tip: You could also choose File > Publish.

6   Click the Publish link in the upper-left corner of the Application window.

7   In the Publish dialog box, click Options. Click the Publish To menu and you will see that you can publish the site to a new site, maybe to try something new without affecting the original testing site, or you could associate the files with another site by selecting another site in the menu. Any other Muse sites that you have previously published are listed in the Publish To menu. You can overwrite

them with the current file, but choose carefully! If you make a mistake, you'll have to open the other site's .muse file and publish it again.

8 Click the Upload menu to see that you can choose to upload all of the files or only those that have been modified. Leave the options at their defaults, and click OK to publish just the modified files. The updated site will be opened in the default browser.

9 Click the ABOUT page menu item in the top navigation to view the ABOUT page, and notice that the text color of the quote in the middle of the ABOUT page has updated to use the FooterBG color. Close the browser, and return to Muse.

Muse, by default, publishes only the content in your site that has been changed. In this case, it publishes the ABOUT page and any other files necessary, such as CSS and scripts. If you add a new image or other asset, that new asset is converted to a web format, if necessary, and uploaded as well as the page, replacing just those files on the server. If you select All Files in the Upload menu, Muse publishes all of the site content and replaces the files on the server.

10 Close the ABOUT page to return to Plan mode.

Upgrading a temporary Business Catalyst site

When you finish testing a site, you can upgrade it to a paid hosting plan. Your account can have multiple sites associated with it, some testing and some paid, depending on what point in the design and testing process they are in.

Note: The following steps will, at one point, require you to make a purchase. Do it when you are ready to upgrade your own site to a paid hosting account. Or, do so when your client is ready for you to publish their site for them, and they have provided you with their credit card information so that you can upgrade the site using their payment information.

Once you upgrade a site, you'll begin paying monthly hosting fees for that one site—and you are free to continue updating the site's content as needed. Upgrading the site gives you many benefits: You can use your own domain name rather than the supplied testing domain name (like kevinkoffeekart.businesscatalyst.com), you can add more admin users, and the site will not expire.

Before embarking on the site upgrade process, review the workflow below to get a better understanding of the steps required:

* Publish a temporary site from Muse (you did that in the previous section).

* Purchase a domain name from a third-party domain name registrar (examples: GoDaddy.com, NetworkSolutions.com, 1and1.com). For the purposes of this book, kevinskart.com was purchased.

With your account set up and domain name purchased, you're ready to convert a trial site to a paid hosting site.

1 Ensure that the site you want to upgrade is open within Muse.

2 Click the Manage link in the upper-left corner of the Application window.

In your default browser, the Business Catalyst Admin Console will open. The first step is to upgrade your site. The Admin Console content that first loads in the browser when you click Manage in Muse is called the Dashboard.

3 Click the Push Site Live button in the main area of the Business Catalyst Admin page.

At this point, another Business Catalyst web page is opened, offering hosting plans ranging from starter to pro plans. You must purchase one of the plans to continue the process. At the time of this writing, you can even choose to bill your client directly, instead of paying yourself then billing the amount back to the client. If you have a Creative Cloud membership, see the sidebar below.

Adobe Creative Cloud membership

Adobe Creative Cloud membership includes hosting for five websites (at the "webBasics" membership level). If you have a membership and have pushed less than the maximum number of sites live, you can simply click the Push Site Live button.

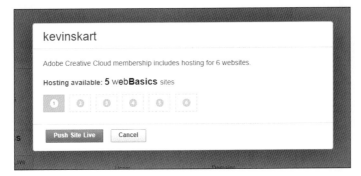

4 After successfully upgrading your site, close the browser and return to Muse.

5 In Muse, with the site open, click Manage to open the Business Catalyst Admin page again in the default browser. Notice that with the Dashboard showing, the Push Site Live button is gone because the site is now paid, and under the Status header, the status has changed from Temporary to Live.

Next, you'll associate the domain name you purchased with the site to change its URL.

6 From the Admin dashboard on the Business Catalyst site, click Add a Domain from the Domains section of the Dashboard.

7 Click the New Domain button in the Site Domains section.

You will now enter the domain name that you purchased.

8 In the Add A New Domain window, enter the Domain name you purchased, choose Home Page from the Start Page menu, select a country if necessary, select a culture from the Culture menu, and click Save, leaving all other default settings in the Add a New Domain dialog box.

9 After successfully associating a domain with your site, you will see the Site Domains section again in the Admin area with a success message in the upper-right corner.

You will now need to go to the website of the registrar that you used when you registered your domain name to point your domain name to the Business Catalyst host servers. For more information on entering the DNS information, contact the registrar where you purchased your domain name.

The following DNS information can be used:

• NS1.WORLDSECURESYSTEMS.COM

• NS2.WORLDSECURESYSTEMS.COM

• NS3.WORLDSECURESYSTEMS.COM

You can add multiple domain names to your site in the Business Catalyst Admin dashboard. For instance, you could specify kevinkart.com and kevinskart.com both to point to the same site. Of course, you must own both domains and have access to the registrar admin to change the DNS information like you saw earlier.

After you've upgraded the site, associated a domain name, and updated the DNS settings of the domain, users will be able to access the site after a maximum of 7 days. Sites can usually be seen within 24 to 48 hours.

Exporting your site as HTML

If you plan on using your own hosting provider, or want to export a folder of conveniently sliced and optimized image files to use for other web purposes (newsletters, social media site updates, e-mail signatures, mobile apps), you can export the site as HTML. When you export, Muse generates the HTML, CSS, JavaScript, and image files necessary to run the site.

1   With the KevinsKoffeeKart site open, choose File > Export As HTML. In the Export to HTML dialog box, click the Location folder icon. In the Select Local Folder To Export dialog box that opens, create a new folder on your Desktop and then click Create. With the folder selected, click Open (Windows) or Select (Mac OS). In the Export To HTML dialog box, click OK.

2   After Muse exports the site, click View Site if you'd like to see the site in a browser or click OK to close the dialog box.

When you export HTML from Muse, the files that Muse generates cannot be read back in. In other words, if you make any changes to the site in Muse, you will need to re-export the HTML.

3   Go to the folder into which you exported the site content to see what Muse created.

Congratulations! You've finished the site, gotten a good grounding in the workings of Muse, and published your site for the world to see.

Review questions

1 What are the two methods for sending your site live in Muse?

2 What purpose does excluding pages from export serve?

3 Name an advantage for upgrading your temporary site to a paid site.

4 Name a reason why you might export as HTML.

Review answers

1 You can either publish the site content to the Business Catalyst host servers, or you can use the File > Export As HTML command to generate the site files in a folder.

2 Excluding pages from export in Muse will not publish or export the designated pages or the content that is unique to excluded pages (image files, etc.). This is useful for pages for design tests or pages that contain a product you are no longer selling, for instance.

3 Upgrading your trial Muse site to a paid site has many benefits, including that a paid site doesn't expire, you can use your own domain name, and you can add other admin users who can also access the site's Dashboard to view site statistics (reports) or help manage the website settings, to name a few.

4 You might export to HTML if you plan on using your own hosting provider or want to hand the site files off to someone else.

INDEX

HTML
    embedding on web pages, 206–211
    exporting site as, 244, 245
    limitations when formatting frames
        containing, 208
HTML Code dialog box, 209
hyperlinks. *See* links
Hyperlinks tab (Site Properties dialog box),
    174, 175

I

icons
    anchor, 178
    embedded HTML, 207
    embedded image, 160
    warning, 151
Illustrator
    copying and pasting images from, 148
    designing web pages in, 12–13
image frames
    about, 146
    applying background image to, 125–126
    formatting Blank slideshow widget,
        229–230
    rotating, 157
Image Import Options dialog box, 149
images, 142–167. *See also* resizing images
    background, 55, 56
    choosing favicon, 33–34
    compatible formats for, 126, 144–146
    copying/pasting into Muse, 117
    cropping, 151, 152–153, 154–155
    drop shadows for, 194
    editing original, 161–162
    embedded, 160
    fixing broken links to, 162–163
    image titles and alternative text, 166, 167
    importing, 146–150
    linking, 160–163, 167, 177
    locking and grouping, 155–156
    optimal resolution for, 50, 87, 144
    pinning content to page, 163–164, 167
    placed, 144, 160, 167
    Rasterized Text Frame Indicator in text
        frames, 118
    relinking, 160–161
    rotating, 156–157

showing on Assets panel, 159
slicing and pasting Photoshop, 148
tips for placing, 147
transforming with Selection tool,
    150–153
using logo in header, 62–64
vertical credits for, 117–118, 119
wrapping text around, 158–159, 167
importing
    images, 146–150
    layered Photoshop files, 149
indenting paragraphs, 104–105
InDesign
    exporting text for use in Muse, 94
    replacing with Muse for website
        design, 10
inline content, 129
inserting
    anchors, 178–179
    text, 90–94
installing
    Classroom in a Book files, 3
    fonts, 2
    Muse, 2
instances, 160
interactivity. *See also* widgets
    designing pages for, 52, 184
internal links
    creating, 170–171
    creating anchors for, 177–179
    defined, 170, 189

J

.jpg files, 145, 146, 147
jumpstarting lessons
    deleting preference files when, 4
    steps for, 5

K

keyboard shortcuts
    adjusting Mac OS X preferences for
        Zoom tool, 26
    changing font size with, 96
    Zoom in/Zoom out, 24, 122
keywords for web pages, 43, 44, 45

placing multiple images with, 149
removing selected image from, 147
text placement with, 92–93
Place Photoshop Button command, 189
placing
images, 146, 147, 148–150
layered Photoshop file, 189
text, 92–93
Plan mode
accessing page properties in, 42
applying master pages in, 87
default master pages in, 53
editing site map in, 35
entering, 16
excluding page from navigation
menu, 66–67
planning site navigation, 51–52
.png files, 145–146
points, 95
positioning
options on Wrap panel, 158–159
unavailable for menus, 80
PPI (pixels per inch), 50
preferences
deleting current, 4
hiding Welcome screen, 14
locating folder for, 3, 4
Preferences dialog box, 237
Preview mode
about, 17
testing widgets in, 217
using, 27–28
viewing web pages in, 13
previewing
active Document window, 28
web pages, 13
websites, 24–25, 27
print design, 50–52
.psd files
converting placed Photoshop, 144
linking placed images to original image
in, 146
placing in Muse, 148–150
Publish dialog box, 236–237
publishing websites, 233–245
about, 13
associating domain names with site,
242–243

changing publish account associated
with, 237
excluding pages from export, 234, 245
exporting site as HTML, 244, 245
making and uploading edits, 238–239
methods for, 245
purchasing domain names for
sites, 240
steps for, 235–237
upgrading temporary sites, 236,
240–243, 245
using Business Catalyst hosting, 234,
235–237
purchasing domain names, 240
Push Site Live button (Business Catalyst
Admin page), 240, 241

R

ranking web pages, 44
Rasterized Text Frame indicators, 118,
181, 197
Rectangle tool
about, 122, 141
creating line with, 127–128
drawing with, 122–123
making dotted lines, 128–130
rectangles
alignment for pasted, 158
giving 100% width characteristics,
123–125
red lines, 76
Redefine Style button, 204
redefining
graphic styles, 203–205
paragraph styles, 109–111
relinking images, 160–161
removing rounded corners, 193
renaming page thumbnails, 37, 38
reordering
master pages, 84
panels, 20–21, 23
required computer knowledge, 2
resetting
default states, 78
page properties, 46, 58
resizing
groups, 156
menu, 71–72

Production Notes

The *Adobe Muse Classroom in a Book* was created electronically using Adobe InDesign CS5. Art was produced using Adobe Illustrator and Adobe Photoshop. The Myriad Pro and Warnock Pro OpenType families of typefaces were used throughout this book.

References to company names in the lessons are for demonstration purposes only and are not intended to refer to any actual organization or person.

Images

Photographic images and illustrations are intended for use with the tutorials.

Typefaces used

Adobe Myriad Pro and Adobe Warnock Pro are used throughout the lessons. For more information about OpenType and Adobe fonts, visit www.adobe.com/type/opentype/.

Team credits

The following individuals contributed to the development of this edition of the *Adobe Muse Classroom in a Book*:

Writer: Brian Wood
Project Editor: Valerie Witte
Developmental and Copy Editor: Linda LaFlamme
Production Editor: Katerina Malone
Technical Editor: Christine Ricks
Technical Analyst: Tommi West
Compositor: David Van Ness
Proofreader: Patricia Pane
Indexer: Rebecca Plunkett
Cover designer: Eddie Yuen
Interior designer: Mimi Heft

Contributor

Brian Wood is an Adobe Certified Instructor in Dreamweaver CS5, Acrobat 9 Pro, and Illustrator CS5. He is the author of seven training books (on Illustrator, InDesign, and Adobe Muse), all published by Peachpit Press, as well as numerous training videos and DVDs on Dreamweaver and CSS, InDesign, Illustrator, and Acrobat, including Acrobat multimedia and forms and others.

In addition to training many clients large and small, Brian speaks regularly at national conferences, such as Adobe MAX, the Getting Started with Dreamweaver and CSS tour, The InDesign Conference, The Web Design Conference, and The Creative Suite Conference, as well as events hosted by AIGA and other industry organizations. To learn more, visit www.askbrianwood.com.

AdobePress

LEARN BY VIDEO

Table of Contents never more than a click away

Up to 15 hours of high-quality video training

Lesson files are included on the DVD

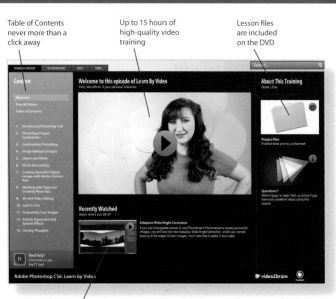

The **Learn by Video** series from video2brain and Adobe Press is the only Adobe-approved video courseware for the Adobe Certified Associate Level certification, and has quickly established itself as one of the most critically acclaimed training products available on the fundamentals of Adobe software.

Learn by Video offers up to 15 hours of high-quality HD video training presented by experienced trainers, as well as lesson files, assessment quizzes, and review materials. The DVD is bundled with a full-color printed booklet that provides supplemental information as well as a guide to the video topics.

Video player remembers which movie you watched last

Watch-and-Work mode shrinks the video into a small window while you work in the software

For more information go to
www.adobepress.com/learnbyvideo

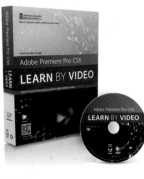

Titles

Adobe Photoshop CS6: Learn by Video: Core Training in Visual Communication
ISBN: 9780321840714

Adobe Illustrator CS6: Learn by Video
ISBN: 9780321840684

Adobe InDesign CS6: Learn by Video
ISBN: 9780321840691

Adobe Flash Professional CS6: Learn by Video: Core Training in Rich Media Communication
ISBN: 9780321840707

Adobe Dreamweaver CS6: Learn by Video: Core Training in Web Communication
ISBN: 9780321840370

Adobe Premiere Pro CS6: Learn by Video: Core Training in Video Communication
ISBN: 9780321840721

Adobe After Effects CS6: Learn by Video
ISBN: 9780321840387